Your Birthday Promise

Workbook, Planner, and Journal

Your Birthday Promise
Workbook, Planner, and Journal

A Yearly Celebration and Monthly Activation of
Your Identity, Role, and Purpose

Rose Martin

Bella Vista, AR

Your Birthday Promise Workbook, Planner, and Journal
Written By Rose Martin

Copyright © 2026 Rose Martin
Book ISBN: 979-8-9934872-1-2
Library of Congress Control Number:

All Rights Reserved. No part of this work may be reproduced or used in any form or by any means - graphic, electronic, or mechanical, including photocopying or information storage and retrieval systems - without written permission from the publisher. Brief passages may be cited for ministry and educational purposes as long as full acknowledgment is given.

Published by: Achievement Publications
PO Box 3321
Bella Vista, AR 72715
United States

Web: www.YourBirthdayPromise.com
Email: YourBirthdayPromise@gmail.com

Copyright Notices:

Unless otherwise noted Scripture quotations are taken from THE HOLY BIBLE, NEW INTERNATIONAL VERSION® NIV® Copyright © 1973, 1978, 1984 by International Bible Society® Used by permission. All rights reserved worldwide.

Scripture quotations marked (BSB) are from The Holy Bible, Berean Study Bible, BSB. Copyright ©2016, 2018 by Bible Hub. Used by Permission. All Rights Reserved Worldwide.

Scripture quotations marked (ESV) are from The ESV® Bible (The Holy Bible, English Standard Version®), copyright © 2001 by Crossway, a publishing ministry of Good News Publishers. Used by permission. All rights reserved.

Scripture taken from the NKJV New King James Version®. Copyright © 1982 by Thomas Nelson. Used by permission. All rights reserved.

Scripture quotations marked NLT are taken from the *Holy Bible*, New Living Translation, Copyright © 1996, 2004, 2015 by Tyndale House Foundation. Used by permission of Tyndale House Publishers, Inc., Carol Stream, Illinois 60188. All rights reserved.

⚠ Disclaimer: This content is for spiritual growth and entertainment purposes only. It does not replace professional medical or psychological advice. Interpret all insights as symbolic and reflective of your personal journey.

Rev 1-12-2026

Dedication

Dedicated to all the children of God
who want to know the reality of who they truly are.

Acknowledgements

Thank you and love to my husband Charles for giving me the space and support for this heartfelt Year-long endeavor.

Table of Contents

A Spiritual Celebration of Your Birthday Promise 1

    Your Birthday Promise 2

    Understanding Your Time and Season 2

    The Month of Your Birth Holds the First Key 3

    God's Seasonal Year 3

    The Energy Flows Down 4

    Calendar Dates for the Seasonal Months of the Year 5

    How to Use Your Birthday Promise Journal 6

    Your Birthday Life Review 7

    To be Used Before, During, After Your Birthday 7

    Starting at Other Times of the Year 8

    Embracing the Traits of Your Birth Month 8

    Become Aware of Who You Are 9

    Evidence of Personal and Spiritual Growth 10

    The Fruit of the Tree of Life 10

    Inspecting the Fruit 11

    Finding the Strong and Weak Areas of Your Life 12

    Key Areas of Life to Consider on Your Birthday 13

    The Wheel of Life 14

    Your Validation and Confirmation 15

Under Which Month Where You Born? 16

Part One 17

Celebrating Your Birthday! 17

Your Birthday Promise Month 18

    Remember, Review, Renew, and Receive Your Gifts 18

    Birthday Life Review Questions 19

Happy Birthday, Aries! 21

Happy Birthday, Taurus! 35

Happy Birthday, Gemini! 49

Happy Birthday, Cancer! 63

Happy Birthday, Leo! 77

Happy Birthday, Virgo! 91

Happy Birthday, Libra! 105

Happy Birthday, Scorpio! 119

Happy Birthday, Sagittarius! 133

Happy Birthday, Capricorn! 147

Happy Birthday, Aquarius! 161

Happy Birthday, Pisces! 175

Yearly Birthday Life Review Questions 189

    My Birthday Life Review 190

    Spiritual Fruit Tending 192

    Journaling the Reflections on the Key Areas of Life 193

    Deep Dive on Your Wheel of Life Findings 194

    Your Birthday Promise Insights 197

Part Two 201

Your Journey Around the Wheel of the Year 201

    Nourishment from Each Month 202

    Each Month Holds New Energies and Insights 202

    Balance and Grow from Each Month's Traits, Qualities, and Challenges 203

    Learn More about Your Friends, Family, Children, and Co-Workers 203

    Self-awareness and Development Over Time 204

    Months That Will Help You Balance 204

    The Area of Life, its Month, its Traits, and its Opposite 206

    It's a Learning Process 207

    Growing Fruit All Throughout the Year 207

The Month of Aries 210

The Month of Taurus 218

The Month of Gemini 226
The Month of Cancer 234
The Month of Leo 242
The Month of Virgo 250
The Month of Libra 258
 The Month of Scorpio 266
The Month of Sagittarius 274
The Month of Capricorn 282
The Month of Aquarius 290
The Month of Pisces 298

Part Three 306
Personal and Spiritual Growth Aides 306
    Your Personal Experience 307
    Design Your Own Ritual 307
    My prayer to Father God for the Coming Year 309
    A Fresh Start Every Month! 311
    Personality Development and Spiritual Growth 312
    The Holy Spirit as Your Guide 313
    Divine Assurances to Edify Your Life 314
    Scripture Birthday Blessings 315
    Your Birthday Promise Supporting Scripture 316
Author's Note 318
In Conclusion, ... 319
Notable Reflections 320
Glossary 321
Journal 323

A Spiritual Celebration of Your Birthday Promise

Some people look forward to their birthday, others approach it with anxiety, and others simply ignore it. No matter how we feel about another trip around the Sun or adding another candle to the cake, Birthdays serve as more than a measure of time but also as a testimony of our progress and continual opportunities.

Many observe the tradition of giving or receiving gifts on Birthdays. These are typically special or sentimental gifts - going out to dinner, taking trips, getting jewelry or something you would not normally do or buy for yourself.

Amazingly there are other important gifts that are not thought about on Birthdays. They are the personal gifts that God gave us on our Birthday! They are the life plan He prepared for us and the gifts, talents, and abilities He gave to equip us for our life on this Earth. These are typically overlooked and not acknowledged on Birthdays, or any other time of the Year.

What if you celebrated those gifts every Year? How would it change your life? Would it give you more confidence? Would it strengthen your identity? Would it empower your life?

In a world where value is measured by wealth, status, and achievements, Birthdays remind us that life itself is a fundamental gift and we have been given individual abilities to live it. Every breath you take, every Year that passes, all of your life experiences bring eternal value to the purpose of your precious life.

It is time to celebrate Your Birthday in its fullness! It is time to remember and acknowledge your God-given gifts! Do you know what they are?

Your Birthday Promise

We are all born with a purpose and a plan that is lived out throughout our lifetime. This is called Your Birthday Promise. It is the Promise God has made with you for your life.

According to this Promise, each person is born with a unique set of God-given characteristics and abilities. Our Creator has given them to us to be used and developed to live out the purposes of our lives. We are administrators of the heavenly gifts and talents God wants us to use here on the Earth for His eternal purposes. As above, so below.

> *Your kingdom come, Your will be done, on earth as it is in heaven.*
> *Matthew 6:10*

Your Birthday Promise consists of your role and the personality traits and abilities, known as gifts and talents, you carry, and the life experiences needed to accomplish your life's purpose and walk your destined path. It is said to be a guide to your life's journey. However, you will not know the complete promise and objective until you have finished your course on Earth, but you can get a glimpse of it.

> *For now we see only a reflection as in a mirror; then we shall see face to face.*
> *Now I know in part; then I shall know fully, even as I am fully known.*
> *1 Corinthians 13:12*

For now, you are able to get a glimpse of yourself through the major indicators of Your Birthday Promise and the attributes you were born with! You can know these right now through understanding the time you were born - specifically the Month under which you were born.

Understanding Your Time and Season

God created time and seasons. There is a time to be born, and a time to die, as Ecclesiastes 3:1-2 BSB tells us.

> *To everything there is a season, and a time for every purpose under heaven:*
> *a time to be born and a time to die...*

You were born at the right time, in the right place, to the right family for you to begin your journey, your mission, on this earth. All of these factors set the stage for your life.

You were crowned with life at the moment of your first breath with a role to carry out for your life and in the world. Your Birthday Month will tell you all about it.

The Month of Your Birth Holds the First Key

The Month that you were born under holds the first key to discovering your role and purpose and is the fastest and easiest way to start seeing yourself as you truly are. It shows who you are at a core level, describing your personality at its center, and the qualities that are seeking expression through you.

The significance of the Month is by no means the only indicator of your gifts, abilities, or purpose but it gives you an immediate, clear idea of who you are at your core. It gives you instant insight into your heart.

In the Biblical understanding, your heart is at the center of your being. It influences your thoughts, emotions, and actions. It is the heart that is the place where you are most yourself. It is the very core and the spiritual center of your being.

Above all else, guard your heart, for everything you do flows from it. Proverbs 4:23

From a spiritual perspective, the heart is considered the place where God's Spirit seeks to dwell and bring about change, inviting those who seek spiritual growth to guard and purify their hearts as they pursue a deeper relationship with Him.

While further details can be obtained from the exact Day on which you were born, and even more specifics from the exact Time and Place of your Birth (which are not covered in this work), discovering the attributes of the Month under which you were born is a simple yet accurate way to start understanding yourself and the primary role you have at this time, for your life and in the world.

God's Seasonal Year

Every Season is different. Every Month has its role. Just as Months and Seasons have their roles, so do each one of us.

Each Month of the Year, as outlined in God's Seasonal Year, has a unique physical and material makeup that He designed for His purposes. Creator God also gave each Seasonal Month spiritual and developmental qualities.

Since Ancient times, the qualities of each Seasonal Month have been studied, observed, and lived by sages, magi, prophets, kings, and priests. They were trained to understand God's signs in the Heavens and through them they learned His ways. These insights are now becoming more available to the everyday person for their study.

God tells us to look up and learn from the Heavens.

Lift up your eyes and look to the heavens: Who created all these? He who brings out the starry host one by one and calls forth each of them by name. Because of his great power and mighty strength, not one of them is missing. Isaiah 40:26

Can you bring forth the constellations in their seasons or lead out the Bear with its cubs? Do you know the laws of the heavens? Can you set up God's dominion over the earth? Job 38:32-33

The heavens declare the glory of God; the skies proclaim the work of his hands. Psalm 19:1

Lifting one's eyes to the Heavens implies a gesture of seeking help and guidance from a higher power symbolizing trust in Divine intervention. God encourages us to look up and receive.

Your purpose is written in the Heavens and is sealed in your life. It is yours to do with what you will. You have free will. You can use it for good, develop it, and become all that you can be with what you have been entrusted to carry out your life's purpose. By doing so you will grow in love and satisfaction each day. You will be building the foundation on which to live your life and experience all that has been planned for you. The reflection of God's love will be shown in your life.

Are you expressing the gifts you have been given, suppressing them, or are you even aware of them?

The Energy Flows Down

Where the Earth was on its trip around the Sun at the time of Your Birth indicates what Month it is under. The Month of your birth is a major indicator of the gifts and talents that you have at the core of your being. The energy of Your Birthday Promise Month flows from The Most High through the Heavens into your being.

The names for the Months of the Seasonal Year are taken from the Starry Hosts, or Constellations, that surround the Earth. They are the markers of the path that the Earth takes on its Yearly journey around the Sun. These Constellations mark the beginning, middle, and end of the Spring, Summer, Fall, and Winter Seasons through the Seasonal Months that are in each.

Each Seasonal Month has its own name to identify it in the Universe. The Seasonal Months' names in order beginning with the first Seasonal Month of Spring are as follows: Aries, Taurus, Gemini, Cancer, Leo, Virgo, Libra, Scorpio, Sagittarius, Capricorn, Aquarius, and Pisces.

Astronomers match God's Seasonal Months with the calendar dates we use today, called the Gregorian Calendar. This is how we can identify the dates of the beginning and end of each Seasonal Month in the Universe. The exact beginning dates may differ slightly depending on the Year, so it's best to double check if Your Birthday is near the start or end of a Seasonal Month.

Calendar Dates for the Seasonal Months of the Year

1 Aries
March 19 – April 20

2 Taurus
April 21 – May 20

3 Gemini
May 21 – June 20

4 Cancer
June 21 – July 22

5 Leo
July 23 – August 22

6 Virgo
August 23 – September 22

7 Libra
September 23 – October 22

8 Scorpio
October 23 – November 21

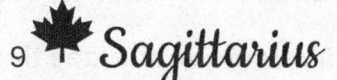
9 Sagittarius
November 22 – December 21

10 Capricorn
December 22 – January 19

11 Aquarius
January 20 – February 18

12 Pisces
February 19 – March 20

How to Use Your Birthday Promise Journal

Recognizing the special energy that surrounds Your Birthday will make a big positive difference in your life. *Your Birthday Promise Workbook, Planner, and Journal* will help you to connect with the time and season of Your Birth and all that it holds for you. It is designed for your personal and spiritual growth throughout the Year. Following the Introduction, it is divided into three main Parts.

Introduction, *A Spiritual Celebration of Your Birthday Promise,* gives you an overview of Your Birthday Promise and how to use this Journal.

Part One, *Your Birthday Promise Month,* is all about your individual Birthday Month and identifying the core qualities of your personality, role, and traits - all a part of your gifts, talents, and abilities.

At the end of Part One you will find **Your Yearly Birthday Life Review Questions** where you can do a deep dive into the ratings you gave yourself on the Fruit of your life, as well as the status of the Key Areas of your life in preparation for the Year ahead.

Part Two, *Journey Around the Wheel of the Year,* is about recognizing the features of each of the twelve Months of the Seasonal Year to learn how they can help nourish and cultivate your personal growth and raise your understanding of those who have their Birthday during those Months.

Part Three, *Personal and Spiritual Growth Aides,* contains helpful tools and insights to guide and assist you during Your Birthday celebration and activation as well as throughout the Year.

This Journal provides the resources you need to evaluate your life, build your self-awareness, grow in your role and become all that you can be!

- ◊ Identify your primary personality traits, as well as gifts and talents.
- ◊ Identify the core role you have been given for your life, as well as your role in the whole of humanity.
- ◊ Understand what you are here to learn through your life experiences.
- ◊ Yearly Birthday Life Review questions and prompts to help you understand the past Year and align you with the current one.
- ◊ Identify Areas of Life that you are satisfied with and any that need attention through the ratings you give yourself on the Wheel of Life.
- ◊ Name the Fruits of the Tree of Life that are operating in your life.
- ◊ Guided reflections will help you understand your patterns, realize breakthroughs, and continually move towards your best self.
- ◊ Scripture and Affirmations to encourage and build you up.

Your Birthday Life Review

This Journal can be started at any time of the Year. However, spending a few days before, during, and after Your Birthday focusing on Your Birthday Life Review is optimal.

At this Yearly appointed time you have a special opportunity to make room for Divine revelation. Your Birthday Life Review is a powerful time to think about your life and the Year ahead. It is an ideal time to...

- Connect with the Living God Who created you.
- Observe and renew the qualities and blessings of Your Birthday Promise.
- Evaluate how you are doing in the Key Areas of your life.
- Get further understanding of the plan for your life.
- Set intentions for growing personally and spiritually.
- Ask for the gifts and talents needed to be activated.
- Receive the current energies of Your Birth Month.
- Get encouragement and direction from the Spirit for the Year ahead.

And that is what you are doing now at Your Birthday season! Reviewing and activating the plan for the Year ahead. This will give you a strong start for the Year!

To be Used Before, During, After Your Birthday

Take the time necessary to get the most meaning out of Your Birthday celebration and activation by starting Your Birthday Life Review 20 days before and continue on 20 days after Your Birthday, in addition to the actual Day of Your Birth. About 20 days before Your Birthday the energies and anticipation are already starting.

Use the days before to review your past Year and the days after to begin to implement and live the intentions you make. Intentions can be compared to resolutions that we make at the calendar New Year.

Select times where you can spend quite time reading through *Your Birthday Promise Workbook, Planner, and Journal.* Find Your Birthday Promise Month in this Journal to become familiar with Your Promise. Read through it all.

You can then continue on throughout the Year to learn more about each successive Month in Part Two of this Journal.

By doing so, you will continue to make real progress all throughout the Year. You will get answers to your life questions and be able to transform confusion into fulfilling experiences. You will be able to make purposeful plans, monitor achievements, and consistently support your well-being each Month as you walk out your life plan. As you work through this Journal you will begin to see for yourself how your life changes for the better.

You do not have to settle for less than a life full of purpose and meaning. Live your life with the end goal of finishing all of your life lessons and hearing, "Well done!"

Your balanced, joyful, meaningful future starts today!

Starting at Other Times of the Year

To start this Journal at a time other than Your Birthday, firstly, familiarize yourself with the traits of Your Birthday Promise Month, and then find the current Month and recognize the characteristic traits of that Month. See if there is an Area of Your Life where those traits will help at this time. Ask for them. Believe you will receive what you need. Follow the rest of the Months through the rest of the Year. Then you will come to Your Birthday Month, and you can start a fresh new Yearly cycle!

Embracing the Traits of Your Birth Month

It's important for you to realize that God loves you and that He has a plan for your life. The God of the Universe is closely involved with all of the details of your life and cares about you very much. He chose the Month of Your Birth and created a personalized blueprint of your journey specifically for you. This includes all the opportunities, trials, and victories in your life!

He planted specific seeds inside of you, including gifts and talents, that He wants you to grow. He is excited for you to discover, develop, and use them to fulfill your purpose and make a difference in the world.

God created and empowered the Seasonal Months and has given every person the ability to excel in as well as overcome the negative characteristics of the Month in which they were born.

"For I know the plans I have for you," declares the LORD, "plans to prosper you and not to harm you, plans to give you hope and a future. Jeremiah 29:11

And God is faithful; he will not let you be tempted beyond what you can bear. But when you are tempted, he will also provide a way out so that you can endure it. 1 Corinthians 10:13

And we know that in all things God works for the good of those who love him, who have been called according to his purpose. Romans 8:28

Although there are many physical and spiritual components of the Heavens contained in each Month, in *Your Birthday Promise Yearly Workbook, Planner, and Journal* we will be focusing on the core personality and role of those born in each of the Months.

You will be contributing to your personal and spiritual growth as you endeavor to learn, understand, and observe the traits of Your Birth Month and become familiar with the cycle of the entire Seasonal Year. Learning to embrace and appreciate the gifts and talents of the Month under which you were born will help you embrace and appreciate yourself.

Become Aware of Who You Are

The purpose of becoming aware of yourself, your role, your purpose, your gifts and talents, is not to take anything away from God's glory. Instead, it is to acknowledge Him in every part of the life you have been given. It is to make the most of the opportunities and life lessons that God has provided for you. It is to connect you to the reality of who you were created to be.

The Yearly Life Review in this Journal guides you in your journey of discovering who you are by providing the tools and direction you need to help you look inward. When you reflect on your own thoughts, behaviors, values, you will come to know yourself and God's plan for your life and experience new growth.

Building self-awareness involves understanding the role, personality and abilities you have been given. Activities like reflection, journaling, prayer, meditation, stillness and daily living can reveal your thoughts, emotions, and behaviors. These activities can deepen self-insight, highlight areas for improvement, and strengthen your relationship with the Spirit of the Living God.

Being aware of yourself leads to better emotional control, improved relationships, and greater overall wellbeing which will lead to personal growth and enhanced decision-making ability. They all work together to fulfill your purpose. This Journal provides the information and prompts you need to build your self-awareness and spirituality.

Evidence of Personal and Spiritual Growth

When you work through the topics shown under your specific Birth Month section you will be able to consider and rate various aspects of your inner self to get an instant reality check on your personal and spiritual growth. You will be able to confirm the aspects of your life that are going well, and identify the aspects that need attention.

Two specific ways that you can get a status check on your life are through rating yourself on the Fruit you produce in your life and the health of the twelve Main Areas of your life. These are explained in Your Birthday Month section.

The Fruit of the Tree of Life

Personal and spiritual growth is linked to the measure of Fruit in all areas of a person's life. The Fruit of our life is evidenced through the visible outcomes or results that are shown in our actions and character. Fruit can also be an indicator of our inner peace.

In addition, in the Book of Revelation 22:1-5, an angel shows John a river of life-giving water flowing down from heaven alongside a Tree which produces Fruit twelve times a Year, once each Month. From a Judeo-Christian viewpoint, these twelve Fruits from the Tree of Life are symbolic fruits, also called the Fruits of the Spirit, or virtues. They include the Fruits listed in the Book of Galatians 5:22-23. Each Fruit also reveals an aspect of God's nature.

These Fruits provide knowledge of truth and give spiritual nourishment as the leaves from this tree serve as healing for all nations. Growing these Fruits in our lives nourish our character and provide healing properties for our souls.

The Fruits of the Spirit are not achieved through our effort alone but are cultivated through a relationship with the Spirit of the living God. A tree needs strong roots to produce fruit, and similarly, developing the Fruits of the Spirit requires a close relationship with the Holy Spirit. This connection is nurtured through spending intentional time with Him.

"I am the vine; you are the branches. If you remain in me and I in you, you will bear much fruit; apart from me you can do nothing." John 15:5

Inspecting the Fruit

The Fruit of the Tree of Life serves as a guide to enhance your personal development and ethical living. Every fruit carries its own special qualities, supporting both physical health and spiritual growth. By displaying these virtues you not only improve your life and spiritual well-being but also contribute positively to your community and the world at large.

These qualities are shown through our daily interactions, our speech, and our impact on others. For instance, love is demonstrated by acts of kindness; joy is conveyed through positive interactions; peace is preserved by exercising patience; and self-control is reflected in the managing of emotions and behaviors. These practical applications of the Fruit of the Spirit can be applied in everyday activities, helping us to live out these virtues throughout our life.

The Fruits of the Spirit help guide you in leading a life full of faith, love, and peace. At the time of Your Yearly Life Review, ask God to increase them in your life for the coming Year. Ask for guidance in revealing areas needing growth and support. Simply praying, *"Lord, help me to be more self-controlled today,"* invites God's presence into your everyday life.

Growing in these Fruits will help you mature in all areas of your life and will be a part of fulfilling your purpose. These characteristics are the goal and fruit of love. Displaying them in your life is a testimony to the Holy Spirit's transformative power.

At the time of your Yearly Birthday Life Review, and throughout the Year, you can use the presence of the Fruits of the Tree of Life as a measuring stick for your personal and spiritual growth and abundance. Gaining insight into their meanings and benefits allows you to build a stronger bond with the Spirit, your inner self, and your fellow man.

Love, joy, peace, patience, kindness, goodness, faithfulness, gentleness, self-control, long-suffering, temperance, wisdom...how are you growing in these virtues? Rate yourself and see!

See The Fruit of the Tree of Life rating chart under your individual Birth Month in Part One to enter your responses.

Finding the Strong and Weak Areas of Your Life

There are Areas of Life that we all have in common. These can be divided into twelve Key Life Areas that make up the categories of our everyday lives. As part of Your Yearly Life Review you can do a checkup to evaluate how you are doing in each Area.

The Key Areas are listed in the following Table along with a key question and the key matters related to that Area. Use this as a guide to reflect on the Key Areas of Life and the concerns related to each one.

As you think about each area, they will speak to you, either as an area you have been struggling with, or as an area you are doing well in. In your mind, give yourself a score from 1-8 on how you feel you are doing in that Area, with 8 being the most satisfying and 1 needing the most attention. From this you will be able to determine the areas where more attention is needed and others where you can rejoice in the progress you have already made. You can highlight those scores on the Wheel of Life found in Your Birthday Month section in Part One.

Stronger areas are defined as balanced, peaceful, developed, and working well. Weaker areas are defined as under-developed, unfulfilled, tense, or otherwise problematic. The Wheel of Life will help you visualize the strengths and weakness related to your overall well-being.

The purpose of this Key Areas of Life Table and the corresponding Wheel of Life is to assess and improve the balance across all the Areas that influence your overall well-being. You can reflect on how the Areas are contributing to or hindering you in living a fulfilled life. Guidance from the Spirit will show you how to improve, heal, handle, or to just keep going as you are where needed.

This evaluation is important for your personal growth.

Key Areas of Life to Consider on Your Birthday

Key Life Area	Reflection Question and Matters Included in Each Area for Evaluation. How am I doing in each Life Area?
Identity	**Who am I?** My appearance, the impression I make on others. the mask I wear as I meet the outside world, my identity, mannerisms, my core personality, self-discovery, personal development.
Resources	**What do I value?** My personal values, resources, finances, possessions, how I relate to money, how I approach earning money, my sense of material security, income from work, resources needed to provide for myself, self-worth, what I value and how I manage my resources.
Communication	**How do I communicate?** My thinking, speaking, writing, learning style, and immediate environment. How I exchange ideas, and interact with my close social circle, including siblings, neighbors, and local community,
Home	**My foundation?** My physical home, family, heritage, roots, private life, my upbringing, intimate relatives, relationship with parental figures, my sense of emotional security and well-being.
Recreation	**My creative self-expression?** My creativity, children, romance, sexual activity, hobbies, vacation, leisure time, zest for life, play, entertainment, where I seek fun, what brings me joy and pleasure.
Routines	**My daily routines?** My health, daily routines, work, service, self-care, habits, fitness, how I take care of my body, how I maintain my well-being, my vocation, schedules, approach to work and service to others, duty, volunteer involvement.
Partnerships	**How do I relate?** My marriage, committed partnerships, one-to-one relationships, how I connect with others in both romantic and business partnerships, cooperation and balance in connections, what I seek in a partner.
Shared Resources	**How do I protect my resources?** My business side of marriage, joint bank accounts, shared investments, financial portfolios, wills, divorces, credit card debt, taxes, royalties, inheritances, commissions, my partner's money, how I handle change, starting over.
Philosophy	**My spiritual path?** My search for meaning, quest for knowledge, higher education, my desire to explore the world, travel to faraway places – spiritually or physically, my beliefs, connection with God, religion, adventure, ethics, philosophy of life.
Public Life	**My social standing?** My career, public image, status, ambitions, my mission, professional path, how I am perceived in the world, my reputation, business, achievement in the world, long-term goals.
Community	**How do I connect with like-minded people?** My group involvement, my friends, social networks, my role in my community, humanitarian causes, clubs, pursuit of my hopes and dreams, social contribution, philanthropy, giving, collaborative endeavors.
Subconscious	**My hidden matters?** My inner concerns, secret fears, ways I may sabotage myself, my private dreams, hidden aspects of myself, my inner world, spiritual growth, endings, secrets I keep, my need to retreat from the world.

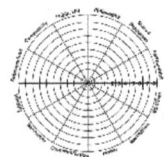

The Wheel of Life

The Wheel of Life Evaluation Tool provides clarity on the Areas of Life that feel aligned and those that are asking for more attention. It is a tool that places the Key Areas of Life around a wheel to help you measure the status of each one. It's a useful way to look at your current situation and recognize which Areas of your life are functioning well and which ones need work. You will become aware of your strengths, find potential blind spots, identify areas for growth, and begin planning practical steps to make progress.

The Wheel of Life

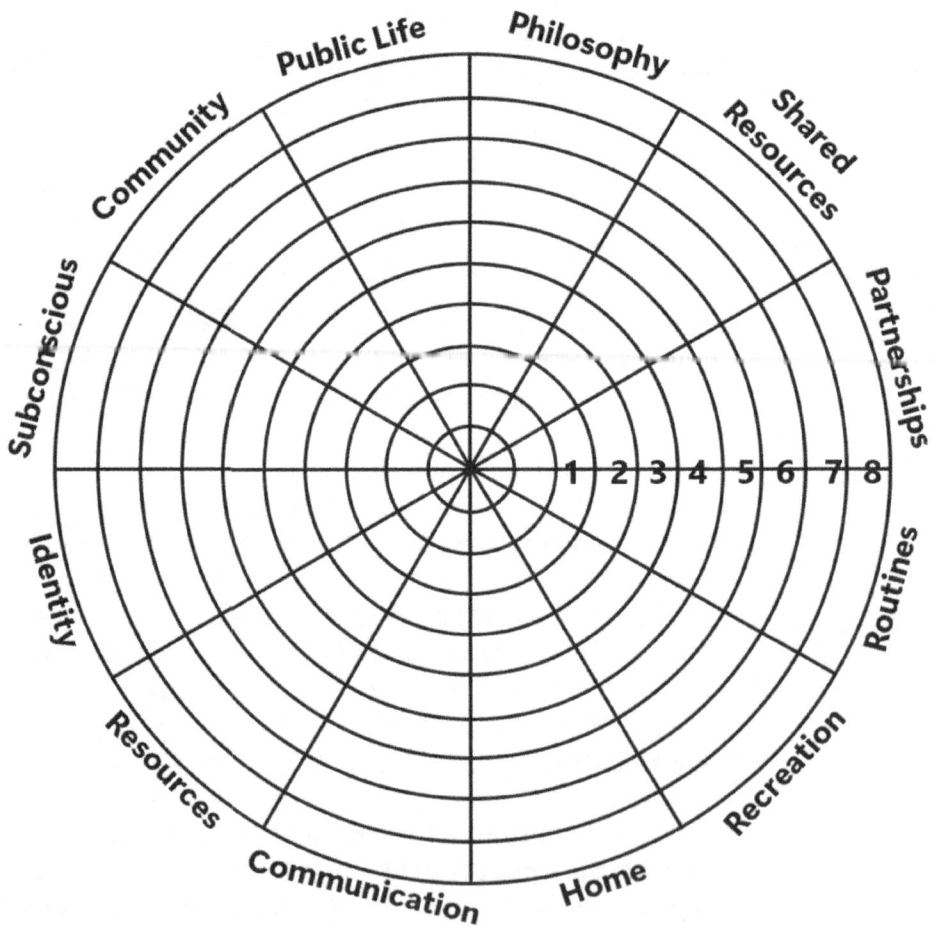

**See the Wheel of Life found in your individual Birthday Month in Part One.
Use it to enter your ratings.**

Your Validation and Confirmation

You are most likely aware that you have certain skills and talents, but self-doubt, life responsibilities, or concerns about changing your behaviors may be preventing you from fully developing your abilities.

When you realize that the traits you see in yourself are many of the same traits associated with the Month you were born under; when you connect the idea that these God-given talents and abilities are associated with the role of that particular Month; and when you comprehend that you were chosen to be born at that specific time, you will receive meaningful confirmation and motivation. You will get a new sense of identity, renewed enthusiasm, and the inspiration you need to confidently start or continue pursuing your goals and visions.

If what you learn from using this Journal resonates deep inside your being, it is not by chance. It is recognition. A part of you has always known this. It has just been waiting for you to remember and name it (and claim it!).

When you recognize that you have a godly purpose, are equipped with what you need, and are worthy and capable of achieving mighty things, you will be encouraged to cultivate your gifts, fulfill your life's purpose, and allow more of God's presence in your life.

It is your responsibility to actively cultivate the gifts and talents you carry that are associated with Your Birthday Promise. God has given you free will. You have the freedom to determine how you react, what you learn, how you heal after traumas, how you handle relationships, how you love, and all the other daily decisions of life, including your relationship with Him.

Rest assured - you don't have to figure everything out! God has your back! Be gentle in your judgment of yourself. To get the most out of each experience learn to replace "Why is this happening to me?," or "What did I do wrong?," with "What is God trying to show me?, "What can I learn from this?," or "How can I do this better next time?"

Under Which Month Where You Born?

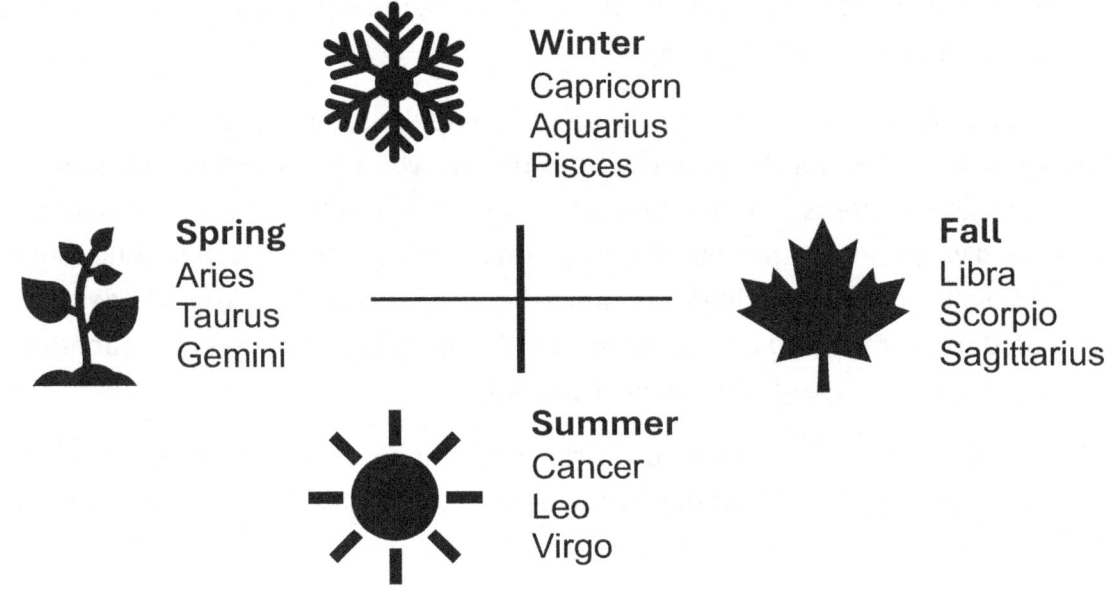

Winter
Capricorn
Aquarius
Pisces

Spring
Aries
Taurus
Gemini

Fall
Libra
Scorpio
Sagittarius

Summer
Cancer
Leo
Virgo

What is Your Role in This World?

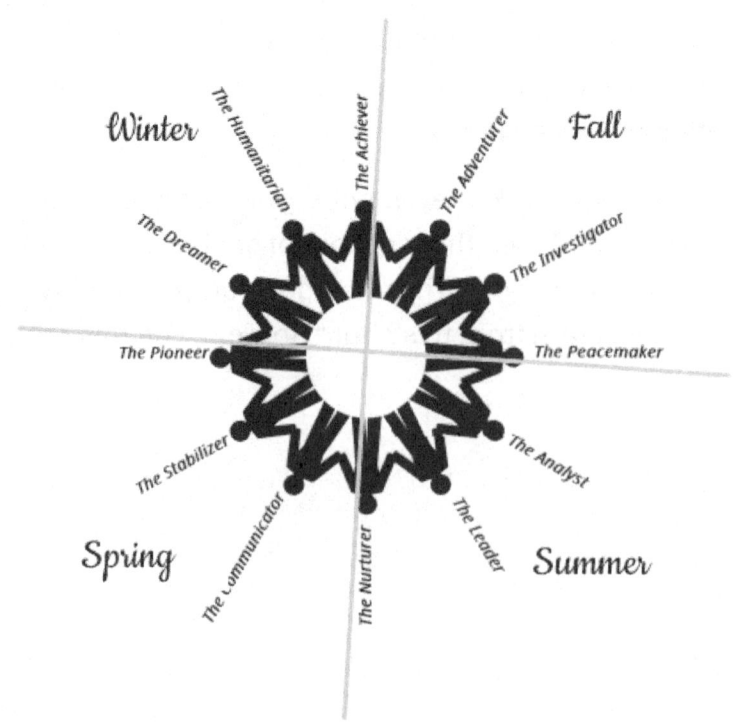

Winter — The Humanitarian, The Achiever
Fall — The Adventurer, The Investigator, The Peacemaker, The Analyst
Summer — The Leader, The Nurturer
Spring — The Communicator, The Stabilizer, The Pioneer, The Dreamer

Part One

Celebrating Your Birthday!

Happy Birthday to you! You have now completed a 365-day trip around the Sun since your last Birthday. Congratulations! Quite a few things have likely happened throughout the Year. Each Year on or around Your Birthday is a good time to review and learn from them and plan for the next Year.

Your Birthday Promise Month

Remember, Review, Renew, and Receive Your Gifts

Each Year the Earth takes one trip around the Sun. At the point it comes to the position in the Heavens where it was when you were born, your personal life's plan's energy is the strongest. Each Birthday provides an opportunity...

- ♦ to remember, review, and renew the qualities you were given at Your Birth.
- ♦ to realign your life with Creator God.
- ♦ to receive your gifts from Him.
- ♦ to assess how you are progressing through a Yearly Birthday Life Review.
- ♦ to symbolically plant seeds for the Year ahead and cultivate all Areas of Your Life.
- ♦ It is a powerful time of Your Year!

In Part One you will find the Seasonal Months in their order with the description of each Month's Birthday Promise, followed by Birthday Life Review Questions.

- ➢ Find the Month under which you were born and read about the traits of Your Birthday Promise Month to get familiar with and be reminded of the core personality traits you were given.

- ➢ Reflect on your life, your purpose, role, lessons to learn, contribution to society based on Your Birth Month descriptions and complete the Birthday Life Review questions that apply to each.

- ➢ Read about the Fruits of the Tree of Life and the Wheel of Life and rate yourself on each of them. Journal your insights.

- ➢ Give some thought to and answer or contemplate all of the questions in the Birthday Life Review Questions section.

- ➢ Jot down insights and revelations you receive as you look forward to Your New Year.

- ➢ Ask for and receive the gifts that are associated with Your Birthday Month – the unique characteristics and abilities to use and develop in your life.

Taking Inventory of the Qualities of Your Life

Birthday Life Review Questions are provided for you at the end of Part One as prompts for a thorough evaluation of your personality, role, and life, the ratings you gave yourself on the Fruit of the Tree of Life, the Wheel of Life, as well as the general insights on your New Year. Go to them after you have read the promises of Your Birth Month. Think of your past Year through the reflections and questions provided.

The questions will prompt you to think about your life. Think of how your life was a Year ago. From the answers and revelations you will be able to see, "What things changed?" "What contributions did I make?" "What challenges did I have?" "What were my victories or defeats?" "What lessons did I learn?" "How do I rate my life?"

During your time of reflection, think of the coming Year. "How do I envision my life one Year from now?" "What skills do I want to continue developing?" "What areas do I want to cut back or balance?"

Through reflecting on these, you will come into a new understanding of yourself, your purpose, and the Year ahead.

Birthday Life Review Questions

My Birthday Life Review
Do you recognize the Birthday Promise qualities in yourself?
Go to Page 190 for Your Birthday Life Review questions.

Spiritual Fruit Tending
Questions and prompts for your quiet time
Go to Page 192 for a deep dive into your Fruit of the Tree of Life ratings.

Deep Dive on Your Wheel of Life Findings
Questions and prompts for your quiet time
Go to Page 194 for a deep dive into your Wheel of Life ratings.

Your Birthday Promise Insights
Reflections on Last Year ✴ Intentions for the Year Ahead
Questions and prompts for your quiet time
Go to Page 197 for a deep dive into your Birthday Promise Insights.

Your Birthday Promise Month

Happy Birthday, Aries!

Aries

THE PIONEER

The Initiating First Month of Spring
March 21 – April 20

Aries! You are bold, fearless, and always ready to face any challenges. You're a natural leader with a strong sense of purpose, and are known to take bold actions for the greater good.

Your Birthday Promise – The Aries Personality

With Your Birthday under the Month of Aries, you were born with the will to succeed and experience life on your own terms. You are bold, self-assertive, make the first move, take chances, and actively lead fearlessly. You need to be in control and do not hesitate in taking the driver's seat.

Your personality is strong, commanding, and impossible to ignore. You may even be seen as arrogant. You have the power to defeat. Even so, you are often the reluctant leader because you possess a passionate sense of moral responsibility for others.

Born in Aries, the first Month of the Seasonal Year, you like to be first and want to achieve your goals. You have a strong need to be in competition with everyone, including yourself. You strive to make great things happen.

Often impatient, headstrong, and competitive, you are direct in your approach and like to move forward without any opposition. You are driven to be seen, initiate future possibilities, and potentials and take action. You take the lead and command change.

You operate in the world of facts. You express your vital energy in a very cut and dried manner and do not like long emotionally tiring situations. You tend to feel uncomfortable in the cloudy world of intuition and emotions.

The opinions of others can easily come second to yours. You are less likely to judge people by their words and more likely to judge them by their actions.

You are a trailblazer and need freedom to start a new project whenever the inspiration strikes. You may find yourself stepping away from a crowd or group when you receive an idea or inspiration or want to take action before others do.

You like new beginnings, are enthusiastic, and can be impulsive. You are adventurous, love challenges and rush to explore. You become bored unless you have a regular adrenaline rush to keep you alert and focused.

Over your lifetime, each life experience will in some way be involved in fulfilling your need to be independent, develop self-awareness, and be The Pioneer, The Warrior, The Instigator, The Fearless Daredevil!

Why have you been given these traits? You carry these traits to equip you with what you need to fulfill your individual life's mission as well as the role you have in all of humanity.

Embracing the characteristics of Your Birthday Promise will help you navigate life with authenticity and purpose.

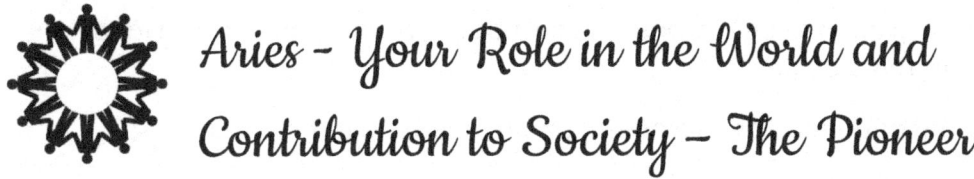

Aries – Your Role in the World and Contribution to Society – The Pioneer

Each of you should use whatever gift you have received to serve others, as faithful stewards of God's grace in its various forms. 1 Peter 4:10

We each have a role to fill for ourselves and for humanity. Born under the Month of Aries, your contribution to the world and society is to lead others into new territories. You are a pioneer and your core purpose in life is to make space for new and better opportunities by shaking things up. You are to inspire others with your unconquerable spirit.

You are never afraid to explore new paths or blaze new trails. Your role is to take the lead in developing anything new for the advancement of society in all fields. You lead the way when it comes to fighting for what you believe and what you want.

With your unconquerable spirit and steadfast determination, your fiery passion ignites the spark of change. You show people that taking risks and being bold can lead to greater rewards. Your ability to take charge and blaze new trails helps guide those around you, motivating them to follow their own paths with confidence. You are a reminder of the importance of courage in the pursuit of success and fulfillment in life.

You inspire people with your courage, enthusiasm, pioneering spirit, and endless energy. While others give up in self-doubt, you rise even higher. You carry a unique ability to motivate and support others, encouraging personal growth and positive change in them. Your energy is contagious and motivates them to do the same.

Aries – What You are Here to Learn

Lessons to Learn to Excel at Your Role

Born under the Month of Aries, throughout your life, you are here to learn:

...what it means to develop self-awareness, independence and the ability to stand up for yourself. Being an individual is crucial for you.

...to analyze why you seek to be the best, as competition is not always the ideal approach for everything in life.

...to weigh the consequences before acting and to evaluate if the cause is worthwhile.

...to balance your need for speed with the calm steadiness required to see things through to completion.

...to develop authentic interest in other peoples' lives.

...to mature your challenging self-involved qualities into greater empathy, compassion, and understanding for others.

... to recover from failure and learn from your mistakes.

...to cultivate bravery and assertiveness while also learning to temper impulsiveness with wisdom.

...to embrace your passions while respecting boundaries.

Aries – Let Your Light Shine

Born under the Month of Aries, the special light you shine is your creative expression and application of your will through your individuality and personality. You have a strong desire to be noticed, take initiative, and create opportunities for the future. You naturally step forward, leading others and encouraging actions that bring about change. Your personality will be used and developed to fulfill your life's purpose.

> *"You are the light of the world. A city set on a hill cannot be hidden. Nor do people light a lamp and put it under a basket, but on a stand, and it gives light to all in the house. In the same way, let your light shine before others, so that they may see your good works and give glory to your Father who is in heaven." Matthew 5:14-16 ESV*

Taking Inventory of the Qualities of Your Life

As you review your life during this time of Your Birthday Month, realize that you are already everything you need to be at this time in your journey. You are not broken or damaged. You are who you were created to be right now. We each have an opportunity to take stock and grow in the gifts and talents we have been given.

At this Yearly time of celebrating Your Birthday, you have an opportunity to get to know and love yourself more fully than you have before. It is a time to trust God in the unfolding and timing of your life and get a better sense of the meaning and purpose of your life.

Aries – My Birthday Life Review

Do you recognize the Birthday Promise qualities in yourself?
If so, are they being used and developed? If you feel you are lacking in any of these, or are out of balance, you can ask the Spirit to help you make the most of them in this New Year. **Go to Page 190 for Your Birthday Life Review questions.**

The Fruit of the Tree of Life for Growth and Healing

Spiritual Fruit Tending - Reflect on These Virtues in Your Life and Rate Them

Fruit of the Spirit	👍 Growing Well?	➕ Needs Fertilizing?	👎 Needs Pruning
Love - A deep and abiding affection and concern for others.			
Joy – A state of happiness and delight, even in the midst of difficult circumstances.			
Peace – A state of tranquility and harmony, both internally and externally.			
Patience – The ability to endure challenges or agitation without becoming angry or upset.			
Kindness – A gentle and kind nature, showing compassion and care for others.			
Goodness – A moral excellence and uprightness of character.			
Faithfulness – Loyalty, trustworthiness, and steadfastness in commitments.			
Gentleness – A kind and considerate demeanor, avoiding harshness or aggression.			
Self-control – The ability to restrain impulses and appetites.			
Long-suffering - The capacity to endure hardship with patience and perseverance.			
Temperance - Moderation and self-restraint in all aspects of life.			
Wisdom - The ability to make sound judgments and decisions based on knowledge and experience.			

Aries - Spiritual Fruit Tending
Questions and prompts for your quiet time
Go to Page 192 for a deep dive into your Fruit of the Tree of Life ratings.

Rate Your Life on the Wheel of Life

Think about the matters of your life shown in the Key Areas of Life Table from Page 13 and evaluate your current level of satisfaction in each Area on a scale from 1-8. The Wheel of Life segments correspond with the topics in this Table. Rate each Area and highlight the number you gave yourself in each Area on the blank Wheel below.

How is your life going? Be sure to rate yourself honestly. This is your reality check. Your honest evaluation will quickly help pinpoint any imbalance. The lower rated areas will show you where you need more focus. No more guessing!

Then, outline the highlighted Wheel of Life ratings with a marker to link them to each other to form a figure within the circle showing the degree of balance in your life, as in the following example.

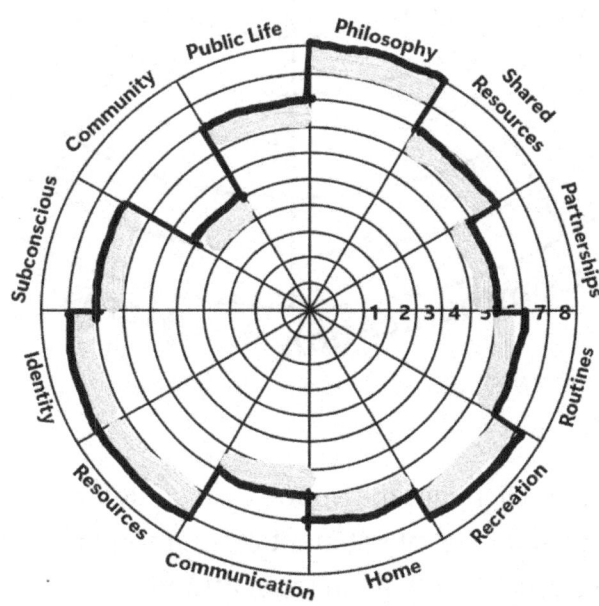

Example of the Wheel of Life with Evaluations

Wheel of Life

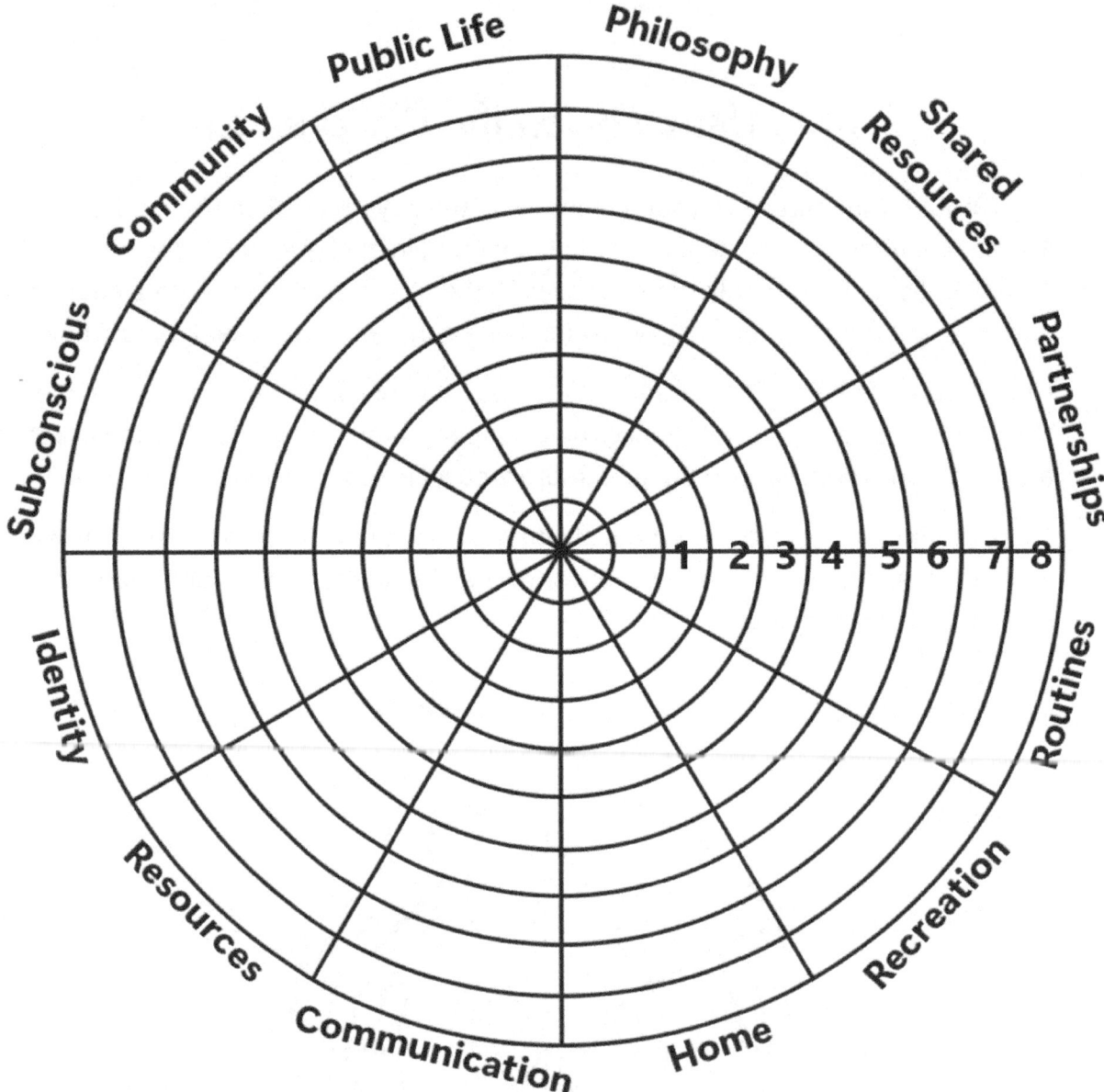

Filling in the Wheel of Life: Highlight the space on a scale from 1-8 under each Key Area that reflects your current level of satisfaction or imbalance in that area, with 8 being the most satisfying and 1 needing the most attention.

Next, interpret the results. How does the balance of your Key Areas of Life look? Analyze the resulting shape to identify the unbalanced areas that require attention and how to improve your satisfaction with them.

With a different color, mark the scores where you would like them to be in the future. Transfer your current and goal scores, as number of stars, to the table below to see where you stand in each category.

Fill in the stars for the Wheel of Life ratings you gave yourself for the current Year and then give yourself stars for next Year's goal.

Wheel of Life Area of Life	How many stars do you give yourself? 1-8 (from your Wheel of Life rating)	
	Current Wheel of Life	Goal for Next Year
Identity	☆☆☆☆☆☆☆☆	☆☆☆☆☆☆☆☆
Resources	☆☆☆☆☆☆☆☆	☆☆☆☆☆☆☆☆
Communication	☆☆☆☆☆☆☆☆	☆☆☆☆☆☆☆☆
Home	☆☆☆☆☆☆☆☆	☆☆☆☆☆☆☆☆
Recreation	☆☆☆☆☆☆☆☆	☆☆☆☆☆☆☆☆
Routines	☆☆☆☆☆☆☆☆	☆☆☆☆☆☆☆☆
Partnerships	☆☆☆☆☆☆☆☆	☆☆☆☆☆☆☆☆
Shared Resources	☆☆☆☆☆☆☆☆	☆☆☆☆☆☆☆☆
Philosophy	☆☆☆☆☆☆☆☆	☆☆☆☆☆☆☆☆
Public Life	☆☆☆☆☆☆☆☆	☆☆☆☆☆☆☆☆
Community	☆☆☆☆☆☆☆☆	☆☆☆☆☆☆☆☆
Subconscious	☆☆☆☆☆☆☆☆	☆☆☆☆☆☆☆☆

Good ratings in the different areas of your life have a major noticeable impact on your overall well-being and quality of life. A well-balanced life can reduce stress and anxiety, improve your mental wellbeing, and make you more productive, and will improve your self-esteem, family life, partnerships, career, and the other areas of

your life. On the other hand, a lack of balance in several areas of your life will cause instability in the other Areas of your life as well.

Make a conscious decision to take better care of your life and make it all that it can be. Start by giving some thought to each Area in the Wheel of Life. What is the status of each one? Reflect on what there is to learn about each one. Work on strengthening the various areas of your life to welcome more peace, purpose, and fulfillment.

Taking Inventory of the Qualities of Your Life

Aries – Deep Dive on Your Wheel of Life Findings
Questions and prompts for your quiet time
Go to Page 194 for a deep dive into your Wheel of Life ratings.

Aries – Your Birthday Promise Insights
Reflections on Last Year ✴ Intentions for the Year Ahead
Questions and prompts for your quiet time
Go to Page 197 for a deep dive into Your Birthday Promise Insights.

God's Birthday Message for Aries....

Dear Aries, as you review your life this Year, remember the unique individual that you have been created to be and the core qualities that you have been given to equip you for your role in life.

Born in the first Month of Spring and the Spiritual Year, Aries represents the spark of creation. As the youngest in order of the Months, you tend to have a strong sense of self. You were given the qualities of leadership, courage, determination, and are known for being first. These equip you for your role as The Pioneer, to fulfill your purpose of leading others into new territories with enthusiasm and a pioneering spirit.

God is calling you to take the lead in initiating anything new for the advancement of society in all fields. Your spiritual journey is about boldness. The time has come to step into your full potential as an innovator. You have the ability to lead boldly and inspire others.

God encourages you to continue initiating new paths and learning to trust your instincts in order to take fearless action and pursue exciting challenges. Your talents are needed to find new solutions.

Your natural courage and inventiveness equip you for greatness. In your determination you need to remember patience. Sometimes you need to pause before charging ahead.

God is calling you to embrace more responsibility and be an inspiration to others. Success will come through remaining persistent in the face of setbacks. You are being forged in the fires of challenge to come out wiser and more discerning.

Spiritual Growth Tips

- ✓ Remember that God is always with you in your battles – you are never alone.
- ✓ Realize that true strength comes not only from action, but from faith.
- ✓ Instead of relying only on your own power lean on your faith when facing obstacles.
- ✓ Before you act, pause and pray. Let the wisdom of God guide your steps.
- ✓ Rather than rushing ahead without thinking, trust in God's timing.

💡 Aries – Take-Aways from Your Deep Dives

Now that you have reflected, meditated, and received insight about all the Areas of Your Life from the Spirit during your time of prayer, meditation, and meeting with the Spirit, journal the revelations, words, and directions that come to mind for the coming Year.

What have you learned about yourself?

What have you learned about God?

What have you learned about the direction and plan for your life?

Finally – Submit Your Plans to God

While we can meet with the Lord, get direction, and set our intentions for the New Year, we ultimately need to submit them to God's Will and timing. We most likely will not understand exactly how things will play out, but we will recognize the general road map showing the Areas of our Life that are being brought into alignment with His ways. While we are honing our gifts and abilities, He will open doors and close doors accordingly and we will flow along with Him on this Year's journey.

Many are the plans in a person's heart, but it is the LORD's purpose that prevails. Proverbs 19:21

A man's heart plans his course, but the LORD determines his steps. Proverbs 16:9 BSB

And we know that in all things God works for the good of those who love him, who have been called according to his purpose. Romans 8:28

To everything there is a season, and a time to every purpose under the heaven: A time to be born, and a time to die; a time to plant, and a time to pluck up that which is planted... Ecclesiastes 3:1-2 NKJV

Biblical Affirmations to Declare Over Your Life

In addition to the specific traits you have been given to fulfill your God-given purpose, there are fundamental truths about who God created you to be. These affirmations confirm the qualities you have been given for your underlying relationship and identity through Him.

Birthday affirmations, declarations, and prayers go beyond mere wishes; they are faith-filled expressions that align with God's Word that speak life, purpose, encouragement, and Divine blessing. The words we speak have power, and for those on a spiritual path, it is important to declare what God says about us. While the world may try to label us by our past, errors, or situations, we should instead rely on the truth found in God's Word.

Use these affirmations, supported by Scripture, to renew your mind, strengthen your faith, and walk confidently in your God-given identity. Repeat them daily and let the truth of His promises transform your life!

Who Am I?

- I am a child of God and an heir to His promises. (Romans 8:17)
- I am fearfully and wonderfully made. (Psalm 139:14)
- I am God's masterpiece, created for good works. (Ephesians 2:10)
- I am chosen, holy, and dearly loved by God. (Colossians 3:12)
- I am bold because the Lord is my helper. (Hebrews 13:6)
- I am confident that God will finish the good work He started in me. (Philippians 1:6)

Promises of God

- This is the day the Lord has made; I will rejoice and be glad in it. (Psalm 118:24)
- Nothing can separate me from God's love. (Romans 8:38-39)
- God's plans for me are good, filled with hope and a future. (Jeremiah 29:11)
- God directs my steps and makes my paths straight. (Proverbs 3:5-6)
- God's power works in me to accomplish far more than I can imagine. (Ephesians 3:20)
- The Lord is faithful to keep His promises to me. (Deuteronomy 7:9)
- The Lord makes everything beautiful in His time. (Ecclesiastes 3:11)

I Am – Aries Personality Declarations

- ♥ I am a leader.
- ♥ I am courageous, naturally ambitious, passionate, and take risks.
- ♥ I want to be first, have an indomitable spirit, unwavering determination, and am headstrong and willful.
- ♥ I am an initiator that is not afraid to take risks.
- ♥ I am determined, bold, and confident .
- ♥ I am not afraid to go after what I want.
- ♥ I stand up for what I believe in.
- ♥ I am determined to succeed.
- ♥ I am able to recover after disasters.
- ♥ I act on my Spirit inspired ideas.
- ♥ I am grateful for all that I have accomplished and all that I will achieve.
- ♥ I am responsible for myself.

Aries – Reminders for Growth and Balance

- + Nothing will keep me down for long.
- + My greatest strengths are my passion and drive.
- + I practice patience and slowing down.
- + I pause before reacting.
- + I am learning anger management skills.
- + I think carefully about the consequences of decisions.
- + I cultivate empathy and self-awareness.
- + I balance self-focus with consideration for others.

And there is more!

For more insight into the traits of Aries go to, "Nourishment from the Month of Aries," in Part Two, *Journey Around the Wheel of the Year*.

Happy Birthday, Taurus!

Taurus

The Stabilizer

The Fixed Middle Month of Spring
April 21 – May 20

Taurus! Your reliability and love for stability give you one of the most grounded roles. You are determined and steadfast, with a strong connection to the earth and a deep appreciation for beauty.

Your Birthday Promise - The Taurus Personality

With Your Birthday under the Month of Taurus, you were born to gather, assimilate, collect, build, stabilize, and create long-term success.

You are a good steward of all things under your care and are considered exceptionally reliable and thorough in all your activities. You have the ability to sense what is worth investing in, be it careers, relationships, or personal growth. You operate in a matter-of-fact way to seek tangible, physical results through steady and stable efforts and hard work.

You were born to find comfort and gratification. However, unlike those who seek immediate results, you understand good things take time. When you sense something is right for you, you can make it happen. You have a powerful inner guidance system.

You find happiness easily because you are not competitive. Your relaxed attitude and common sense ultimately lead you towards fulfilment, even though you are not the number one, even though you do not move quickly. Your patience and persistence produce strong, steadfast, sustainable efforts that can withstand any pitfalls and ultimately make your dreams a reality.

Of all the Months, Taurus has the most common sense. You are good at offering helpful advice and instinctively know the needs of those you love. You are practical and are concerned with the basic needs of physical life, such as food, shelter, love, and the money to buy what is needed. What is needed is determined by your individual personal values and whether you are being practical or lavish.

You tend to be an eternal optimist. Nothing seems to get you upset. However, when pushed to a certain point, you have a strong temper. You are fiercely loyal and value loyalty in others. You are extremely intolerant of disloyalty.

You enjoy worldly comforts and can get too comfortable and stagnate, not wanting to change in a given situation. You like to be at home in your own familiar environment. You seek stability in all realms of life be it physical, emotional, or spiritual. You want peace and harmony and stay away from disruptive situations.

You dislike changes in general and once you have taken care of the few major unavoidable challenges in the course of your life, you are back on track. Once you have made a decision, nothing, nor anyone, can make you change your mind. Because of your hard-headedness you can often come across as unsentimental.

Taurus' basic impulse is acquisition. You have great potential for accumulating resources. You tend to be materialistic in order to protect yourself. You can be possessive and keep things for life. If unbalanced, you can become a pack rat holding on to all your possessions.

Each life experience over your lifetime will in some way be involved in fulfilling your need to be resourceful, productive, and stable to be The Stabilizer, The Builder, and The Patient Strategist.

Why have you been given these traits? You carry these traits to equip you with what you need to fulfill your individual life's mission as well as the role you have in all of humanity.

Embracing the characteristics of Your Birthday Promise will help you navigate life with authenticity and purpose.

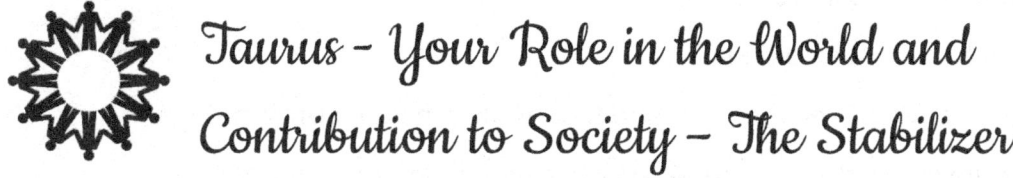

Taurus – Your Role in the World and Contribution to Society – The Stabilizer

Each of you should use whatever gift you have received to serve others as faithful stewards of God's grace in its various forms. 1 Peter 4:10

We each have a role to fill for ourselves and for humanity. Born under the Month of Taurus, your contribution to society is to be a dependable foundation for yourself and others. You are the steady, constant presence that people can rely on. Your Taurus purpose is focused on establishing predictability in an unstable world.

Your purpose in life is to teach people the value of remaining firmly rooted in the grounds of honesty and of staying focused on their goals with patience and perseverance. You motivate people to work hard and honestly, and to avoid taking short cuts to success.

Your role is designed to create more beauty, peace, and stability in life. You have a gift of creating a safe and comfortable space for others. Through acts of kindness and care you reflect God's love. You have a natural ability to restore balance and promote well-being.

The Month of Taurus indicates you may be good at handling and making money, and would be excellent at advising others on how to improve their financial matters.

Taurus – What You are Here to Learn

Lessons to Learn to Excel at Your Role

Born under the Month of Taurus, throughout your life, you are here to learn:

- to embrace change as a path to growth.

- to avoid clinging stubbornly to your beliefs and ideals.

- to cultivate your sense of security.

- to value your worth without proving it through possessions.

- to recognize the value of vulnerability.

- to lessen the attachment to comfort and certainty.

- to stay open to new possibilities.

- to slow down, cultivate awareness, and find beauty in your surroundings.

- to build a solid foundation in your life while savoring every moment.

Taurus – Let Your Light Shine

Born under the Month of Taurus, the special light you shine is through constructive and beneficial ways to generate and use your resources. You seek physical, tangible results and work steadily and practically to achieve them. Your resources will be used and developed to fulfill your life purpose.

> *"You are the light of the world. A city set on a hill cannot be hidden. Nor do people light a lamp and put it under a basket, but on a stand, and it gives light to all in the house. In the same way, let your light shine before others, so that they may see your good works and give glory to your Father who is in heaven." Matthew 5:14-16 ESV*

 # Taking Inventory of the Qualities of Your Life

As you review your life during this time of Your Birthday Month, realize that you are already everything you need to be at this time in your journey. You are not broken or damaged. You are who you were created to be right now. We each have an opportunity to take stock and grow in the gifts and talents we have been given.

At this Yearly time of celebrating Your Birthday, you have an opportunity to get to know and love yourself more fully than you have before. It is a time to trust God in the unfolding and timing of your life and get a better sense of the meaning and purpose of your life.

 ## Taurus – My Birthday Life Review

Do you recognize the Birthday Promise qualities in yourself?
If so, are they being used and developed? If you feel you are lacking in any of these, or are out of balance, you can ask the Spirit to help you make the most of them in this New Year. **Go to Page 190 for Your Birthday Life Review questions.**

The Fruit of the Tree of Life for Growth and Healing

Spiritual Fruit Tending - Reflect on These Virtues in Your Life and Rate Them

Fruit of the Spirit	👍 Growing Well?	➕ Needs Fertilizing?	👎 Needs Pruning
Love - A deep and abiding affection and concern for others.			
Joy – A state of happiness and delight, even in the midst of difficult circumstances.			
Peace – A state of tranquility and harmony, both internally and externally.			
Patience – The ability to endure challenges or agitation without becoming angry or upset.			
Kindness – A gentle and kind nature, showing compassion and care for others.			
Goodness – A moral excellence and uprightness of character.			
Faithfulness – Loyalty, trustworthiness, and steadfastness in commitments.			
Gentleness – A kind and considerate demeanor, avoiding harshness or aggression.			
Self-control – The ability to restrain impulses and appetites.			
Long-suffering - The capacity to endure hardship with patience and perseverance.			
Temperence - Moderation and self-restraint in all aspects of life.			
Wisdom - The ability to make sound judgments and decisions based on knowledge and experience.			

Taurus - Spiritual Fruit Tending
Questions and prompts for your quiet time
Go to Page 192 for a deep dive into your Fruit of the Tree of Life ratings.

Rate Your Life on the Wheel of Life

Think about the matters of your life shown in the Key Areas of Life Table from Page 13 and evaluate your current level of satisfaction in each Area on a scale from 1-8. The Wheel of Life segments correspond with the topics in this Table. Rate each Area and highlight the number you gave yourself in each Area on the blank Wheel below.

How is your life going? Be sure to rate yourself honestly. This is your reality check. Your honest evaluation will quickly help pinpoint any imbalance. The lower rated areas will show you where you need more focus. No more guessing!

Then, outline the highlighted Wheel of Life ratings with a marker to link them to each other to form a figure within the circle showing the degree of balance in your life, as in the following example.

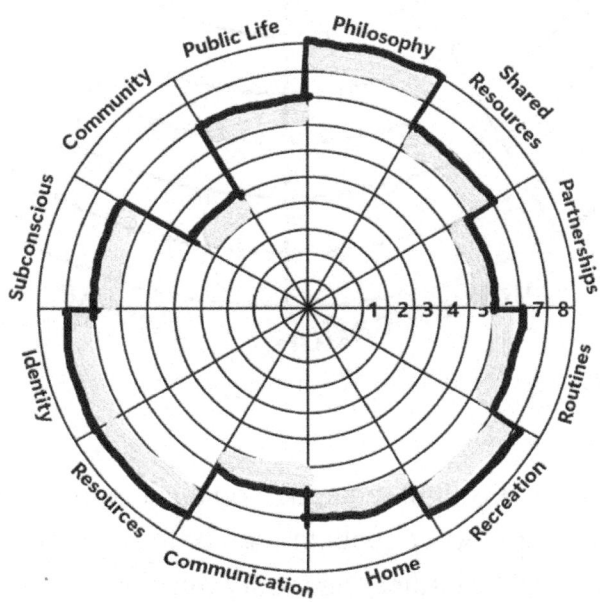

Example of the Wheel of Life with Evaluations

Wheel of Life

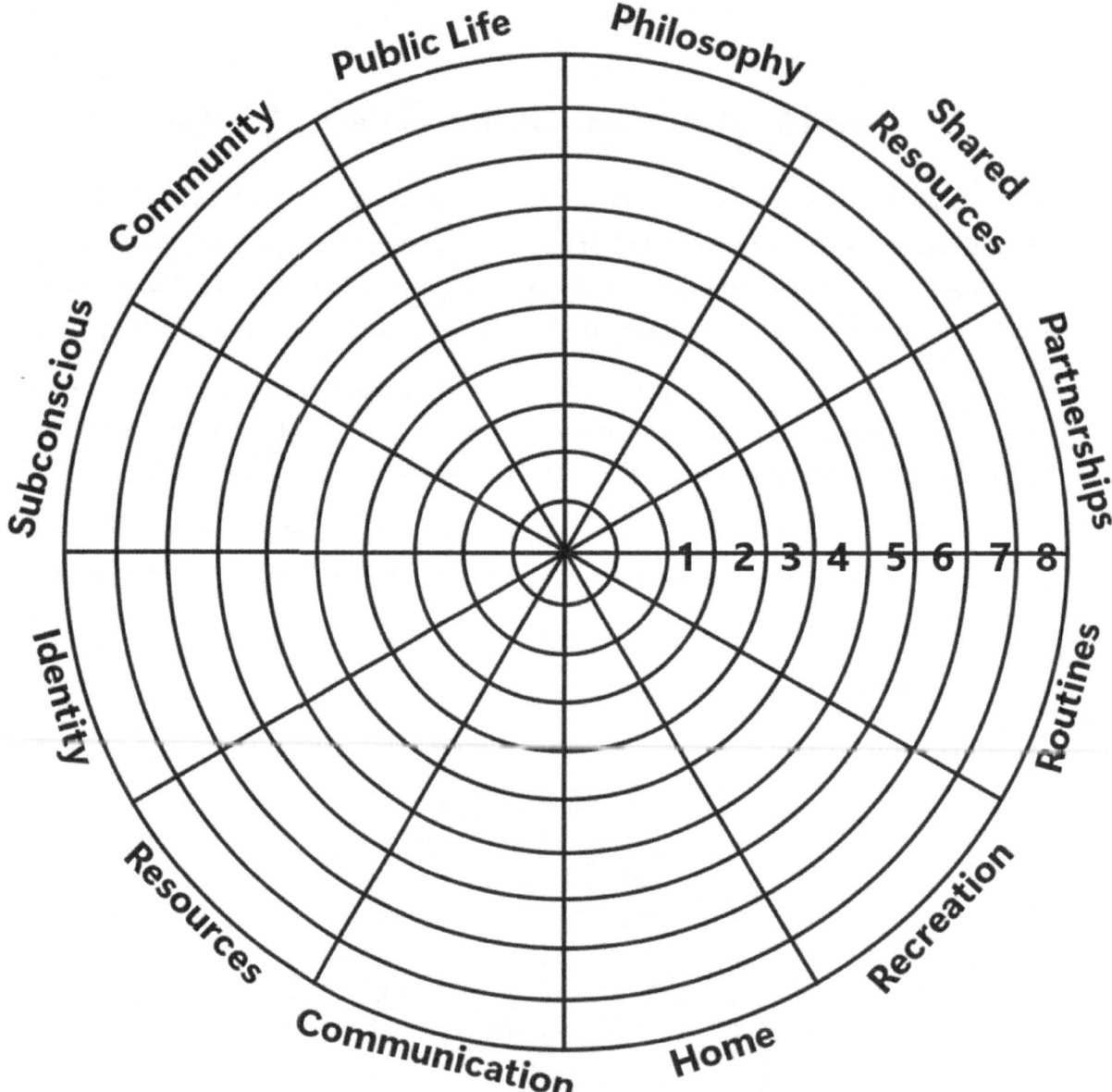

Filling in the Wheel of Life: Highlight the space on a scale from 1-8 under each Key Area that reflects your current level of satisfaction or imbalance in that area, with 8 being the most satisfying and 1 needing the most attention.

Next, interpret the results. How does the balance of your Key Areas of Life look? Analyze the resulting shape to identify the unbalanced areas that require attention and how to improve your satisfaction with them.

With a different color, mark the scores where you would like them to be in the future. Transfer your current and goal scores, as number of stars, to the table below to see where you stand in each category.

Fill in the stars for the Wheel of Life ratings you gave yourself for the current Year and then give yourself stars for next Year's goal.

Wheel of Life Area of Life	How many stars do you give yourself? 1-8 (from your Wheel of Life rating)	
	Current Wheel of Life	Goal for Next Year
Identity	☆☆☆☆☆☆☆☆	☆☆☆☆☆☆☆☆
Resources	☆☆☆☆☆☆☆☆	☆☆☆☆☆☆☆☆
Communication	☆☆☆☆☆☆☆☆	☆☆☆☆☆☆☆☆
Home	☆☆☆☆☆☆☆☆	☆☆☆☆☆☆☆☆
Recreation	☆☆☆☆☆☆☆☆	☆☆☆☆☆☆☆☆
Routines	☆☆☆☆☆☆☆☆	☆☆☆☆☆☆☆☆
Partnerships	☆☆☆☆☆☆☆☆	☆☆☆☆☆☆☆☆
Shared Resources	☆☆☆☆☆☆☆☆	☆☆☆☆☆☆☆☆
Philosophy	☆☆☆☆☆☆☆☆	☆☆☆☆☆☆☆☆
Public Life	☆☆☆☆☆☆☆☆	☆☆☆☆☆☆☆☆
Community	☆☆☆☆☆☆☆☆	☆☆☆☆☆☆☆☆
Subconscious	☆☆☆☆☆☆☆☆	☆☆☆☆☆☆☆☆

Good ratings in the different areas of your life have a major noticeable impact on your overall well-being and quality of life. A well-balanced life can reduce stress and anxiety, improve your mental wellbeing, and make you more productive, and will improve your self-esteem, family life, partnerships, career, and the other areas of

your life. On the other hand, a lack of balance in several areas of your life will cause instability in the other Areas of your life as well.

Make a conscious decision to take better care of your life and make it all that it can be. Start by giving some thought to each Area in the Wheel of Life. What is the status of each one? Reflect on what there is to learn about each one. Work on strengthening the various areas of your life to welcome more peace, purpose, and fulfillment.

 ## Taking Inventory of the Qualities of Your Life

Taurus – Deep Dive on Your Wheel of Life Findings
Questions and prompts for your quiet time
Go to Page 194 for a deep dive into your Wheel of Life ratings.

Taurus – Your Birthday Promise Insights
Reflections on Last Year ✴ Intentions for the Year Ahead
Questions and prompts for your quiet time
Go to Page 197 for a deep dive into Your Birthday Promise Insights.

God's Birthday Message for Taurus...

Dear Taurus, as you review your life this Year, remember the unique individual that you have been created to be and the core qualities that you have been given to equip you for your role in life.

Born in Taurus, the second Month of Spring, you were given the qualities of stability and predictability that give you a steadfast and reliable spirit. These equip you for your role as The Stabilizer, to fulfill your purpose of being consistent in your efforts, holding your ground, and being the rock for those around you.

Your loyalty, patience, and commitment are much needed traits. You are unswerving in your efforts to reach your goals. Your fixed nature gives you a streak of stubbornness.

God encourages you to enjoy life's simple pleasures of the physical world while keeping your connection to the spiritual. You appreciate nature, art, and sensory experiences, so being in nature, walking barefoot and gardening will help you to keep yourself grounded.

While you value your relationships and belongings and are a good steward of what you are responsible for, God wants you to value your own worth. By loving yourself, you can better share that love with others.

Your stubbornness can be beneficial, but God encourages you to be careful of becoming too inflexible. It is important to be receptive to new ideas, viewpoints, and methods because the world is constantly changing. Adaptability can help prevent you from being left behind. You may be a slow learner, but once you grasp something you retain it.

Spiritual Growth Tips

✓ Be open to God's leading in new directions, even when they come as a surprise.

✓ Develop inner stability by working on emotional and physical healing.

✓ Remember that success involves both effort and faith in God's plan.

✓ Release material possessions and direct your attention toward spiritual richness.

✓ Practice surrendering control in your life.

💡 Taurus – Take-Aways from Your Deep Dives

Now that you have reflected, meditated, and received insight from the Spirit from your time of prayer, meditation, and meeting with the Spirit about all Areas of Your Life, journal the revelations, words, and directions that come to mind for the coming Year.

What have you learned about yourself?

What have you learned about God?

What have you learned about the direction and plan for your life?

Finally – Submit Your Plans to God

While we can meet with the Lord and get direction and set intentions for the New Year, we ultimately need to submit to His Will and timing. We may not understand how things play out, but we will recognize areas of our life that we can intentionally bring into alignment with His ways. While we are honing our gifts and abilities, He will open doors and close doors accordingly and we will flow along with Him on this Year's journey.

Many are the plans in a person's heart, but it is the LORD's purpose that prevails.
Proverbs 19:21

A man's heart plans his course, but the LORD determines his steps.
Proverbs 16:9 BSB

And we know that in all things God works for the good of those who love him, who have been called according to his purpose. Romans 8:28

To everything there is a season, and a time to every purpose under the heaven: A time to be born, and a time to die; a time to plant, and a time to pluck up that which is planted... Ecclesiastes 3:1-2 NKJV

Biblical Affirmations to Declare Over Your Life

In addition to the specific traits you have been given to fulfill your God-given purpose, there are underlying truths about who God created you to be. These affirmations confirm the qualities you have been given for your underlying relationship and identity through Him.

Birthday affirmations, declarations, and prayers go beyond mere wishes; they are faith-filled expressions that align with God's Word that speak life, purpose, encouragement, and Divine blessing. The words we speak have power, and for those on a spiritual path, it is important to declare what God says about us. While the world may try to label us by our past, errors, or situations, we should instead rely on the truth found in God's Word.

Use these affirmations, supported by Scripture, to renew your mind, strengthen your faith and walk confidently in your God-given identity. Repeat them daily and let the truth of His promises transform your life!

Who Am I?

- I am a child of God and an heir to His promises. (Romans 8:17)
- I am fearfully and wonderfully made. (Psalm 139:14)
- I am God's masterpiece, created for good works. (Ephesians 2:10)
- I am chosen, holy, and dearly loved by God. (Colossians 3:12)
- I am bold because the Lord is my helper. (Hebrews 13:6)
- I am confident that God will finish the good work He started in me. (Philippians 1:6)

Promises of God

- This is the day the Lord has made; I will rejoice and be glad in it. (Psalm 118:24)
- Nothing can separate me from God's love. (Romans 8:38-39)
- God's plans for me are good, filled with hope and a future. (Jeremiah 29:11)
- God directs my steps and makes my paths straight. (Proverbs 3:5-6)
- God's power works in me to accomplish far more than I can imagine. (Ephesians 3:20)
- The Lord is faithful to keep His promises to me. (Deuteronomy 7:9)
- The Lord makes everything beautiful in His time. (Ecclesiastes 3:11)

I Am – Taurus Personality Declarations

- ♥ I am a stabilizer.
- ♥ I am steadfast, grounded, and practical.
- ♥ I am responsible, stable, and devoted.
- ♥ I am constant and tenacious.
- ♥ I am slow to anger.
- ♥ I am focused and productive.
- ♥ I am patient and persevere.
- ♥ I am a lover of nature.
- ♥ I have common sense.
- ♥ I am good at offering advice.

Taurus – Reminders for Growth and Balance

- + I am strong and push through any challenges.
- + I am worthy of success and financial security.
- + I forgive others as well as myself.
- + I realize change is a path to growth.
- + I remain open to new possibilities.
- + I honor my worth without proving it through my possessions.
- + I heal by being in nature.
- + I appreciate the beauty and pleasures of my life.
- + I enjoy being creative and working with my hands.
- + I value the spiritual values of life.
- + I learn to take other people's views into consideration.

And there is more!

For more insight into the traits of Taurus go to, "Nourishment from the Month of Taurus," in Part Two, *Journey Around the Wheel of the Year*.

Happy Birthday, Gemini!

The Communicator

The Transitional Last Month of Spring
May 21 – June 20

Gemini! You are curious, talkative, and a seeker of every day knowledge. With your excellent communication and social skills, as well as your versatile nature, you love to connect with people to debate, share ideas, and build bridges.

Your Birthday Promise - The Gemini Personality

With Your Birthday under the Month of Gemini, you were born to be a student of life and communicate to others the many bits of knowledge you have acquired. You are curious about all things, not only learning new information but also sharing it.

Born under the Month of Gemini you are interested in the world of ideas. You are an instinctive communicator and can easily exchange ideas. You associate well with people and are popular. You can adapt to any situation you find yourself in, and you have the capacity to stay objective while also enjoying the lighter side of life.

You spend a lot of time asking questions and answering them. Your curiosity and your quick-wittedness are insatiable. Your mind is in constant motion, hopping from one topic to another, solving problems, and accumulating anecdotes and knowledge within a short range of time. Your mind moves faster than most.

Driven by multiple ideas, potentialities, and wishes, Gemini's are transparent and intellectually motivated. You are inquisitive and learn quickly. Quickly is the way to describe the way you decide, respond, and change. You go with the flow.

Your mobility is primarily mental, allowing you to engage in various activities that may not be related. You can collect information and react to it at the same time. Your exceptional capability to adapt and shift your energy swiftly is frequently overlooked. Your mental agility is unparalleled and your mental database is filled with a lot of information.

You have a short attention span and can be easily distracted. As long as there is movement and engagement with others, your mind remains active and everything functions well. You thrive on constant change, whether it is switching jobs, relationships, or living situations.

Gemini is the 'jack of all trades master of none' and knows a little about a lot of things. You can be opinionated and hold your own opinion high. You cultivate a wide variety of interests. This makes you a fine teacher because of the richness of information you possess and your ability to recall it.

Unlike those born in other Months that may become entangled in their emotions or circumstances, Gemini possesses a natural talent for reframing situations, adapting quickly, and finding opportunities where others see obstacles.

Gemini is sociable and interacts with many people and does not want to deal with jealousy or possessiveness. They have a great independent streak.

There are always two sides to your Gemini nature. You are hard to pin down, because as soon as it is decided you are one way, you demonstrate the totally opposite personality. You have an amazing mind for remembering the past and outstanding understanding of current events.

The Month of Gemini is associated with communication, curiosity and intellect. It is natural for you to express yourself and want to go places. You love traveling and learning new things.

Each life experience over your lifetime will in some way be involved in fulfilling your need to communicate with and learn from others and be The Communicator, The Social Butterfly, and The Jack-of-all-Trades.

Why have you been given these traits? You carry these traits to equip you with what you need to fulfill your individual life's mission as well as the role you have in all of humanity.

Embracing the characteristics of Your Birthday Promise will help you navigate life with authenticity and purpose.

Gemini - Your Role in the World and Contribution to Society - The Communicator

Each of you should use whatever gift you have received to serve others as faithful stewards of God's grace in its various forms. 1 Peter 4:10

We each have a role to fill for ourselves and for humanity. Born under the Month of Gemini, your contribution to society is to spread awareness and unite people. You unwittingly act as the glue that unites all mankind through your communication skills.

You were born to be a great communicator conveying information and telling stories. Your curiosity and quick wit enable you to share knowledge in a way that is both engaging and enlightening. Your purpose is to liberate people from the stagnancy of ignorance and routine, and lead them to new and fresh insights.

You help others understand complex ideas and encourage learning. You use your words to share the truth to inspire, educate, and stimulate others. By being able to grasp different viewpoints, you build connections and earn respect.

Your gift is used to pass information on to the next generation while at the same time striving to upgrade your skills for even more challenging yet rewarding opportunities. You must keep learning and apply your gift of communication to inspire and uplift other people.

Gemini – What You are Here to Learn
Lessons to Learn to Excel at Your Role

Born under the Month of Gemini, throughout your life, you are here to learn:

...to stop over-thinking, over-evaluating, over-processing.

...to learn the power of words, thoughts, and messages.

...to avoid speaking before considering the effect your words may have.

...to become more trusting of internal messages.

...to intentionally focus on long-term priorities.

...to consciously remind yourself to come into the present.

...the pleasure of commitment in order to grow and become a loyal and devoted friend.

Gemini – Let Your Light Shine

Born under the Month of Gemini, the special light you shine is through your ability to express and communicate your ideas and knowledge. You are motivated by multiple ideas, potentialities, and wishes. You are intellectually driven and seek to shift minds and perspectives. Your communication and intellect will be used and developed to fulfill your life's purpose.

> "You are the light of the world. A city set on a hill cannot be hidden. Nor do people light a lamp and put it under a basket, but on a stand, and it gives light to all in the house. In the same way, let your light shine before others, so that they may see your good works and give glory to your Father who is in heaven." *Matthew 5:14-16 ESV*

Taking Inventory of the Qualities of Your Life

As you review your life during this time of Your Birthday Month, realize that you are already everything you need to be at this time in your journey. You are not broken or damaged. You are who you were created to be right now. We each have an opportunity to take stock and grow in the gifts and talents we have been given.

At this Yearly time of celebrating Your Birthday, you have an opportunity to get to know and love yourself more fully than you have before. It is a time to trust God in the unfolding and timing of your life and get a better sense of the meaning and purpose of your life.

Gemini – My Birthday Life Review

Do you recognize the Birthday Promise qualities in yourself?
If so, are they being used and developed? If you feel you are lacking in any of these, or are out of balance, you can ask the Spirit to help you make the most of them in this New Year. **Go to Page 190 for Your Birthday Life Review questions.**

The Fruit of the Tree of Life for Growth and Healing

Spiritual Fruit Tending - Reflect on These Virtues in Your Life and Rate Them

Fruit of the Spirit	👍 Growing Well?	➕ Needs Fertilizing?	👎 Needs Pruning
Love - A deep and abiding affection and concern for others.			
Joy – A state of happiness and delight, even in the midst of difficult circumstances.			
Peace – A state of tranquility and harmony, both internally and externally.			
Patience – The ability to endure challenges or agitation without becoming angry or upset.			
Kindness – A gentle and kind nature, showing compassion and care for others.			
Goodness – A moral excellence and uprightness of character.			
Faithfulness – Loyalty, trustworthiness, and steadfastness in commitments.			
Gentleness – A kind and considerate demeanor, avoiding harshness or aggression.			
Self-control – The ability to restrain impulses and appetites.			
Long-suffering - The capacity to endure hardship with patience and perseverance.			
Temperence - Moderation and self-restraint in all aspects of life.			
Wisdom - The ability to make sound judgments and decisions based on knowledge and experience.			

Gemini - Spiritual Fruit Tending
Questions and prompts for your quiet time
Go to Page 192 for a deep dive into your Fruit of the Tree of Life ratings.

Rate Your Life on the Wheel of Life

Think about the matters of your life shown in the Key Areas of Life Table from Page 13 and evaluate your current level of satisfaction in each Area on a scale from 1-8. The Wheel of Life segments correspond with the topics in this Table. Rate each Area and highlight the number you gave yourself in each Area on the blank Wheel below.

How is your life going? Be sure to rate yourself honestly. This is your reality check. Your honest evaluation will quickly help pinpoint any imbalance. The lower rated areas will show you where you need more focus. No more guessing!

Then, outline the highlighted Wheel of Life ratings with a marker to link them to each other to form a figure within the circle showing the degree of balance in your life, as in the following example.

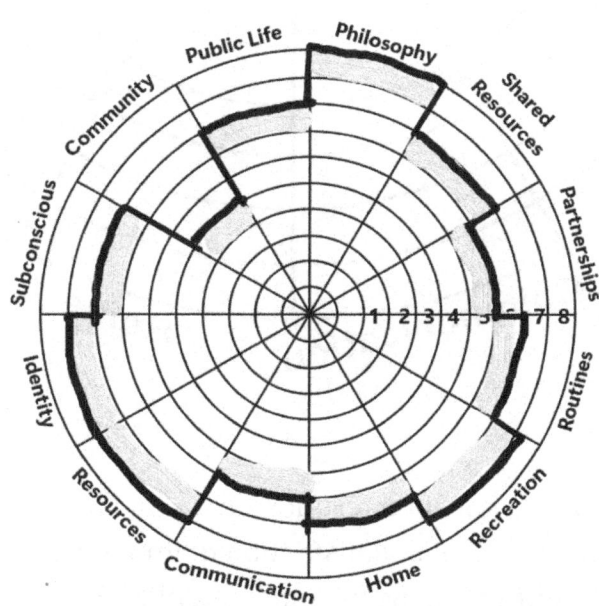

Example of the Wheel of Life with Evaluations

55

Wheel of Life

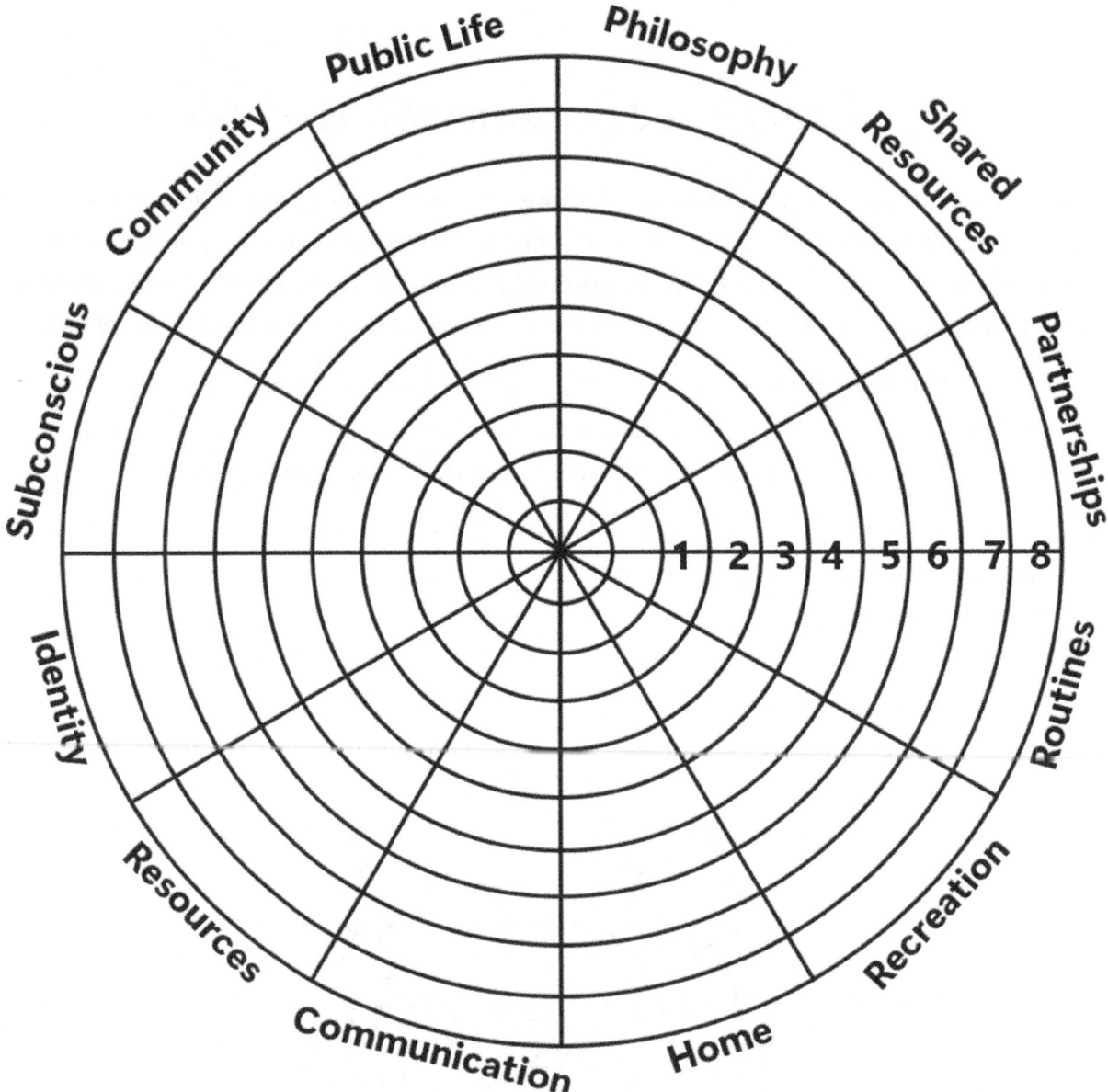

Filling in the Wheel of Life: Highlight the space on a scale from 1-8 under each Key Area that reflects your current level of satisfaction or imbalance in that area, with 8 being the most satisfying and 1 needing the most attention.

Next, interpret the results. How does the balance of your Key Areas of Life look? Analyze the resulting shape to identify the unbalanced areas that require attention and how to improve your satisfaction with them.

With a different color, mark the scores where you would like them to be in the future. Transfer your current and goal scores, as number of stars, to the table below to see where you stand in each category.

Fill in the stars for the Wheel of Life ratings you gave yourself for the current Year and then give yourself stars for next Year's goal.

Wheel of Life Area of Life	How many stars do you give yourself? 1-8 (from your Wheel of Life rating)	
	Current Wheel of Life	Goal for Next Year
Identity	☆☆☆☆☆☆☆☆	☆☆☆☆☆☆☆☆
Resources	☆☆☆☆☆☆☆☆	☆☆☆☆☆☆☆☆
Communication	☆☆☆☆☆☆☆☆	☆☆☆☆☆☆☆☆
Home	☆☆☆☆☆☆☆☆	☆☆☆☆☆☆☆☆
Recreation	☆☆☆☆☆☆☆☆	☆☆☆☆☆☆☆☆
Routines	☆☆☆☆☆☆☆☆	☆☆☆☆☆☆☆☆
Partnerships	☆☆☆☆☆☆☆☆	☆☆☆☆☆☆☆☆
Shared Resources	☆☆☆☆☆☆☆☆	☆☆☆☆☆☆☆☆
Philosophy	☆☆☆☆☆☆☆☆	☆☆☆☆☆☆☆☆
Public Life	☆☆☆☆☆☆☆☆	☆☆☆☆☆☆☆☆
Community	☆☆☆☆☆☆☆☆	☆☆☆☆☆☆☆☆
Subconscious	☆☆☆☆☆☆☆☆	☆☆☆☆☆☆☆☆

Good ratings in the different areas of your life have a major noticeable impact on your overall well-being and quality of life. A well-balanced life can reduce stress and anxiety, improve your mental wellbeing, and make you more productive, and will improve your self-esteem, family life, partnerships, career, and the other areas of

your life. On the other hand, a lack of balance in several areas of your life will cause instability in the other Areas of your life as well.

Make a conscious decision to take better care of your life and make it all that it can be. Start by giving some thought to each Area in the Wheel of Life. What is the status of each one? Reflect on what there is to learn about each one. Work on strengthening the various areas of your life to welcome more peace, purpose, and fulfillment.

Taking Inventory of the Qualities of Your Life

Gemini – Deep Dive on Your Wheel of Life Findings
Questions and prompts for your quiet time
Go to Page 194 for a deep dive into your Wheel of Life ratings.

Gemini – Your Birthday Promise Insights
Reflections on Last Year ✶ Intentions for the Year Ahead
Questions and prompts for your quiet time
Go to Page 197 for a deep dive into Your Birthday Promise Insights.

God's Birthday Message for Gemini...

Dear Gemini, as you review your life this Year, remember the unique individual that you have been created to be and the core qualities that you have been given to equip you for your role in life.

Born in Gemini, the third Month of Spring, you were given the qualities of learning and communication to equip you for your role of The Communicator, to fulfill your purpose of educating and uniting others. You are known for being curious, adaptable, outgoing, with a social spirit. You thrive on learning and sharing wisdom.

God is calling you to master your mental energy to be a powerhouse in communication and intellectual pursuits. Your natural curiosity, wit, intellectual depthm, and sociability give you the ability to connect with others to deliver your messages through words and ideas.

God encourages you to approach life with an active, and engaged mind that stays open and curious about the world. Avoid scattering your mental energy and diluting your efforts. Learn to focus and continue to use your curious mind to expand your knowledge and experiences more effectively.

God's message to you is to not become so focused on accumulating facts and ideas that you overlook their deeper meaning. Remain adaptable, open, and attentive to deeper insights about yourself and the world around you. When you share your discoveries with others, you can foster understanding, unity, and progress.

Spiritual Growth Tips

✓ Keep learning.

✓ Speak with kindness and lift others up.

✓ Avoid engaging in gossip or unnecessary arguments.

✓ Be mindful of how your words impact those around you, sometimes words can be reckless.

✓ Use your gift of communication to spread wisdom and faith.

✓ Before saying something, ask yourself: "Will these words bring truth and light?" If not, rethink them!

💡 Gemini – Take-Aways from Your Deep Dives

Now that you have reflected, meditated, and received insight from the Spirit from your time of prayer, meditation, and meeting with the Spirit about all Areas of Your Life, journal the revelations, words, and directions that come to mind for the coming Year.

What have you learned about yourself?

What have you learned about God?

What have you learned about the direction and plan for your life?

Finally – Submit Your Plans to God

While we can meet with the Lord and get direction and set intentions for the New Year, we ultimately need to submit to His Will and timing. We may not understand how things play out, but we will recognize areas of our life that we can intentionally bring into alignment with His ways. While we are honing our gifts and abilities, He will open doors and close doors accordingly and we will flow along with Him on this Year's journey.

> *Many are the plans in a person's heart, but it is the LORD's purpose that prevails.*
> *Proverbs 19:21*

> *A man's heart plans his course, but the LORD determines his steps.*
> *Proverbs 16:9 BSB*

> *And we know that in all things God works for the good of those who love him, who have been called according to his purpose. Romans 8:28*

> *To everything there is a season, and a time to every purpose under the heaven: A time to be born, and a time to die; a time to plant, and a time to pluck up that which is planted... Ecclesiastes 3:1-2 NKJV*

Biblical Affirmations to Declare Over Your Life

In addition to the specific traits you have been given to fulfill your God-given purpose, there are underlying truths about who God created you to be. These affirmations confirm the qualities you have been given for your underlying relationship and identity through Him.

Birthday affirmations, declarations, and prayers go beyond mere wishes; they are faith-filled expressions that align with God's Word that speak life, purpose, encouragement, and Divine blessing. The words we speak have power, and for those on a spiritual path, it is important to declare what God says about us. While the world may try to label us by our past, errors, or situations, we should instead rely on the truth found in God's Word.

Use these affirmations, supported by Scripture, to renew your mind, strengthen your faith and walk confidently in your God-given identity. Repeat them daily and let the truth of His promises transform your life!

Who Am I?

- I am a child of God and an heir to His promises. (Romans 8:17)
- I am fearfully and wonderfully made. (Psalm 139:14)
- I am God's masterpiece, created for good works. (Ephesians 2:10)
- I am chosen, holy, and dearly loved by God. (Colossians 3:12)
- I am bold because the Lord is my helper. (Hebrews 13:6)
- I am confident that God will finish the good work He started in me. (Philippians 1:6)

Promises of God

- This is the day the Lord has made; I will rejoice and be glad in it. (Psalm 118:24)
- Nothing can separate me from God's love. (Romans 8:38-39)
- God's plans for me are good, filled with hope and a future. (Jeremiah 29:11)
- God directs my steps and makes my paths straight. (Proverbs 3:5-6)
- God's power works in me to accomplish far more than I can imagine. (Ephesians 3:20)
- The Lord is faithful to keep His promises to me. (Deuteronomy 7:9)
- The Lord makes everything beautiful in His time. (Ecclesiastes 3:11)

I Am – Gemini Personality Declarations

- ♥ I am a communicator.
- ♥ I am a connector of resources.
- ♥ I am a student of life.
- ♥ I am interested in the world of ideas.
- ♥ I can easily exchange ideas.
- ♥ I am inquisitive and learn quickly.
- ♥ I have diverse interests.
- ♥ I am a multi-tasker.
- ♥ I have healthy, loving relationships.
- ♥ I am heard and understood.

Gemini – Reminders for Growth and Balance

- + I maintain a good mental attitude.
- + I enjoy helping others.
- + I need diversity and exciting challenges.
- + I take time to delve into topics instead of only skimming the surface.
- + I like short-term activities with a lot of options.
- + I go with the flow.
- + I know a little about a lot of things.
- + I hold my own opinion high.
- + I receive the information I need to further my goals.

And there is more!

For more insight into the traits of Gemini go to, "Nourishment from the Month of Gemini," in Part Two, *Journey Around the Wheel of the Year*.

Happy Birthday, Cancer!

The Nurturer

The Initiating First Month of Summer

June 21 – July 22

Cancer! Your deep emotions and nurturing nature make you the ultimate caregiver. You have a strong desire to care for others. Through your empathy, you embody compassion, and bring hope and healing to others.

Your Birthday Promise – The Cancer Personality

With Your Birthday under the Month of Cancer, you were born to feel, love and nurture. Your caring nature is healing, sensitive and emotional. You enjoy exchanging feelings and were born to learn to master yours.

The meaning of 'home' carries a lot of sentiment for you. You are deeply intertwined with emotions, family, and home. You find comfort and well-being through a nostalgic connection to the past and maintaining strong connections with your mother and/or family.

Of all the Months, those born under the Month of Cancer are the most emotional and the shyest. You are protective, sensitive, nurturing, mothering, patriotic, and safety oriented with a defensive nature. Unlike others who may suppress or overlook their emotions, you approach them with openness and awareness, enabling you to gain valuable insight that is not commonly received.

Your strong capacity for feeling emotions is not a weakness but rather a source of insight, intuition, and transformation. This ability can be harnessed to convert emotions into knowledge, resilience, and personal authority.

Cancers have a well-earned reputation for being moody and not liking change. You are dependent upon others' moods and motives and operate in the world of feeling and inner experiences. Emotional and physical safety are important to you. You look for security in material comforts and have a pronounced need for self-protection from external influences. You withdraw into your shell when you get the slightest criticism or rejection from others. You tend to avoid risks and prioritize security. You take three steps forward and two steps backward when venturing into new endeavors. Your ability to perceive the true character of individuals makes you aware of the darker aspects of reality. You may experience melancholy due to your highly intuitive nature.

Your softness and vulnerability can expose you to the challenging aspects of life. You often learn the hard way that not everyone can be trusted and to be highly selective about who you allow into your internal world and experiences. Over time, you will become discerning about who you allow access to and who has your best interests at heart.

You seek emotional security by initiating connections. You have a desire to form emotional bonds and share your personal experiences openly. Even so, it is difficult for others to get to know you well. Cancers typically reveal their authentic selves only to those they trust.

Cancer individuals often identify as empaths or highly sensitive people who connect with and absorb the energy around them. As a result, you may ignore your own needs and prioritize others, particularly if your own emotions, sensitivities, and talents are not recognized or valued.

Cancers have strong feelings for family. The ancestry and the roots from which you came from give you security in your life. It is natural for you to be very protective of your family and sensitive to the feelings of others. You promote the need for care and nurturance.

Each life experience over your lifetime will in some way be involved in fulfilling your need to give and receive emotional warmth and security and be The Nurturer, The Mother, and The Emotional Heart of the Group.

Why have you been given these traits? You carry these traits to equip you with what you need to fulfill your individual life's mission as well as the role you have in all of humanity.

Embracing the characteristics of Your Birthday Promise will help you navigate life with authenticity and purpose.

Cancer – Your Role in the World and Contribution to Society – The Nurturer

*Each of you should use whatever gift you have received to serve others
as faithful stewards of God's grace in its various forms. 1 Peter 4:10*

We each have a role to fill for ourselves and for humanity. Born under the Month of Cancer, your contribution to society is to show others the power of unconditional love, caring for and loving your family through thick and thin, and spreading your nurturing instincts to all living beings. You set an example of care and compassion through unconditional love. Your empathy and nurturing instincts are truly gifts to this world as you work to diminish suffering.

You are the one people go to when they feel devalued and ignored. People naturally trust you, rely on you, and love to confide in you. You are always there for your loved ones when they need you.

Your ability to feel others' emotions as your own enables you to easily connect with the feelings of others, offering comfort and support during times of distress when they need it most. You help others to understand and manage their own overwhelming emotions.

You bring a personal kind-hearted energy to people's busy everyday lives. Your gentle touch and steadfast support create a safe harbor where healing can take place. You do everything you can to help someone who is being ignored in a conversation or a project to feel included.

By filling your role you give support to others in need. You offer a steady shoulder to cry upon when things get tough.

Cancer – What You are Here to Learn
Lessons to Learn to Excel at Your Role

Born under the Month of Cancer, throughout your life, you are here to learn:

...to live with a caring nature and an open heart while keeping healthy boundaries.

...how to trust what you feel as one of your unique gifts.

...to not be so trusting of others – realizing that not everyone can be trusted.

...to avoid being defensive or hyper-sensitive to external energies.

...to work through emotional challenges and turn emotions into strength.

...to care for others without needing to support them or mother them.

Cancer – Let Your Light Shine

Born under the Month of Cancer, the special light you shine is through establishing a secure home, foundation, and family. You seek bonds with family for emotional security. A foundation based on home, family, and traditions will be used and developed to fulfill your purpose.

"You are the light of the world. A city set on a hill cannot be hidden. Nor do people light a lamp and put it under a basket, but on a stand, and it gives light to all in the house. In the same way, let your light shine before others, so that they may see your good works and give glory to your Father who is in heaven." Matthew 5:14-16 ESV

 ## Taking Inventory of the Qualities of Your Life

As you review your life during this time of Your Birthday Month, realize that you are already everything you need to be at this time in your journey. You are not broken or damaged. You are who you were created to be right now. We each have an opportunity to take stock and grow in the gifts and talents we have been given.

At this Yearly time of celebrating Your Birthday, you have an opportunity to get to know and love yourself more fully than you have before. It is a time to trust God in the unfolding and timing of your life and get a better sense of the meaning and purpose of your life.

 ### Cancer – My Birthday Life Review

Do you recognize the Birthday Promise qualities in yourself?
If so, are they being used and developed? If you feel you are lacking in any of these, or are out of balance, you can ask the Spirit to help you make the most of them in this New Year. **Go to Page 190 for Your Birthday Life Review questions.**

The Fruit of the Tree of Life for Growth and Healing

Spiritual Fruit Tending - Reflect on These Virtues in Your Life and Rate Them

Fruit of the Spirit	👍 Growing Well?	➕ Needs Fertilizing?	👎 Needs Pruning
Love - A deep and abiding affection and concern for others.			
Joy – A state of happiness and delight, even in the midst of difficult circumstances.			
Peace – A state of tranquility and harmony, both internally and externally.			
Patience – The ability to endure challenges or agitation without becoming angry or upset.			
Kindness – A gentle and kind nature, showing compassion and care for others.			
Goodness – A moral excellence and uprightness of character.			
Faithfulness – Loyalty, trustworthiness, and steadfastness in commitments.			
Gentleness – A kind and considerate demeanor, avoiding harshness or aggression.			
Self-control – The ability to restrain impulses and appetites.			
Long-suffering - The capacity to endure hardship with patience and perseverance.			
Temperance - Moderation and self-restraint in all aspects of life.			
Wisdom - The ability to make sound judgments and decisions based on knowledge and experience.			

Cancer - Spiritual Fruit Tending
Questions and prompts for your quiet time
Go to Page 192 for a deep dive into your Fruit of the Tree of Life ratings.

Rate Your Life on the Wheel of Life

Think about the matters of your life shown in the Key Areas of Life Table from Page 13 and evaluate your current level of satisfaction in each Area on a scale from 1-8. The Wheel of Life segments correspond with the topics in this Table. Rate each Area and highlight the number you gave yourself in each Area on the blank Wheel below.

How is your life going? Be sure to rate yourself honestly. This is your reality check. Your honest evaluation will quickly help pinpoint any imbalance. The lower rated areas will show you where you need more focus. No more guessing!

Then, outline the highlighted Wheel of Life ratings with a marker to link them to each other to form a figure within the circle showing the degree of balance in your life, as in the following example.

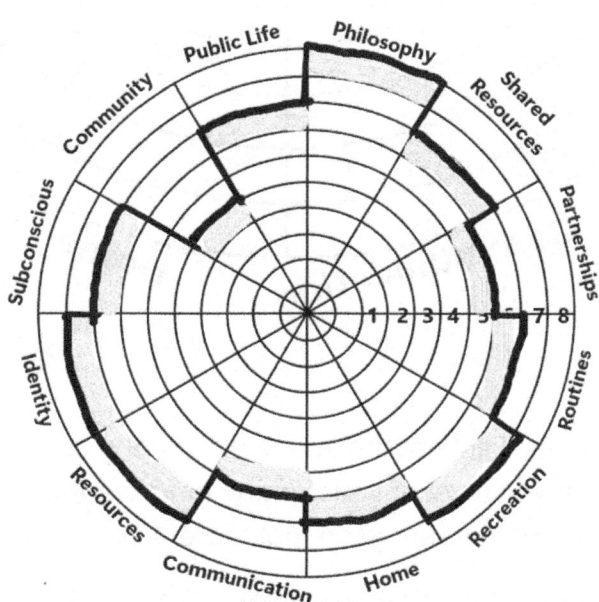

Example of the Wheel of Life with Evaluations

Wheel of Life

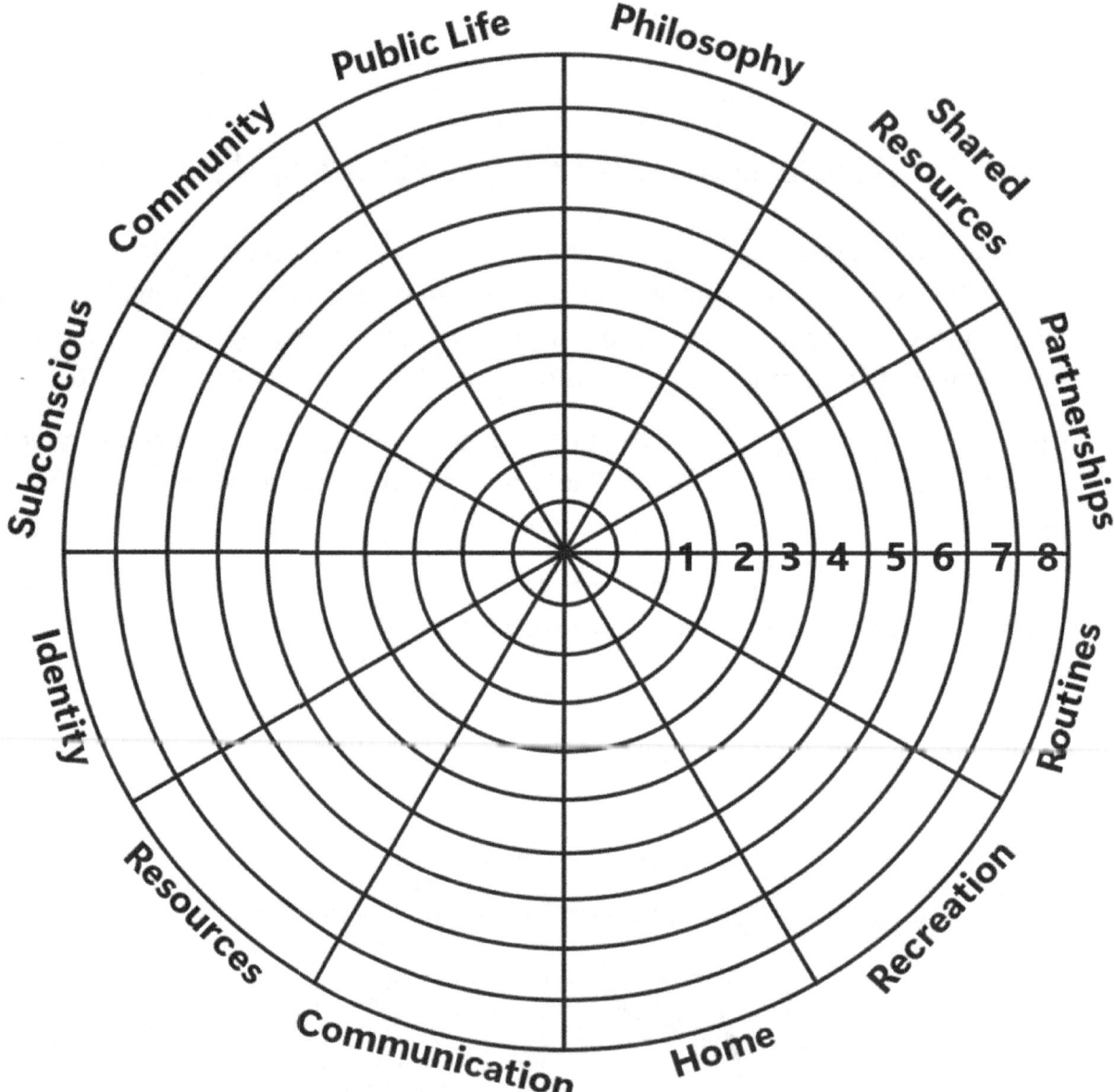

Filling in the Wheel of Life: Highlight the space on a scale from 1-8 under each Key Area that reflects your current level of satisfaction or imbalance in that area, with 8 being the most satisfying and 1 needing the most attention.

Next, interpret the results. How does the balance of your Key Areas of Life look? Analyze the resulting shape to identify the unbalanced areas that require attention and how to improve your satisfaction with them.

With a different color, mark the scores where you would like them to be in the future. Transfer your current and goal scores, as number of stars, to the table below to see where you stand in each category.

Fill in the stars for the Wheel of Life ratings you gave yourself for the current Year and then give yourself stars for next Year's goal.

Wheel of Life Area of Life	How many stars do you give yourself? 1-8 (from your Wheel of Life rating)	
	Current Wheel of Life	Goal for Next Year
Identity	☆☆☆☆☆☆☆☆	☆☆☆☆☆☆☆☆
Resources	☆☆☆☆☆☆☆☆	☆☆☆☆☆☆☆☆
Communication	☆☆☆☆☆☆☆☆	☆☆☆☆☆☆☆☆
Home	☆☆☆☆☆☆☆☆	☆☆☆☆☆☆☆☆
Recreation	☆☆☆☆☆☆☆☆	☆☆☆☆☆☆☆☆
Routines	☆☆☆☆☆☆☆☆	☆☆☆☆☆☆☆☆
Partnerships	☆☆☆☆☆☆☆☆	☆☆☆☆☆☆☆☆
Shared Resources	☆☆☆☆☆☆☆☆	☆☆☆☆☆☆☆☆
Philosophy	☆☆☆☆☆☆☆☆	☆☆☆☆☆☆☆☆
Public Life	☆☆☆☆☆☆☆☆	☆☆☆☆☆☆☆☆
Community	☆☆☆☆☆☆☆☆	☆☆☆☆☆☆☆☆
Subconscious	☆☆☆☆☆☆☆☆	☆☆☆☆☆☆☆☆

Good ratings in the different areas of your life have a major noticeable impact on your overall well-being and quality of life. A well-balanced life can reduce stress and anxiety, improve your mental wellbeing, and make you more productive, and will improve your self-esteem, family life, partnerships, career, and the other areas of

your life. On the other hand, a lack of balance in several areas of your life will cause instability in the other Areas of your life as well.

Make a conscious decision to take better care of your life and make it all that it can be. Start by giving some thought to each Area in the Wheel of Life. What is the status of each one? Reflect on what there is to learn about each one. Work on strengthening the various areas of your life to welcome more peace, purpose, and fulfillment.

 Taking Inventory of the Qualities of Your Life

Cancer – Deep Dive on Your Wheel of Life Findings
Questions and prompts for your quiet time
Go to Page 194 for a deep dive into your Wheel of Life ratings.

Cancer – Your Birthday Promise Insights
Reflections on Last Year ✴ Intentions for the Year Ahead
Questions and prompts for your quiet time
Go to Page 197 for a deep dive into Your Birthday Promise Insights.

God's Birthday Message for Cancer...

Dear Cancer, as you review your life this Year, remember the unique individual that you have been created to be and the core qualities that you have been given to equip you for your role in life.

Born in Cancer, the first Month of Summer, you were given the qualities of nurturing, empathy, and intuition. These equip you for your role as The Nurturer to fulfill your purpose of showing others the power of love, vulnerability, and the importance of home.

Your sensitive nature is your unique gift. You are empathetic and protective over your loved ones. God is calling you to take the lead in demonstrating compassion towards others, a quality that is needed in the world today.

Your spiritual path is deeply tied to emotions. You absorb other people's energy easily, so learning to set boundaries is key. God encourages you not to neglect your own soul's needs while taking care of others. Compassion towards others starts with compassion for yourself. Self-care is not selfish.

God's message to you is to give yourself time for rest, creativity, and bonding with loved ones to nurture your spirit. When you have replenished your own soul you can continue shining your healing light out into the world.

Spiritual Growth Tips

✓ Keep showing love and concern to others around you.

✓ Help others but set boundaries – do not lose yourself.

✓ Remember that you do not have to carry everything alone.

✓ God's loving presence and consoling words are always with you.

✓ Trust God to handle what is beyond your control and let go of anxiety.

✓ Even when other's may not, remember that God sees and values your heart.

💡 Cancer – Take-Aways from Your Deep Dives

Now that you have reflected, meditated, and received insight from the Spirit from your time of prayer, meditation, and meeting with the Spirit about all Areas of Your Life, journal the revelations, words, and directions that come to mind for the coming Year.

What have you learned about yourself?

What have you learned about God?

What have you learned about the direction and plan for your life?

Finally – Submit Your Plans to God

While we can meet with the Lord and get direction and set intentions for the New Year, we ultimately need to submit to His Will and timing. We may not understand how things play out, but we will recognize areas of our life that we can intentionally bring into alignment with His ways. While we are honing our gifts and abilities, He will open doors and close doors accordingly and we will flow along with Him on this Year's journey.

*Many are the plans in a person's heart, but it is the LORD's purpose that prevails.
Proverbs 19:21*

*A man's heart plans his course, but the LORD determines his steps.
Proverbs 16:9 BSB*

And we know that in all things God works for the good of those who love him, who have been called according to his purpose. Romans 8:28

*To everything there is a season, and a time to every purpose under the heaven:
A time to be born, and a time to die; a time to plant,
and a time to pluck up that which is planted... Ecclesiastes 3:1-2 NKJV*

Biblical Affirmations to Declare Over Your Life

In addition to the specific traits you have been given to fulfill your God-given purpose, there are underlying truths about who God created you to be. These affirmations confirm the qualities you have been given for your underlying relationship and identity through Him.

Birthday affirmations, declarations, and prayers go beyond mere wishes; they are faith-filled expressions that align with God's Word that speak life, purpose, encouragement, and Divine blessing. The words we speak have power, and for those on a spiritual path, it is important to declare what God says about us. While the world may try to label us by our past, errors, or situations, we should instead rely on the truth found in God's Word.

Use these affirmations, supported by Scripture, to renew your mind, strengthen your faith and walk confidently in your God-given identity. Repeat them daily and let the truth of His promises transform your life!

Who Am I?

- I am a child of God and an heir to His promises. (Romans 8:17)
- I am fearfully and wonderfully made. (Psalm 139:14)
- I am God's masterpiece, created for good works. (Ephesians 2:10)
- I am chosen, holy, and dearly loved by God. (Colossians 3:12)
- I am bold because the Lord is my helper. (Hebrews 13:6)
- I am confident that God will finish the good work He started in me. (Philippians 1:6)

Promises of God

- This is the day the Lord has made; I will rejoice and be glad in it. (Psalm 118:24)
- Nothing can separate me from God's love. (Romans 8:38-39)
- God's plans for me are good, filled with hope and a future. (Jeremiah 29:11)
- God directs my steps and makes my paths straight. (Proverbs 3:5-6)
- God's power works in me to accomplish far more than I can imagine. (Ephesians 3:20)
- The Lord is faithful to keep His promises to me. (Deuteronomy 7:9)
- The Lord makes everything beautiful in His time. (Ecclesiastes 3:11)

I Am – Cancer Personality Declarations

- ♥ I am a nurturer.
- ♥ I am compassionate and kind.
- ♥ I am emotionally sensitive.
- ♥ I am sensitive to the feelings of others.
- ♥ I am devoted and tenacious.
- ♥ I am loyal and protective.
- ♥ I am intuitive.
- ♥ I am nurturing of myself and others.
- ♥ I am generous.

Cancer – Reminders for Growth and Balance

- + I am loved by my family.
- + I forgive those who have wronged me.
- + I ask forgiveness from those I have injured.
- + I focus on my home and family and am very protective of them.
- + I have a closed inner circle.
- + I trust those I love.
- + I balance my emotions. I think positive thoughts.
- + I monitor myself by asking, "How much can I give without become depleted?"
- + I develop emotional regulation practices.
- + I like to spend time alone.
- + I am accepted by the people I care about.

And there is more!

For more insight into the traits of Cancer go to, "Nourishment from the Month of Cancer," in Part Two, *Journey Around the Wheel of the Year*.

Happy Birthday, Leo!

The Leader

The Fixed Middle Month of Summer

July 23 – August 22

Leo! You possess a dynamic and charismatic personality. You love the spotlight. Your natural charisma attracts and inspires people. You are a natural leader who inspires others through your strength and passion.

Your Birthday Promise - The Leo Personality

With Your Birthday under the Month of Leo you were born to lead, organize, and delegate to those around you. You are a natural leader and your presence is meant to be seen, experienced, and remembered. You are someone who has a great deal of fortitude and courage. You are not afraid to take risks.

You are meant to motivate others with your confidence, presence, and bold personality. What makes you different from any other leadership Month is that you don't just lead - you inspire. You stabilize future possibilities and potentials and your commanding leadership leads to inspired action.

Born under the Month of Leo you are dignified, proud, and honorable. You broadcast your self-assurance to the world. You relate to being outgoing, social, popular, and you are honest, generous, sincere, and loyal. You are driven to be seen.

Organization is important to you and you need a sense of order and control in your life. You are strong-willed and seldom ask for help because you do not feel you need it. Your authority and dignity earn you unquestioned respect and loyalty from your followers. You demand respect and will dismiss anyone who treats you otherwise.

You were born to seek the spotlight and you see others around you in supporting roles. You often take the stage with grace and energy wherever you go. You create your own sparkle of light that captivates others. Although you can be performative, your heart is true.

You love fun and have a childlike nature and wonder of the world. You take life on in a wholehearted manner, love fun, and can be dramatic.

Of all Months, Leos are the most creative and artistic. You possess a never-ending stream of ideas and put your own unique stamp on them. You have a lot to give and offer to this world.

Leos are confident, giving, and natural leaders. Your confidence and charm lure people toward yourself. You have an ability to influence and empower others through your self-expression.

Each life experience over your lifetime will in some way be involved in fulfilling your need to express yourself creatively and be The Charismatic Leader, The Performer, and The Creator.

Why have you been given these traits? You carry these traits to equip you with what you need to fulfill your individual life's mission as well as the role you have in all of humanity.

Embracing the characteristics of Your Birthday Promise will help you navigate life with authenticity and purpose.

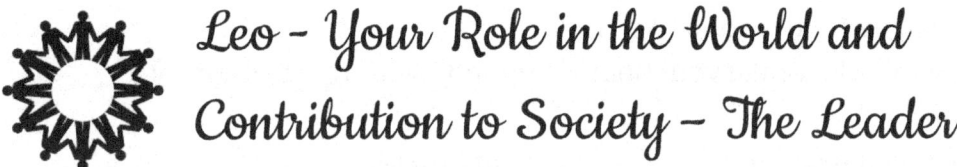

Leo – Your Role in the World and Contribution to Society – The Leader

Each of you should use whatever gift you have received to serve others as faithful stewards of God's grace in its various forms. 1 Peter 4:10

We each have a role to fill for ourselves and for humanity. Born under the Month of Leo, your contribution to society is to develop your creative brilliance and take center stage or lead the pack. Your individuality and need for self-expression must be reflected in your work.

You have a natural talent to charm and guide others, making you an ideal leader. You are drawn to leadership roles as a showcase for your courageous spirit and the ability to take charge. You are to become the best version of yourself and inspire others with your example. You attract loyalty in return for your inspiration, support, and strength.

Leos are known for their vibrant creativity and their talents inspire others to tap into their own inner light and express themselves, and to be strong and courageous in all situations. You encourage these qualities in others and feel that you are the father and teacher of all mankind. You have the power to brighten the lives of others. Your gift is to encourage people, and validate their value and potential. Your energy is contagious and you make others feel braver, bolder, and more expressive. You motivate people to become their full authentic selves and take action just because they see you doing it.

The true purpose of your life is to use your unique gifts to shine brightly in the world and encourage others. You fulfill your destiny when you lead courageously with a selfless spirit, inspiring those around you to do the same, creating a ripple effect of positivity.

Leo – What You are Here to Learn

Lessons to Learn to Excel at Your Role

Born under the Month of Leo, throughout your life, you are here to learn:

- to use your leadership skills and courageous spirit with heart.
- to know that there is no need to compete with others when they are shining in their own light and creativity.
- to let other people in at a deep level.
- to actively seek out strong connections instead of trusting that they will form on their own.
- to use your gifts for the good of others.
- to develop the wisdom of your heart to match the magnetism of your personality.
- to rely less on the opinions and feedback of others.
- to develop healthy pride and sense of self.
- to develop the confidence to stand strong in yourself.
- to cultivate confidence while remaining humble and generous.

Leo – Let Your Light Shine

Born under the Month of Leo, the special light you shine is through your love of life and a powerful desire toward creative self-expression. You need to be a visible leader in order to establish your inspired actions. The expression of your will, your being, and your creativity will be used and developed to fulfill the purpose of your life.

> "You are the light of the world. A city set on a hill cannot be hidden. Nor do people light a lamp and put it under a basket, but on a stand, and it gives light to all in the house. In the same way, let your light shine before others, so that they may see your good works and give glory to your Father who is in heaven." Matthew 5:14-16 ESV

Taking Inventory of the Qualities of Your Life

As you review your life during this time of Your Birthday Month, realize that you are already everything you need to be at this time in your journey. You are not broken or damaged. You are who you were created to be right now. We each have an opportunity to take stock and grow in the gifts and talents we have been given.

At this Yearly time of celebrating Your Birthday, you have an opportunity to get to know and love yourself more fully than you have before. It is a time to trust God in the unfolding and timing of your life and get a better sense of the meaning and purpose of your life.

Leo – My Birthday Life Review

Do you recognize the Birthday Promise qualities in yourself?
If so, are they being used and developed? If you feel you are lacking in any of these, or are out of balance, you can ask the Spirit to help you make the most of them in this New Year. **Go to Page 190 for Your Birthday Life Review questions.**

The Fruit of the Tree of Life for Growth and Healing

Spiritual Fruit Tending - Reflect on These Virtues in Your Life and Rate Them

Fruit of the Spirit	👍 Growing Well?	➕ Needs Fertilizing?	👎 Needs Pruning
Love - A deep and abiding affection and concern for others.			
Joy – A state of happiness and delight, even in the midst of difficult circumstances.			
Peace – A state of tranquility and harmony, both internally and externally.			
Patience – The ability to endure challenges or agitation without becoming angry or upset.			
Kindness – A gentle and kind nature, showing compassion and care for others.			
Goodness – A moral excellence and uprightness of character.			
Faithfulness – Loyalty, trustworthiness, and steadfastness in commitments.			
Gentleness – A kind and considerate demeanor, avoiding harshness or aggression.			
Self-control – The ability to restrain impulses and appetites.			
Long-suffering - The capacity to endure hardship with patience and perseverance.			
Temperence - Moderation and self-restraint in all aspects of life.			
Wisdom - The ability to make sound judgments and decisions based on knowledge and experience.			

Leo - Spiritual Fruit Tending
Questions and prompts for your quiet time
Go to Page 192 for a deep dive into your Fruit of the Tree of Life ratings.

Rate Your Life on the Wheel of Life

Think about the matters of your life shown in the Key Areas of Life Table from Page 13 and evaluate your current level of satisfaction in each Area on a scale from 1-8. The Wheel of Life segments correspond with the topics in this Table. Rate each Area and highlight the number you gave yourself in each Area on the blank Wheel below.

How is your life going? Be sure to rate yourself honestly. This is your reality check. Your honest evaluation will quickly help pinpoint any imbalance. The lower rated areas will show you where you need more focus. No more guessing!

Then, outline the highlighted Wheel of Life ratings with a marker to link them to each other to form a figure within the circle showing the degree of balance in your life, as in the following example.

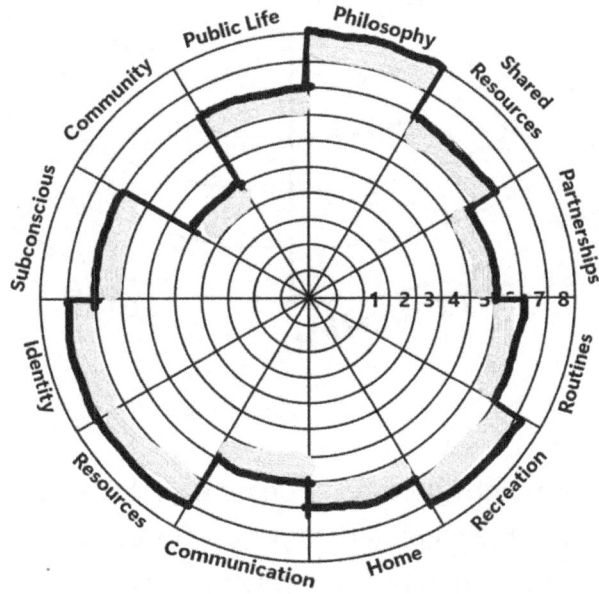

Example of the Wheel of Life with Evaluations

83

Wheel of Life

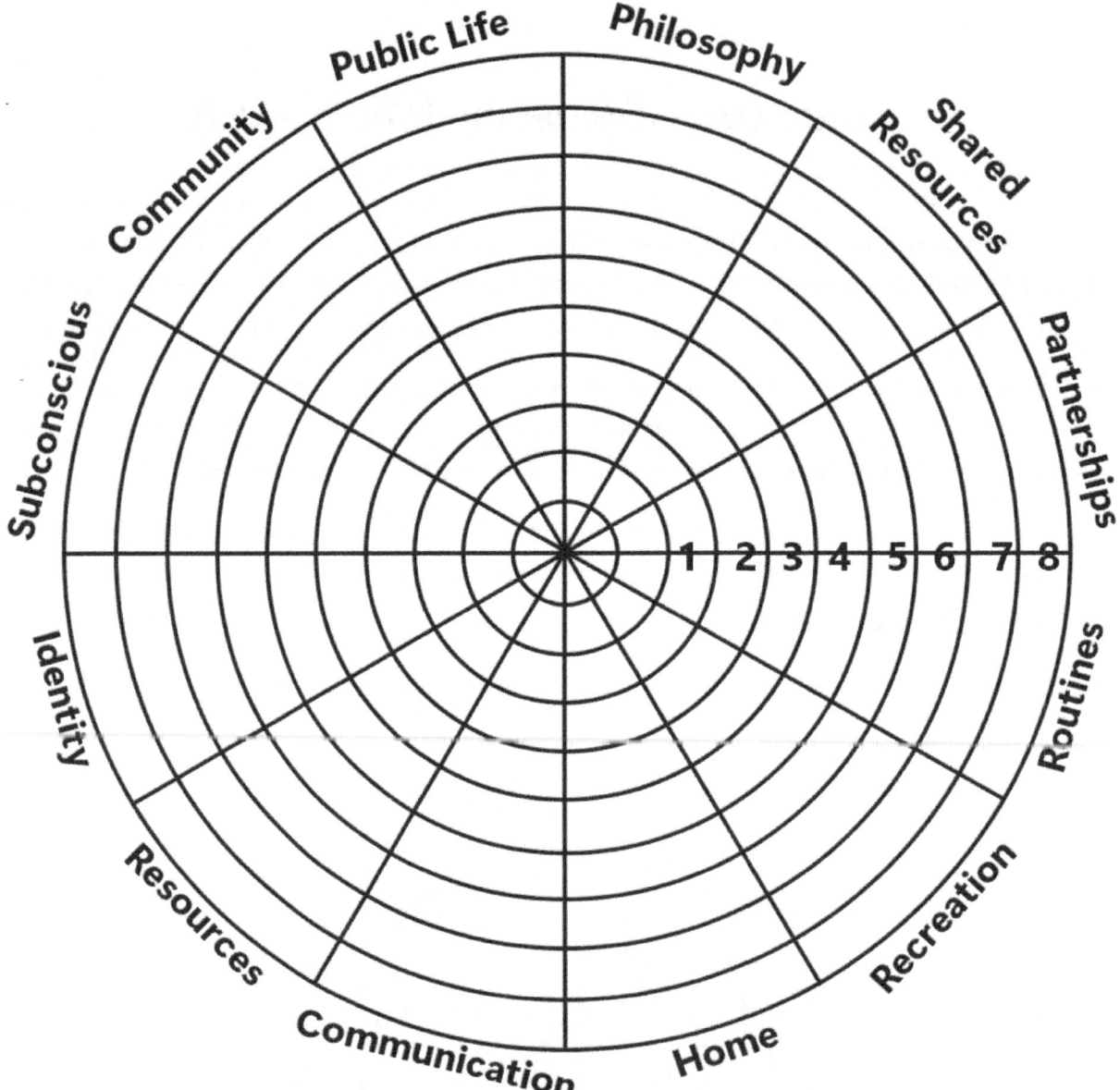

Filling in the Wheel of Life: Highlight the space on a scale from 1-8 under each Key Area that reflects your current level of satisfaction or imbalance in that area, with 8 being the most satisfying and 1 needing the most attention.

Next, interpret the results. How does the balance of your Key Areas of Life look? Analyze the resulting shape to identify the unbalanced areas that require attention and how to improve your satisfaction with them.

With a different color, mark the scores where you would like them to be in the future. Transfer your current and goal scores, as number of stars, to the table below to see where you stand in each category.

Fill in the stars for the Wheel of Life ratings you gave yourself for the current Year and then give yourself stars for next Year's goal.

Wheel of Life Area of Life	How many stars do you give yourself? 1-8 (from your Wheel of Life rating)	
	Current Wheel of Life	Goal for Next Year
Identity	☆☆☆☆☆☆☆☆	☆☆☆☆☆☆☆☆
Resources	☆☆☆☆☆☆☆☆	☆☆☆☆☆☆☆☆
Communication	☆☆☆☆☆☆☆☆	☆☆☆☆☆☆☆☆
Home	☆☆☆☆☆☆☆☆	☆☆☆☆☆☆☆☆
Recreation	☆☆☆☆☆☆☆☆	☆☆☆☆☆☆☆☆
Routines	☆☆☆☆☆☆☆☆	☆☆☆☆☆☆☆☆
Partnerships	☆☆☆☆☆☆☆☆	☆☆☆☆☆☆☆☆
Shared Resources	☆☆☆☆☆☆☆☆	☆☆☆☆☆☆☆☆
Philosophy	☆☆☆☆☆☆☆☆	☆☆☆☆☆☆☆☆
Public Life	☆☆☆☆☆☆☆☆	☆☆☆☆☆☆☆☆
Community	☆☆☆☆☆☆☆☆	☆☆☆☆☆☆☆☆
Subconscious	☆☆☆☆☆☆☆☆	☆☆☆☆☆☆☆☆

Good ratings in the different areas of your life have a major noticeable impact on your overall well-being and quality of life. A well-balanced life can reduce stress and anxiety, improve your mental wellbeing, and make you more productive, and will improve your self-esteem, family life, partnerships, career, and the other areas of

your life. On the other hand, a lack of balance in several areas of your life will cause instability in the other Areas of your life as well.

Make a conscious decision to take better care of your life and make it all that it can be. Start by giving some thought to each Area in the Wheel of Life. What is the status of each one? Reflect on what there is to learn about each one. Work on strengthening the various areas of your life to welcome more peace, purpose, and fulfillment.

Taking Inventory of the Qualities of Your Life

Leo – Deep Dive on Your Wheel of Life Findings
Questions and prompts for your quiet time
Go to Page 194 for a deep dive into your Wheel of Life ratings.

Leo – Your Birthday Promise Insights
Reflections on Last Year ✶ Intentions for the Year Ahead
Questions and prompts for your quiet time
Go to Page 197 for a deep dive into Your Birthday Promise Insights.

God's Birthday Message for Leo...

Dear Leo, as you review your life this Year, remember the unique individual that you have been created to be and the core qualities that you have been given to equip you for your role in life.

Born in Leo, the second Month of Summer, you were given the qualities of fixed leadership, generosity, and creativity. These equip you for your role as The Leader to fulfill your purpose of giving direction and leadership to others during these changing times.

You are known as a natural-born leader with charisma and a strong sense of confidence and authority. Your mission is to shine boldly. You remind others that true self-expression includes joy, creativity, and self-love. Continue to display these gifts to motivate others.

You have natural bravery, conviction, and leadership capabilities. God encourages you to use your influence and charisma for the greater good rather than for yourself. God cautions you against pridefulness and reminds you that true leaders lift others up. You can thrive when you are able to rally people together around a common purpose or cause bigger than yourself.

God's message for you is to balance your courage and humility. Confidence is godly, but arrogance prevents progress. You can shine and produce the most fruit when you also display modesty, patience, and the desire to elevate others.

Spiritual Growth Tips

✓ Let your inner light and deeds inspire others.

✓ Shine in a way that honors God, not just personal recognition.

✓ Encourage others with your kindness and lead with humility.

✓ Use your charisma to bring people closer to faith.

💡 Leo – Take-Aways from Your Deep Dives

Now that you have reflected, meditated, and received insight from the Spirit from your time of prayer, meditation, and meeting with the Spirit about all Areas of Your Life, journal the revelations, words, and directions that come to mind for the coming Year.

What have you learned about yourself?

What have you learned about God?

What have you learned about the direction and plan for your life?

Finally – Submit Your Plans to God

While we can meet with the Lord and get direction and set intentions for the New Year, we ultimately need to submit to His Will and timing. We may not understand how things play out, but we will recognize areas of our life that we can intentionally bring into alignment with His ways. While we are honing our gifts and abilities, He will open doors and close doors accordingly and we will flow along with Him on this Year's journey.

Many are the plans in a person's heart, but it is the LORD's purpose that prevails.
Proverbs 19:21

A man's heart plans his course, but the LORD determines his steps.
Proverbs 16:9 BSB

And we know that in all things God works for the good of those who love him, who have been called according to his purpose. Romans 8:28

To everything there is a season, and a time to every purpose under the heaven: A time to be born, and a time to die; a time to plant, and a time to pluck up that which is planted... Ecclesiastes 3:1-2 NKJV

Biblical Affirmations to Declare Over Your Life

In addition to the specific traits you have been given to fulfill your God-given purpose, there are underlying truths about who God created you to be. These affirmations confirm the qualities you have been given for your underlying relationship and identity through Him.

Birthday affirmations, declarations, and prayers go beyond mere wishes; they are faith-filled expressions that align with God's Word that speak life, purpose, encouragement, and Divine blessing. The words we speak have power, and for those on a spiritual path, it is important to declare what God says about us. While the world may try to label us by our past, errors, or situations, we should instead rely on the truth found in God's Word.

Use these affirmations, supported by Scripture, to renew your mind, strengthen your faith and walk confidently in your God-given identity. Repeat them daily and let the truth of His promises transform your life!

Who Am I?

- I am a child of God and an heir to His promises. (Romans 8:17)
- I am fearfully and wonderfully made. (Psalm 139:14)
- I am God's masterpiece, created for good works. (Ephesians 2:10)
- I am chosen, holy, and dearly loved by God. (Colossians 3:12)
- I am bold because the Lord is my helper. (Hebrews 13:6)
- I am confident that God will finish the good work He started in me. (Philippians 1:6)

Promises of God

- This is the day the Lord has made; I will rejoice and be glad in it. (Psalm 118:24)
- Nothing can separate me from God's love. (Romans 8:38-39)
- God's plans for me are good, filled with hope and a future. (Jeremiah 29:11)
- God directs my steps and makes my paths straight. (Proverbs 3:5-6)
- God's power works in me to accomplish far more than I can imagine. (Ephesians 3:20)
- The Lord is faithful to keep His promises to me. (Deuteronomy 7:9)
- The Lord makes everything beautiful in His time. (Ecclesiastes 3:11)

I Am – Leo Personality Declarations

- ♥ I am a natural leader.
- ♥ I am confident and charismatic.
- ♥ I am responsible.
- ♥ I am a great organizer.
- ♥ I am determined and strong-willed.
- ♥ I am creative.
- ♥ I am ambitious.
- ♥ I am proud.
- ♥ I am warm-hearted and generous.
- ♥ I am fiery and daring.
- ♥ I am passionate and loving.
- ♥ I am strong and resilient.
- ♥ I know my value.

Leo – Reminders for Growth and Balance

- + My creativity is one of my greatest strengths.
- + I like to take center stage.
- + I realize that not all attention is good intention.
- + I celebrate other people's light as much as my own.
- + I shine without needing approval from anyone else.
- + I am developing a genuine concern for others.
- + I enjoy helping others.
- + I always look at the bright side of things.
- + I lead humbly and honor God using my confidence.

And there is more!

For more insight into the traits of Leo go to, "Nourishment from the Month of Leo," in Part Two, *Journey Around the Wheel of the Year*.

Happy Birthday, Virgo!

The Analyst

The Transitional Last Month of Summer
August 23 – September 22

Virgo! You are a perfectionist with a strong sense of duty.
You are diligent, dedicated, and analytical and love helping others.
You get to the heart of the matter, avoid disorder,
and make the overall process run efficiently.

Your Birthday Promise - The Virgo Personality

With Your Birthday under the Month of Virgo, you were born with a continual quest for detail, order, and perfection. You are meant to analyze, refine, and focus on details. You operate and think on a micro level. Your mind is attuned to identifying patterns, solutions, and details that may not be evident to others. You are conscientious of all the details, because you value all aspects equally and believe that nothing is unimportant.

At your core, you excel as a problem solver, an expert in efficiency, and a catalyst for transformation. While others may become overwhelmed by complexity, you provide clarity, structure, and mastery to any situation. You have a lot of energy and need to have an outlet.

You possess a unique ability to discern order within chaos. Unlike others that may struggle with disorder, you possess the ability to analyze scattered ideas and streamline the information, removing what is unnecessary and organizing ideas effectively

You prefer to serve and would rather take orders and carry out assignments rather than be the boss. You help others from the viewpoint of what they need, not what you want. You seldom ask 'why,' only 'how?' You can always be counted on to make good on your promises, and you are a true master of all things related to organization and analysis.

You are sensible, avoid drama, and are very realistic. You do not understand the meaning of escapism. You don't believe you can avoid reality. You tend to look for a holistic approach to a situation. You are generally skeptical at first and slow to believe. You move through cold, hard facts to eliminate excess, preferring results that promote duality and refinement.

You take your time and won't be rushed. You will always do your own due diligence. Before you take action, you cautiously ponder over the situation and review all possible alternatives and reactions. You systematically strive to find the best possible response to any given problem. You operate in a practical way seeking results through effort and hard work in both seen and unseen activities.

You are able to go through life with confidence and calmness and people wonder how you manage challenging situations so well! They don't realize that you have spent Years perfecting this art of living.

Even though you love helping others, you sometimes become overly critical of both yourself and those around you. You want perfection in your life and you try to help others improve as well. However, your perfectionism often causes you to overanalyze things and could prevent you from grasping the bigger picture. Virgo is also concerned with health and can become overly health conscious. You may experience bouts of hypochondria.

Your attention to detail and practicality is manifested in the gift of service. You meet the needs of others with a conscientiousness and humility that reflects the love and unselfishness of God.

Each life experience over your lifetime will in some way be involved in fulfilling your need to analyze, discriminate and function efficiently to be The Organizer, The Devoted Servant, The Tactical Planner.

Why have you been given these traits? You carry these traits to equip you with what you need to fulfill your individual life's mission as well as the role you have in the whole of humanity.

Embracing the characteristics of Your Birthday Promise will help you navigate life with authenticity and purpose.

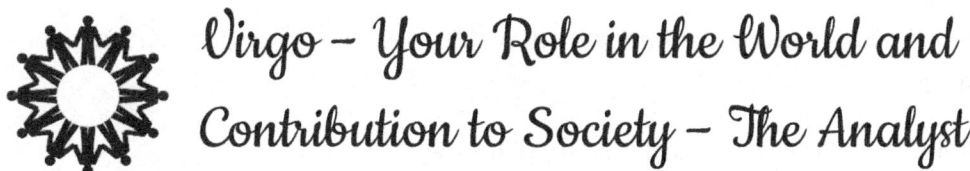

Virgo – Your Role in the World and Contribution to Society – The Analyst

Each of you should use whatever gift you have received to serve others as faithful stewards of God's grace in its various forms. 1 Peter 4:10

We each have a role to fill for ourselves and for humanity. Born under the Month of Virgo, your contribution to society is to hone your chosen craft – to learn a trade and perfect a skill that will provide you opportunities to play an important role in any work situation.

You are a hard worker, a critical thinker, and a natural problem solver who can find errors and their solutions. Your job is to get to the heart of the matter and make things work better and more efficiently. You excel at finding step-by-step solutions for even the most complicated problems and can quickly identify how to improve systems and streamline processes, making life easier for everyone around you.

You enjoy routine responsibilities and are often placed in supporting roles. You become known for making things work more efficiently. You teach people how to set high standards for themselves and work toward their goals by rising above their hardships.

You see beyond the external and understand the true nature of situations and people. This ability helps you make wise decisions and offer guidance to others, ensuring they stay on the right path. You bring peace among people.

Your deep understanding of the human body and mind enable you to provide precise and effective remedies. Your keen eye for imperfections and your ability to identify underlying problems can make you an exceptional natural healer. Your dedication and compassionate manner make you an invaluable ally on the road to recovery.

Virgo – What You are Here to Learn
Lessons to Learn to Excel at Your Role

Born under the Month of Virgo, throughout your life, you are here to learn:

...to discern lifestyle habits that support your daily energy and health needs.

...to not be overly critical of what you perceive to be wrong or not working.

...to check first and make sure your feedback is welcome, to not intrude where you're not wanted.

... to be adaptable to life's unexpected circumstances.

...to not expect everything to proceed in a straight line or fit into a convenient container.

...to achieve peaceful harmony even if the circumstances are not always perfect.

...to trust in your own ideas.

...to navigate the complexities of your thoughts.

...to balance perfectionism with compassion, towards yourself and others.

Virgo – Let Your Light Shine

Born under the Month of Virgo, the special light you shine is through your work and service to others. You are practical and seek results through effort and hard work. Your service to others and taking care of your health will be used and developed to fulfill the purpose of your life.

> *"You are the light of the world. A city set on a hill cannot be hidden. Nor do people light a lamp and put it under a basket, but on a stand, and it gives light to all in the house. In the same way, let your light shine before others, so that they may see your good works and give glory to your Father who is in heaven." Matthew 5:14-16 ESV*

Taking Inventory of the Qualities of Your Life

As you review your life during this time of Your Birthday Month, realize that you are already everything you need to be at this time in your journey. You are not broken or damaged. You are who you were created to be right now. We each have an opportunity to take stock and grow in the gifts and talents we have been given.

At this Yearly time of celebrating Your Birthday, you have an opportunity to get to know and love yourself more fully than you have before. It is a time to trust God in the unfolding and timing of your life and get a better sense of the meaning and purpose of your life.

❓ Virgo – My Birthday Life Review

Do you recognize the Birthday Promise qualities in yourself?
If so, are they being used and developed? If you feel you are lacking in any of these, or are out of balance, you can ask the Spirit to help you make the most of them in this New Year. **Go to Page 190 for Your Birthday Life Review questions.**

The Fruit of the Tree of Life for Growth and Healing

Spiritual Fruit Tending - Reflect on These Virtues in Your Life and Rate Them

Fruit of the Spirit	👍 Growing Well?	➕ Needs Fertilizing?	👎 Needs Pruning
Love - A deep and abiding affection and concern for others.			
Joy – A state of happiness and delight, even in the midst of difficult circumstances.			
Peace – A state of tranquility and harmony, both internally and externally.			
Patience – The ability to endure challenges or agitation without becoming angry or upset.			
Kindness – A gentle and kind nature, showing compassion and care for others.			
Goodness – A moral excellence and uprightness of character.			
Faithfulness – Loyalty, trustworthiness, and steadfastness in commitments.			
Gentleness – A kind and considerate demeanor, avoiding harshness or aggression.			
Self-control – The ability to restrain impulses and appetites.			
Long-suffering - The capacity to endure hardship with patience and perseverance.			
Temperence - Moderation and self-restraint in all aspects of life.			
Wisdom - The ability to make sound judgments and decisions based on knowledge and experience.			

❓ Virgo - Spiritual Fruit Tending
Questions and prompts for your quiet time
Go to Page 192 for a deep dive into your Fruit of the Tree of Life ratings.

Rate Your Life on the Wheel of Life

Think about the matters of your life shown in the Key Areas of Life Table from Page 13 and evaluate your current level of satisfaction in each Area on a scale from 1-8. The Wheel of Life segments correspond with the topics in this Table. Rate each Area and highlight the number you gave yourself in each Area on the blank Wheel below.

How is your life going? Be sure to rate yourself honestly. This is your reality check. Your honest evaluation will quickly help pinpoint any imbalance. The lower rated areas will show you where you need more focus. No more guessing!

Then, outline the highlighted Wheel of Life ratings with a marker to link them to each other to form a figure within the circle showing the degree of balance in your life, as in the following example.

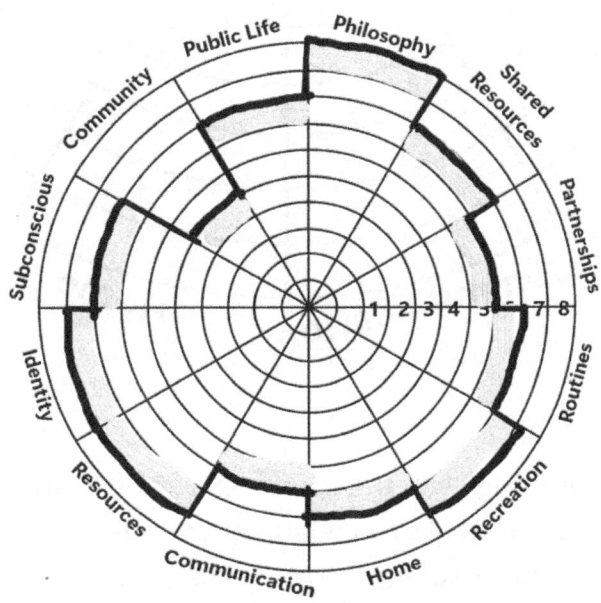

Example of the Wheel of Life with Evaluations

97

Wheel of Life

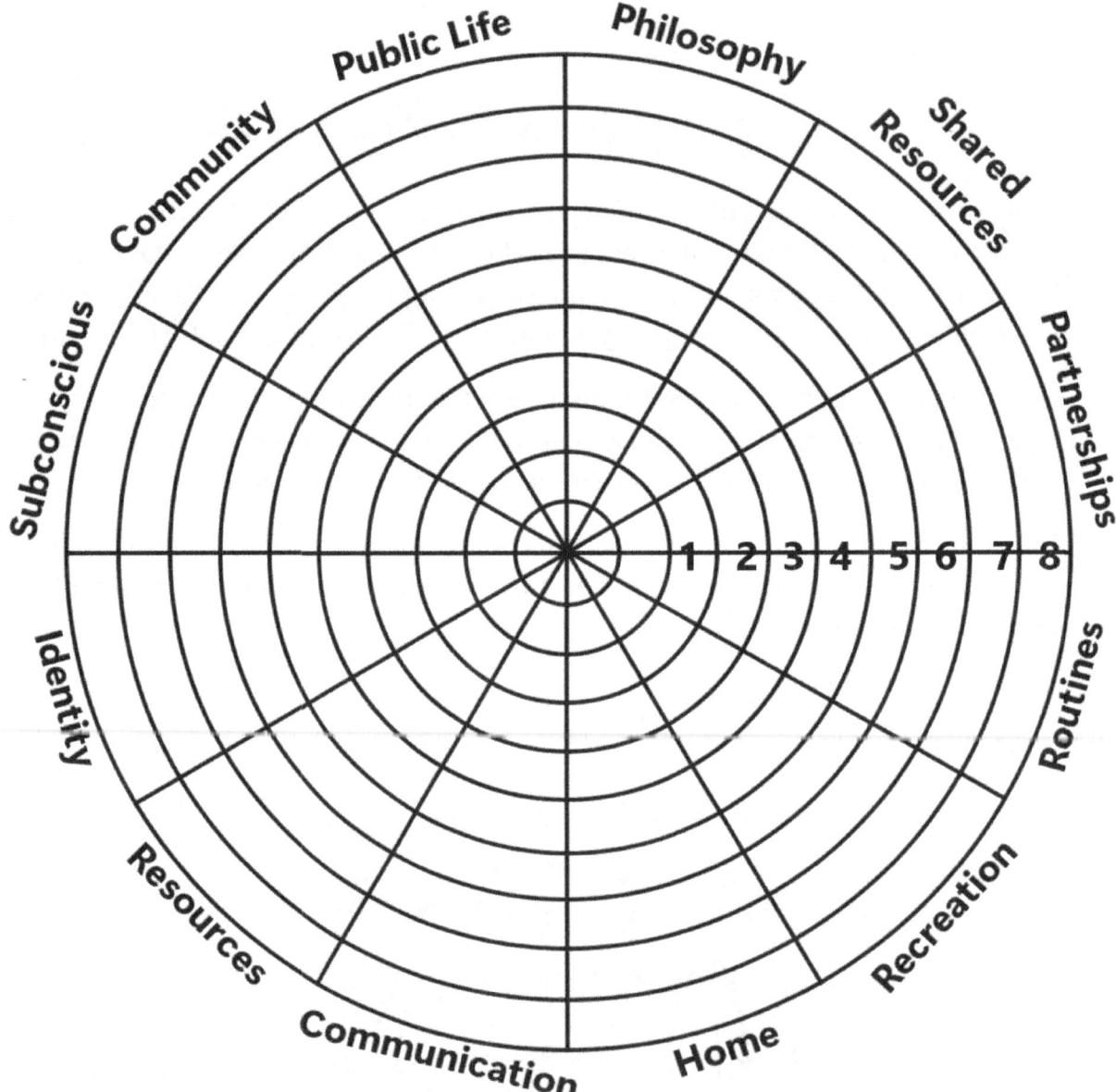

Filling in the Wheel of Life: Highlight the space on a scale from 1-8 under each Key Area that reflects your current level of satisfaction or imbalance in that area, with 8 being the most satisfying and 1 needing the most attention.

Next, interpret the results. How does the balance of your Key Areas of Life look? Analyze the resulting shape to identify the unbalanced areas that require attention and how to improve your satisfaction with them.

With a different color, mark the scores where you would like them to be in the future. Transfer your current and goal scores, as number of stars, to the table below to see where you stand in each category.

Fill in the stars for the Wheel of Life ratings you gave yourself for the current Year and then give yourself stars for next Year's goal.

Wheel of Life Area of Life	How many stars do you give yourself? 1-8 (from your Wheel of Life rating)	
	Current Wheel of Life	Goal for Next Year
Identity	☆☆☆☆☆☆☆☆	☆☆☆☆☆☆☆☆
Resources	☆☆☆☆☆☆☆☆	☆☆☆☆☆☆☆☆
Communication	☆☆☆☆☆☆☆☆	☆☆☆☆☆☆☆☆
Home	☆☆☆☆☆☆☆☆	☆☆☆☆☆☆☆☆
Recreation	☆☆☆☆☆☆☆☆	☆☆☆☆☆☆☆☆
Routines	☆☆☆☆☆☆☆☆	☆☆☆☆☆☆☆☆
Partnerships	☆☆☆☆☆☆☆☆	☆☆☆☆☆☆☆☆
Shared Resources	☆☆☆☆☆☆☆☆	☆☆☆☆☆☆☆☆
Philosophy	☆☆☆☆☆☆☆☆	☆☆☆☆☆☆☆☆
Public Life	☆☆☆☆☆☆☆☆	☆☆☆☆☆☆☆☆
Community	☆☆☆☆☆☆☆☆	☆☆☆☆☆☆☆☆
Subconscious	☆☆☆☆☆☆☆☆	☆☆☆☆☆☆☆☆

Good ratings in the different areas of your life have a major noticeable impact on your overall well-being and quality of life. A well-balanced life can reduce stress and anxiety, improve your mental wellbeing, and make you more productive, and will improve your self-esteem, family life, partnerships, career, and the other areas of

your life. On the other hand, a lack of balance in several areas of your life will cause instability in the other Areas of your life as well.

Make a conscious decision to take better care of your life and make it all that it can be. Start by giving some thought to each Area in the Wheel of Life. What is the status of each one? Reflect on what there is to learn about each one. Work on strengthening the various areas of your life to welcome more peace, purpose, and fulfillment.

 *Taking Inventory of the Qualities of Your Life*

Virgo – Deep Dive on Your Wheel of Life Findings
Questions and prompts for your quiet time
Go to Page 194 for a deep dive into your Wheel of Life ratings.

Virgo – Your Birthday Promise Insights
Reflections on Last Year ✴ Intentions for the Year Ahead
Questions and prompts for your quiet time
Go to Page 197 for a deep dive into Your Birthday Promise Insights.

God's Birthday Message to Virgo...

Dear Virgo, as you review your life this Year, remember the unique individual that you have been created to be and the core qualities that you have been given to equip you for your role in life.

Born in Virgo, the last Month of Summer, you were given the qualities of thoroughness, service, and labor. These equip you for your role as The Analyzer to fulfill your purpose to support, organize, and improve processes in a constructive manner.

You are known for your gifts of analysis, attention to detail, and a servant's heart. God is calling you to continue to use these gifts and your servant's heart to help others. Acts of service contribute to both your personal development and alignment with your purpose.

God sees the care and devotion you pour into your work and relationships. Though you tend to be a perfectionist, He cautions you to not become too critical, anxious, and bogged down in minor details. Do not let the search for perfection keep you from accepting yourself and others. Sometimes being good enough is good enough. Progress, not perfection, is what God desires.

God's message is that it is important to consider the underlying significance of details. Put the emphasis on serving others beyond simply fulfilling assigned tasks. Remain adaptable and receptive to new perspectives and opportunities. Striking a balance between diligence and acceptance can make your abilities shine.

Spiritual Growth Tips

✓ Consider ways you can help those around you, support your community, and make a positive impact in the world as a whole with your servant's heart.

✓ Remember that service should come from joy, not frustration.

✓ Do something of service behind the scenes.

✓ Think of how you can refine your own internal growth, well-being, and happiness instead of always fixing external situations.

Virgo – Take-Aways from Your Deep Dives

Now that you have reflected, meditated, and received insight from the Spirit from your time of prayer, meditation, and meeting with the Spirit about all Areas of Your Life, journal the revelations, words, and directions that come to mind for the coming Year.

What have you learned about yourself?

What have you learned about God?

What have you learned about the direction and plan for your life?

Finally – Submit Your Plans to God

While we can meet with the Lord and get direction and set intentions for the New Year, we ultimately need to submit to His Will and timing. We may not understand how things play out, but we will recognize areas of our life that we can intentionally bring into alignment with His ways. While we are honing our gifts and abilities, He will open doors and close doors accordingly and we will flow along with Him on this Year's journey.

Many are the plans in a person's heart, but it is the LORD's purpose that prevails.
Proverbs 19:21

A man's heart plans his course, but the LORD determines his steps.
Proverbs 16:9 BSB

And we know that in all things God works for the good of those who love him, who have been called according to his purpose. Romans 8:28

To everything there is a season, and a time to every purpose under the heaven: A time to be born, and a time to die; a time to plant, and a time to pluck up that which is planted... Ecclesiastes 3:1-2 NKJV

Biblical Affirmations to Declare Over Your Life

In addition to the specific traits you have been given to fulfill your God-given purpose, there are underlying truths about who God created you to be. These affirmations confirm the qualities you have been given for your underlying relationship and identity through Him.

Birthday affirmations, declarations, and prayers go beyond mere wishes; they are faith-filled expressions that align with God's Word that speak life, purpose, encouragement, and Divine blessing. The words we speak have power, and for those on a spiritual path, it is important to declare what God says about us. While the world may try to label us by our past, errors, or situations, we should instead rely on the truth found in God's Word.

Use these affirmations, supported by Scripture, to renew your mind, strengthen your faith and walk confidently in your God-given identity. Repeat them daily and let the truth of His promises transform your life!

Who Am I?

- I am a child of God and an heir to His promises. (Romans 8:17)
- I am fearfully and wonderfully made. (Psalm 139:14)
- I am God's masterpiece, created for good works. (Ephesians 2:10)
- I am chosen, holy, and dearly loved by God. (Colossians 3:12)
- I am bold because the Lord is my helper. (Hebrews 13:6)
- I am confident that God will finish the good work He started in me. (Philippians 1:6)

Promises of God

- This is the day the Lord has made; I will rejoice and be glad in it. (Psalm 118:24)
- Nothing can separate me from God's love. (Romans 8:38-39)
- God's plans for me are good, filled with hope and a future. (Jeremiah 29:11)
- God directs my steps and makes my paths straight. (Proverbs 3:5-6)
- God's power works in me to accomplish far more than I can imagine. (Ephesians 3:20)
- The Lord is faithful to keep His promises to me. (Deuteronomy 7:9)
- The Lord makes everything beautiful in His time. (Ecclesiastes 3:11)

I Am - Virgo Personality Declarations

- ♥ I am an organizer.
- ♥ I am a critical thinker and analyst .
- ♥ I am an analytical fact-finder with meticulous attention to detail .
- ♥ I am dedicated to service to humanity.
- ♥ I am a problem solver and a fact-checker.
- ♥ I am well-organized and detail oriented.
- ♥ I am tidy and health conscious.
- ♥ I am health conscious.
- ♥ I have healing abilities.
- ♥ I am trustworthy and honest.
- ♥ I am shy, modest, and reserved.
- ♥ I am responsible and competent.
- ♥ I am kind and helpful.

Virgo - Reminders for Growth and Balance

- + I love to read, learn, and do detailed work.
- + I offer my advice without over doing it.
- + I balance doing with being.
- + I remember that I am a human being and am enough.
- + I tune in to the messages coming from my body.
- + I learn ways to take care of myself.
- + I take a step back when I feel overwhelmed.
- + I realize perfection is impossible.
- + I practice relaxation techniques to alleviate stress.
- + I prioritize my health by eating healthy food.
- + I release worry over things I can't control.

And there is more!

For more insight into the traits of Virgo go to, "Nourishment from the Month of Virgo," in Part Two, *Journey Around the Wheel of the Year*.

Happy Birthday, Libra!

The Peacemaker

The Initiating First Month of Fall
September 23 – October 22

Libra! You are a natural mediator, always seeking fairness. You can see both sides which gives you a strong sense of fairness and a desire for peace. You are diplomatic and hate conflict. You strive to find balance in all aspects of life.

Your Birthday Promise - The Libra Personality

With Your Birthday under the Month of Libra you were born to see other people's perspectives. You were born to create harmony, balance, and encourage connection. You help others see things from a different perspective.

The need to relate is a strong element of your personality. You are fair-minded. Social skills are particularly important to you. You have good manners, are a welcomed guest, have thoughtful remarks, and can provide fresh ideas. You are a natural at speaking and sharing your thoughts and are inclined to involve others in conversations on a regular basis. You are a good sounding board and people confide in you.

Those born under the Month of Libra can be a bit sinister at times. You want to know the truth and that there is factual background information to make claims credible. You like to have the facts straight before making an important decision.

You are delicate, charming, sociable, and perpetually compromising. You always give the other side equal time and mediate to avoid conflict. For this reason, you may sometimes come across as hesitant and weak because you dare not insist or give your opinion. You prefer to act as a unifier, an element of understanding and equity, even if it is detrimental to your own assertiveness.

You can effectively bridge gaps between opposing sides by bringing objectivity into complicated circumstances where a fair-minded, common-sense and well-mannered attitude is needed. You are the initiator of actions toward teamwork, marriage, and business partnerships or close associations.

While you may enjoy peace, you can easily cause chaos and uneasiness because of your need for balance. You are often more concerned with the appearance of harmony and justice than true harmony or justice. You hate violence, you spare no efforts for the sake of pacification, and you adjust to the situation with flexibility and charm.

You are driven to inspire ideas, potentialities, and wishes and are intellectually motivated to initiate relationships. You care about everyone and their opinions, and you see both sides of every story. Because of this, making decisions can be difficult for you. Life can be a balancing act where you weigh all your options and have a hard time making up your mind. Indecision may be your worst fault.

You seek to look after everyone else's well-being. Companionship is important and you are miserable when alone. You have many loves but will not feel love deeply until you have grown in experience.

Libras have artistic skills and are known for their talents in the humanities and fashion. Communication of all kinds is vital to your energies. You are naturally beautiful and seek pleasure and comfort.

You are concerned with equality, compromise, symmetry, and peace. You can be persuasive, civil, courteous, and elegant. You are someone who sees alternate sides of every situation, who values justice as a virtue, and who cares a great deal about equality.

Each life experience over your lifetime will in some way be involved in fulfilling your need to cooperate with others and create harmony and balance in your life and be The Peacemaker, The Diplomat, The Smooth Negotiator.

Why have you been given these traits? You carry these traits to equip you with what you need to fulfill your individual life's mission as well as the role you have in all of humanity.

Embracing the characteristics of Your Birthday Promise will help you navigate life with authenticity and purpose.

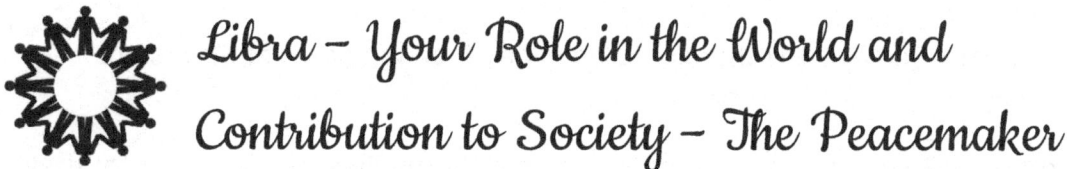 Libra – Your Role in the World and Contribution to Society – The Peacemaker

Each of you should use whatever gift you have received to serve others as faithful stewards of God's grace in its various forms. 1 Peter 4:10

We each have a role to fill for ourselves and for humanity. Born under the Month of Libra, your contribution to society is to bring peace to situations where common sense and a balanced approach is required.

You personify and promote harmony and the art of civilized living. Your role is often the middleman in relationships because you are able to navigate situations with grace and to bring peace in circumstances when needed.

You are the peacemaker who always tries to consider everyone's point of view in a debate or to lead in a reconciliation. You stand for equality, fairness, and harmony. You are here to promote the cause of goodwill and justice for all.

You strongly support world peace and humanitarian work, and use an unbiased and fair attitude to fight for the practical causes of the world and make it become a better place. You establish friendliness and fairness in a world where most everyone tries to step on others to get ahead.

You are able to relate to others and exchange ideas in a fair and even way. You are the most social of all the Months. You are naturally attuned to the needs of others and your desire for harmony and balance motivates you to offer kindness and understanding to everyone you meet. You create peaceful environments where others feel loved and supported.

Libra – What You are Here to Learn
Lessons to Learn to Excel at Your Role

Born under the Month of Libra, throughout your life, you are here to learn:

...to avoid always doing what other people need, want, or expect.

...to prioritize your own needs and desires when considering those of others.

...not to subordinate your own needs to what you fear others may think or agree with.

...not to compare yourself to others or to be overly focused on what others are doing or saying.

... to let others solve their own problems and hold themselves accountable for their own behavior.

...to stand your ground and accept the discomfort of asserting your own wants and needs.

...to realize that you are just as worthy of having your needs met as those around you.

...how to grow a harmonious relationship while also keeping your individual identity and power.

Libra – Let Your Light Shine

Born under the Month of Libra, the special light you shine is through your close personal relationships with others. You thrive on sparking ideas and encouraging possibilities and aspirations. Your intellectual curiosity leads you to build connections with others. You seek out partnerships, aim for harmony, and strive to foster fairness and positive relations. Partnership and close relationships will be used and developed to fulfill your life purpose.

"You are the light of the world. A city set on a hill cannot be hidden. Nor do people light a lamp and put it under a basket, but on a stand, and it gives light to all in the house. In the same way, let your light shine before others, so that they may see your good works and give glory to your Father who is in heaven." Matthew 5:14-16 ESV

Taking Inventory of the Qualities of Your Life

As you review your life during this time of Your Birthday Month, realize that you are already everything you need to be at this time in your journey. You are not broken or damaged. You are who you were created to be right now. We each have an opportunity to take stock and grow in the gifts and talents we have been given.

At this Yearly time of celebrating Your Birthday, you have an opportunity to get to know and love yourself more fully than you have before. It is a time to trust God in the unfolding and timing of your life and get a better sense of the meaning and purpose of your life.

❓ Libra – My Birthday Life Review

Do you recognize the Birthday Promise qualities in yourself?
If so, are they being used and developed? If you feel you are lacking in any of these, or are out of balance, you can ask the Spirit to help you make the most of them in this New Year. **Go to Page 190 for Your Birthday Life Review questions.**

The Fruit of the Tree of Life for Growth and Healing

Spiritual Fruit Tending - Reflect on These Virtues in Your Life and Rate Them

Fruit of the Spirit	👍 Growing Well?	➕ Needs Fertilizing?	👎 Needs Pruning
Love - A deep and abiding affection and concern for others.			
Joy – A state of happiness and delight, even in the midst of difficult circumstances.			
Peace – A state of tranquility and harmony, both internally and externally.			
Patience – The ability to endure challenges or agitation without becoming angry or upset.			
Kindness – A gentle and kind nature, showing compassion and care for others.			
Goodness – A moral excellence and uprightness of character.			
Faithfulness – Loyalty, trustworthiness, and steadfastness in commitments.			
Gentleness – A kind and considerate demeanor, avoiding harshness or aggression.			
Self-control – The ability to restrain impulses and appetites.			
Long-suffering - The capacity to endure hardship with patience and perseverance.			
Temperence - Moderation and self-restraint in all aspects of life.			
Wisdom - The ability to make sound judgments and decisions based on knowledge and experience.			

Libra - Spiritual Fruit Tending
Questions and prompts for your quiet time
Go to Page 192 for a deep dive into your Fruit of the Tree of Life ratings.

Rate Your Life on the Wheel of Life

Think about the matters of your life shown in the Key Areas of Life Table from Page 13 and evaluate your current level of satisfaction in each Area on a scale from 1-8. The Wheel of Life segments correspond with the topics in this Table. Rate each Area and highlight the number you gave yourself in each Area on the blank Wheel below.

How is your life going? Be sure to rate yourself honestly. This is your reality check. Your honest evaluation will quickly help pinpoint any imbalance. The lower rated areas will show you where you need more focus. No more guessing!

Then, outline the highlighted Wheel of Life ratings with a marker to link them to each other to form a figure within the circle showing the degree of balance in your life, as in the following example.

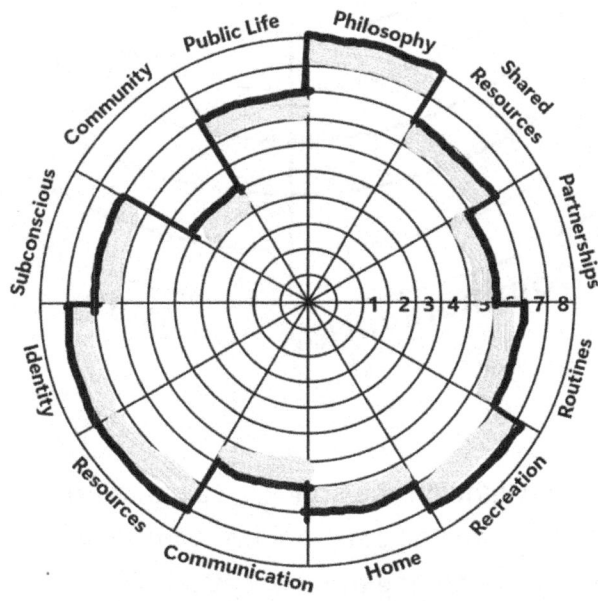

Example of the Wheel of Life with Evaluations

111

Wheel of Life

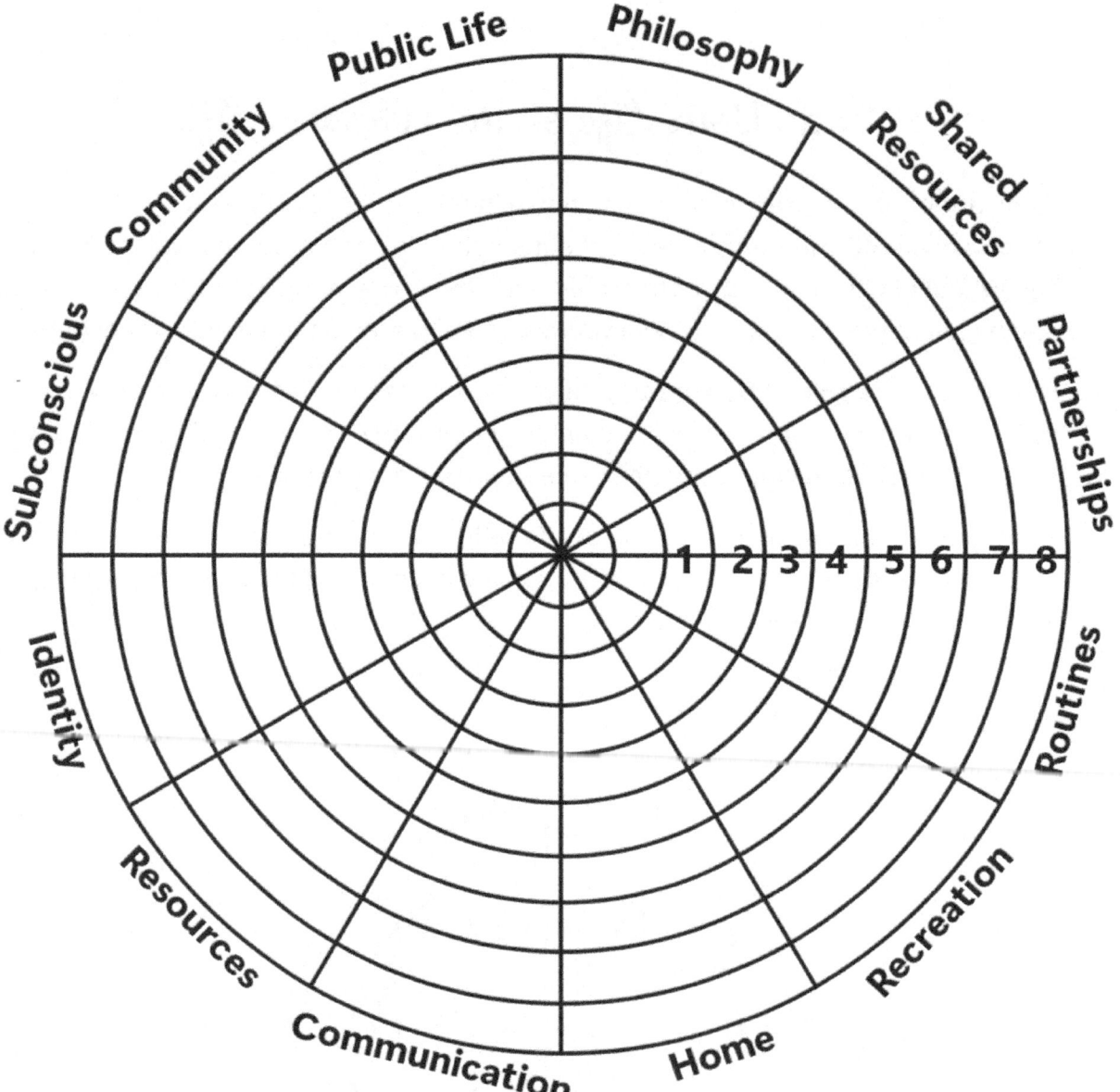

Filling in the Wheel of Life: Highlight the space on a scale from 1-8 under each Key Area that reflects your current level of satisfaction or imbalance in that area, with 8 being the most satisfying and 1 needing the most attention.

Next, interpret the results. How does the balance of your Key Areas of Life look? Analyze the resulting shape to identify the unbalanced areas that require attention and how to improve your satisfaction with them.

With a different color, mark the scores where you would like them to be in the future. Transfer your current and goal scores, as number of stars, to the table below to see where you stand in each category.

Fill in the stars for the Wheel of Life ratings you gave yourself for the current Year and then give yourself stars for next Year's goal.

Wheel of Life Area of Life	How many stars do you give yourself? 1-8 (from your Wheel of Life rating)	
	Current Wheel of Life	Goal for Next Year
Identity	☆☆☆☆☆☆☆☆	☆☆☆☆☆☆☆☆
Resources	☆☆☆☆☆☆☆☆	☆☆☆☆☆☆☆☆
Communication	☆☆☆☆☆☆☆☆	☆☆☆☆☆☆☆☆
Home	☆☆☆☆☆☆☆☆	☆☆☆☆☆☆☆☆
Recreation	☆☆☆☆☆☆☆☆	☆☆☆☆☆☆☆☆
Routines	☆☆☆☆☆☆☆☆	☆☆☆☆☆☆☆☆
Partnerships	☆☆☆☆☆☆☆☆	☆☆☆☆☆☆☆☆
Shared Resources	☆☆☆☆☆☆☆☆	☆☆☆☆☆☆☆☆
Philosophy	☆☆☆☆☆☆☆☆	☆☆☆☆☆☆☆☆
Public Life	☆☆☆☆☆☆☆☆	☆☆☆☆☆☆☆☆
Community	☆☆☆☆☆☆☆☆	☆☆☆☆☆☆☆☆
Subconscious	☆☆☆☆☆☆☆☆	☆☆☆☆☆☆☆☆

Good ratings in the different areas of your life have a major noticeable impact on your overall well-being and quality of life. A well-balanced life can reduce stress and anxiety, improve your mental wellbeing, and make you more productive, and will improve your self-esteem, family life, partnerships, career, and the other areas of

your life. On the other hand, a lack of balance in several areas of your life will cause instability in the other Areas of your life as well.

Make a conscious decision to take better care of your life and make it all that it can be. Start by giving some thought to each Area in the Wheel of Life. What is the status of each one? Reflect on what there is to learn about each one. Work on strengthening the various areas of your life to welcome more peace, purpose, and fulfillment.

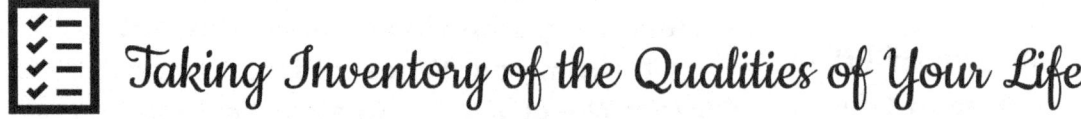

Taking Inventory of the Qualities of Your Life

Libra – Deep Dive on Your Wheel of Life Findings
Questions and prompts for your quiet time
Go to Page 194 for a deep dive into your Wheel of Life ratings.

Libra – Your Birthday Promise Insights
Reflections on Last Year ✳ Intentions for the Year Ahead
Questions and prompts for your quiet time
Go to Page 197 for a deep dive into Your Birthday Promise Insights.

God's Birthday Message for Libra...

Dear Libra, as you review your life this Year, remember the unique individual that you have been created to be and the core qualities that you have been given to equip you for your role in life.

Born in Libra, the first Month of Fall, you were given the qualities of cooperation, gracefulness, charm, and diplomacy. These equip you for your role of being The Peacemaker. Your purpose is to bring differing perspectives together into a harmonious whole. You seek balance and harmony in all things.

God is encouraging you to use your natural gifts of fairness and maintaining equilibrium in all areas of life. Take the initiative to build bridges, resolve conflicts, and bring balance wherever there is discord. Through this you will teach others about fairness, beauty, and peaceful relationships.

The tendency to prioritize harmony and weigh all options may at times result in indecision or putting others' needs ahead of your own. It is important to be aware of how external opinions can influence your choices at the expense of remaining true to your own truth.

God is calling you to be confident in your beliefs while staying open-minded. Share your fairness, charm, and harmony with others and don't hold back out of fear or making the wrong decision. Your spirit grows when you trust your decisions.

Spiritual Growth Tips

✓ Use your sense of justice to help bring about fairness and harmony in your dealings.

✓ Remember that your desire for peace is a Divine gift.

✓ Use your diplomacy to unite people in love and understanding.

✓ Even when it feel uncomfortable, stand up for what is right.

✓ Look for peace through faith, not just human agreement.

💡 Libra – Take-Aways from Your Deep Dives

Now that you have reflected, meditated, and received insight from the Spirit from your time of prayer, meditation, and meeting with the Spirit about all Areas of Your Life, journal the revelations, words, and directions that come to mind for the coming Year.

What have you learned about yourself?

What have you learned about God?

What have you learned about the direction and plan for your life?

Finally – Submit Your Plans to God

While we can meet with the Lord and get direction and set intentions for the New Year, we ultimately need to submit to His Will and timing. We may not understand how things play out, but we will recognize areas of our life that we can intentionally bring into alignment with His ways. While we are honing our gifts and abilities, He will open doors and close doors accordingly and we will flow along with Him on this Year's journey.

> *Many are the plans in a person's heart, but it is the LORD's purpose that prevails.*
> *Proverbs 19:21*

> *A man's heart plans his course, but the LORD determines his steps.*
> *Proverbs 16:9 BSB*

> *And we know that in all things God works for the good of those who love him, who have been called according to his purpose. Romans 8:28*

> *To everything there is a season, and a time to every purpose under the heaven: A time to be born, and a time to die; a time to plant, and a time to pluck up that which is planted... Ecclesiastes 3:1-2 NKJV*

Biblical Affirmations to Declare Over Your Life

In addition to the specific traits you have been given to fulfill your God-given purpose, there are underlying truths about who God created you to be. These affirmations confirm the qualities you have been given for your underlying relationship and identity through Him.

Birthday affirmations, declarations, and prayers go beyond mere wishes; they are faith-filled expressions that align with God's Word that speak life, purpose, encouragement, and Divine blessing. The words we speak have power, and for those on a spiritual path, it is important to declare what God says about us. While the world may try to label us by our past, errors, or situations, we should instead rely on the truth found in God's Word.

Use these affirmations, supported by Scripture, to renew your mind, strengthen your faith and walk confidently in your God-given identity. Repeat them daily and let the truth of His promises transform your life!

Who Am I?

- I am a child of God and an heir to His promises. (Romans 8:17)
- I am fearfully and wonderfully made. (Psalm 139:14)
- I am God's masterpiece, created for good works. (Ephesians 2:10)
- I am chosen, holy, and dearly loved by God. (Colossians 3:12)
- I am bold because the Lord is my helper. (Hebrews 13:6)
- I am confident that God will finish the good work He started in me. (Philippians 1:6)

Promises of God

- This is the day the Lord has made; I will rejoice and be glad in it. (Psalm 118:24)
- Nothing can separate me from God's love. (Romans 8:38-39)
- God's plans for me are good, filled with hope and a future. (Jeremiah 29:11)
- God directs my steps and makes my paths straight. (Proverbs 3:5-6)
- God's power works in me to accomplish far more than I can imagine. (Ephesians 3:20)
- The Lord is faithful to keep His promises to me. (Deuteronomy 7:9)
- The Lord makes everything beautiful in His time. (Ecclesiastes 3:11)

I Am – Libra Personality Declarations

- ♥ I am a natural peacemaker.
- ♥ I am cooperative, graceful, and charming.
- ♥ I am sociable and diplomatic.
- ♥ I am analytically and intellectually inclined.
- ♥ I am a gifted mediator.
- ♥ I am creative and stylish.
- ♥ I am fair and equitable.
- ♥ I am romantic, idealistic, and imaginative.
- ♥ I am concerned with balance in all areas of life.
- ♥ I am able to see both sides of the story.
- ♥ I am able to make decisions regarding my life.

Libra – Reminders for Growth and Balance

- + I enjoy partnerships.
- + I help people see the other side of the story.
- + I like balance and justice.
- + I speak my needs without guilt.
- + I honor what I need.
- + I realize I am not responsible for everyone else.
- + I resist people-pleasing and avoiding conflicts.
- + I shine when addressing imbalances of power.
- + I will advocate for others if I sense injustice.
- + I make agreements with those close to me.
- + I have a natural ability to talk with anyone about nearly anything.
- + I value my partnerships.
- + I avoid conflict when possible.

And there is more!

For more insight into the traits of Libra go to, "Nourishment from the Month of Libra," in Part Two, *Journey Around the Wheel of the Year*.

Happy Birthday, Scorpio!

The Investigator

The Fixed Middle Month of Fall
October 23 – November 21

Scorpio! You are a deep thinker with intense emotions that often bring personal transformation. You often receive insight and understanding that others may miss.
Your inner strength gives you the ability to navigate through life's challenges with resilience and determination.

Your Birthday Promise - The Scorpio Personality

With Your Birthday under the Month of Scorpio you were born to search for deep truth even if it involves issues which are taboo. While others avoid uncomfortable topics you have the rare gift of diving deep into them, knowing that power comes from knowing the truth. You were born to transform, give power to, and face the truth.

You give a lot of thought, study, and practice to any situation. You desire deep thought, deep study, and deep practice. Your role is to be the private eye, detective, scientific and spiritual researcher. You enjoy getting to the heart of the matter.

Scorpio is the most intense, passionate of all Months. You have deep emotions and desires. You are either fully committed to something or not committed at all. There is no middle ground. You are all in, heart, soul, and body. Your nature needs intensity that must be balanced with letting go.

You have intense life experiences that provide for continuous transformation and personal growth. As you dig into what you are experiencing in your inner being, you can discover how to wisely and gracefully turn your experiences and resources into valuable insights and assets.

You are constantly struggling to assert yourself. You have a need for power and control and can learn to manipulate in order to maintain it. You can have a tendency to be aggressive and ready to fight battles. You want to change things.

You have your own mind, are driven by power, and you never, ever give up. You are goal oriented, determined, and will dig deep to find the truth. You have an incredible gift for getting results and are typically one who becomes highly accomplished in life.

Scorpio is a Month obsessed with privacy and secrets. You are attracted to hidden and mysterious topics. You are someone who navigates that unseen space between the physical world and the spiritual world with ease. You are likely to reach a deep understanding of esoteric subjects.

You seek emotional security by forming relationships with very strong boundaries or through excessive closeness. You can seem overpowering and you may intimidate others, but under that exterior is a reserved and cautious person. You need to guard against the extremes of becoming obsessive, possessive, or dictatorial.

Scorpios never forget a slight.

Each life experience over your lifetime will in some way be involved in fulfilling your need for deep involvements and intense transformative experiences and be The Investigator, The Secret One, The Deep Thinker, and The Intense Schemer.

Why have you been given these traits? You carry these traits to equip you with what you need to fulfill your individual life's mission as well as the role you have in all of humanity.

Embracing the characteristics of Your Birthday Promise will help you navigate life with authenticity and purpose.

 Scorpio – Your Role in the World and Contribution to Society – The Investigator

Each of you should use whatever gift you have received to serve others as faithful stewards of God's grace in its various forms. 1 Peter 4:10

We each have a role to fill for ourselves and for humanity. Born under the Month of Scorpio, your contribution to society is to make people stronger than their problems. With your intense passion and unwavering determination to overcome, you help others confront their deepest fears and shed their old selves to embrace their true potential. You are often the one to whom others turn to share their deepest thoughts and experiences.

You are eager to learn and you have extraordinary boldness and courage to face difficult truths about human nature that others avoid, and then share your insights with those around you.

You see beyond the superficial, recognizing truths that transform. Each time you are transformed you gain healing tools that you can use to guide yourself and others throughout your life. When you are able to harness your intense emotional energy for good, you become an invaluable healer and wisdom keeper for your community.

 # Scorpio – What You are Here to Learn

Lessons to Learn to Excel at Your Role

Born under the Month of Scorpio, throughout your life, you are here to learn:

...to maintain a sense of personal power and truth that is forthcoming and wise.

...to heal wounds around thoughts of scarcity, and move into a mindset of abundance.

...to trust what you feel, sense, and perceive with or without confirmation or reaction from others.

...how to manage your powerful feelings.

...to balance the energies of intensity and release.

...to skillfully work with your emotions, turning what was once overwhelming into a source of energy and power.

...to turn your difficulties into life lessons.

...to embrace change as a catalyst for personal growth.

Scorpio – Let Your Light Shine

Born under the Month of Scorpio, the special light you shine is through deep personal transformations and self-improvement. Your focus tends to be on your internal emotional experiences. The deeper mysteries of life such as death, rebirth, and survival are of interest to you and will be used and developed to fulfill your life's purpose, especially in your later Years.

> *"You are the light of the world. A city set on a hill cannot be hidden. Nor do people light a lamp and put it under a basket, but on a stand, and it gives light to all in the house. In the same way, let your light shine before others, so that they may see your good works and give glory to your Father who is in heaven." Matthew 5:14-16 ESV*

 Taking Inventory of the Qualities of Your Life

As you review your life during this time of Your Birthday Month, realize that you are already everything you need to be at this time in your journey. You are not broken or damaged. You are who you were created to be right now. We each have an opportunity to take stock and grow in the gifts and talents we have been given.

At this Yearly time of celebrating Your Birthday, you have an opportunity to get to know and love yourself more fully than you have before. It is a time to trust God in the unfolding and timing of your life and get a better sense of the meaning and purpose of your life.

 Scorpio – My Birthday Life Review

Do you recognize the Birthday Promise qualities in yourself?
If so, are they being used and developed? If you feel you are lacking in any of these, or are out of balance, you can ask the Spirit to help you make the most of them in this New Year. **Go to Page 190 for Your Birthday Life Review questions.**

The Fruit of the Tree of Life for Growth and Healing

Spiritual Fruit Tending - Reflect on These Virtues in Your Life and Rate Them

Fruit of the Spirit	👍 Growing Well?	➕ Needs Fertilizing?	👎 Needs Pruning
Love - A deep and abiding affection and concern for others.			
Joy – A state of happiness and delight, even in the midst of difficult circumstances.			
Peace – A state of tranquility and harmony, both internally and externally.			
Patience – The ability to endure challenges or agitation without becoming angry or upset.			
Kindness – A gentle and kind nature, showing compassion and care for others.			
Goodness – A moral excellence and uprightness of character.			
Faithfulness – Loyalty, trustworthiness, and steadfastness in commitments.			
Gentleness – A kind and considerate demeanor, avoiding harshness or aggression.			
Self-control – The ability to restrain impulses and appetites.			
Long-suffering - The capacity to endure hardship with patience and perseverance.			
Temperance - Moderation and self-restraint in all aspects of life.			
Wisdom - The ability to make sound judgments and decisions based on knowledge and experience.			

Scorpio - Spiritual Fruit Tending
Questions and prompts for your quiet time
Go to Page 192 for a deep dive into your Fruit of the Tree of Life ratings.

Rate Your Life on the Wheel of Life

Think about the matters of your life shown in the Key Areas of Life Table from Page 13 and evaluate your current level of satisfaction in each Area on a scale from 1-8. The Wheel of Life segments correspond with the topics in this Table. Rate each Area and highlight the number you gave yourself in each Area on the blank Wheel below.

How is your life going? Be sure to rate yourself honestly. This is your reality check. Your honest evaluation will quickly help pinpoint any imbalance. The lower rated areas will show you where you need more focus. No more guessing!

Then, outline the highlighted Wheel of Life ratings with a marker to link them to each other to form a figure within the circle showing the degree of balance in your life, as in the following example.

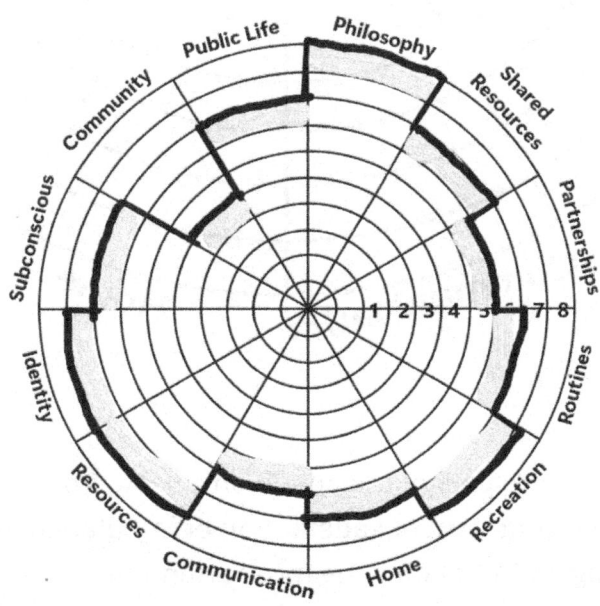

Example of the Wheel of Life with Evaluations

Wheel of Life

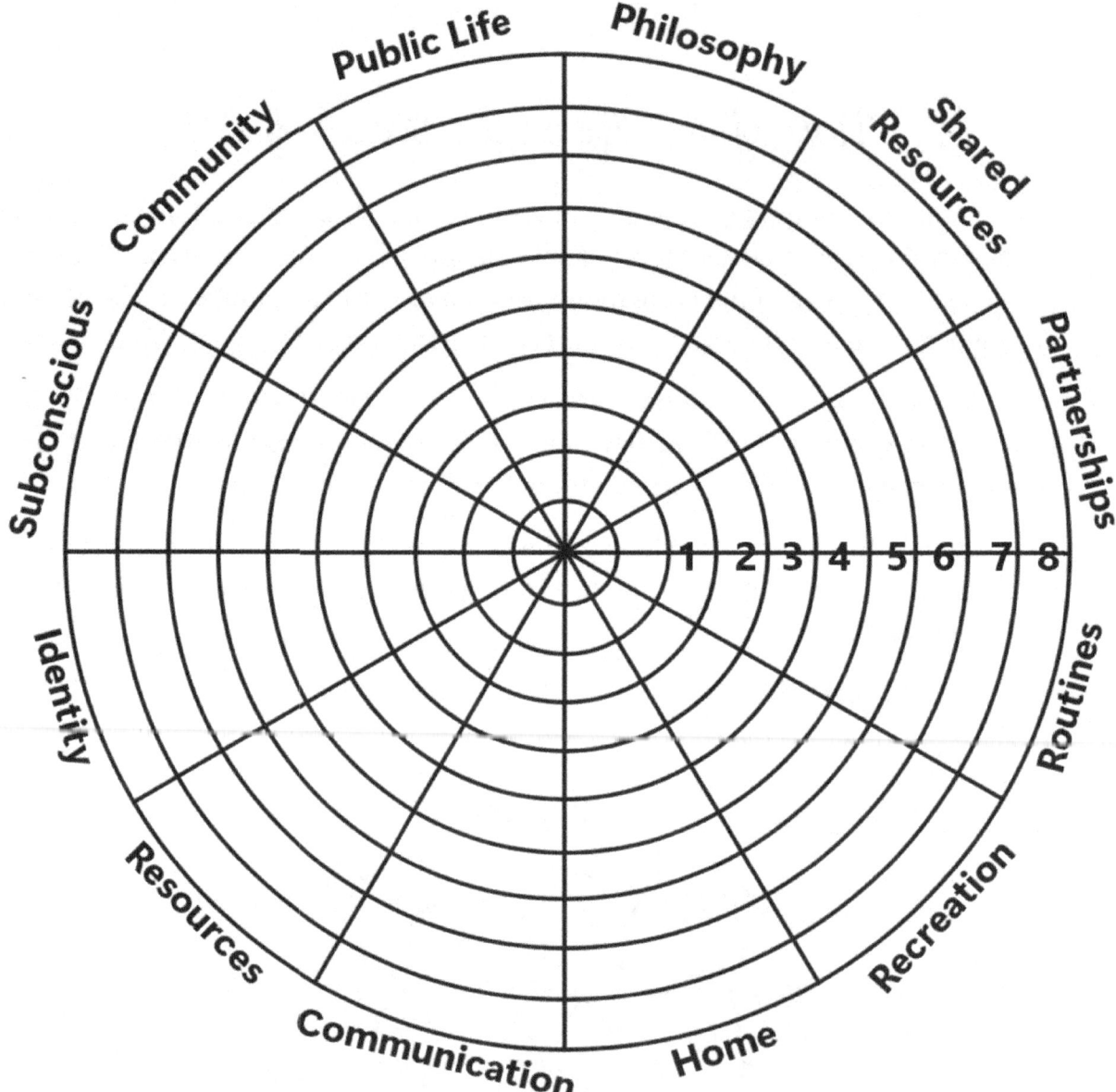

Filling in the Wheel of Life: Highlight the space on a scale from 1-8 under each Key Area that reflects your current level of satisfaction or imbalance in that area, with 8 being the most satisfying and 1 needing the most attention.

Next, interpret the results. How does the balance of your Key Areas of Life look? Analyze the resulting shape to identify the unbalanced areas that require attention and how to improve your satisfaction with them.

With a different color, mark the scores where you would like them to be in the future. Transfer your current and goal scores, as number of stars, to the table below to see where you stand in each category.

Fill in the stars for the Wheel of Life ratings you gave yourself for the current Year and then give yourself stars for next Year's goal.

Wheel of Life Area of Life	How many stars do you give yourself? 1-8 (from your Wheel of Life rating)	
	Current Wheel of Life	Goal for Next Year
Identity	☆☆☆☆☆☆☆☆	☆☆☆☆☆☆☆☆
Resources	☆☆☆☆☆☆☆☆	☆☆☆☆☆☆☆☆
Communication	☆☆☆☆☆☆☆☆	☆☆☆☆☆☆☆☆
Home	☆☆☆☆☆☆☆☆	☆☆☆☆☆☆☆☆
Recreation	☆☆☆☆☆☆☆☆	☆☆☆☆☆☆☆☆
Routines	☆☆☆☆☆☆☆☆	☆☆☆☆☆☆☆☆
Partnerships	☆☆☆☆☆☆☆☆	☆☆☆☆☆☆☆☆
Shared Resources	☆☆☆☆☆☆☆☆	☆☆☆☆☆☆☆☆
Philosophy	☆☆☆☆☆☆☆☆	☆☆☆☆☆☆☆☆
Public Life	☆☆☆☆☆☆☆☆	☆☆☆☆☆☆☆☆
Community	☆☆☆☆☆☆☆☆	☆☆☆☆☆☆☆☆
Subconscious	☆☆☆☆☆☆☆☆	☆☆☆☆☆☆☆☆

Good ratings in the different areas of your life have a major noticeable impact on your overall well-being and quality of life. A well-balanced life can reduce stress and anxiety, improve your mental wellbeing, and make you more productive, and will improve your self-esteem, family life, partnerships, career, and the other areas of

your life. On the other hand, a lack of balance in several areas of your life will cause instability in the other Areas of your life as well.

Make a conscious decision to take better care of your life and make it all that it can be. Start by giving some thought to each Area in the Wheel of Life. What is the status of each one? Reflect on what there is to learn about each one. Work on strengthening the various areas of your life to welcome more peace, purpose, and fulfillment.

 Taking Inventory of the Qualities of Your Life

Scorpio – Deep Dive on Your Wheel of Life Findings
Questions and prompts for your quiet time
Go to Page 194 for a deep dive into your Wheel of Life ratings.

Scorpio – Your Birthday Promise Insights
Reflections on Last Year ✴ Intentions for the Year Ahead
Questions and prompts for your quiet time
Go to Page 197 for a deep dive into Your Birthday Promise Insights.

God's Birthday Message for Scorpio...

Dear Scorpio, as you review your life this Year, remember the unique individual that you have been created to be and the core qualities that you have been given to equip you for your role in life.

Born in Scorpio, the second Month of Fall, you have been given the qualities of resilience, mystery, investigative power, and emotional intensity. These equip you for your role as The Investigator to fulfill your purpose of gaining an understanding of the hidden things of life while helping people along the way. You are unafraid to dive into the areas of life uncovering truths that others find taboo.

You are known for your drive, laser focus, and emotional depth. God cautions you not to let this intensity tip into obsession or darkness. Your probing mind often suspects and anticipates the worst in others and you isolate yourself for protection. With a fixed personality you tend to hold on to past hurts and betrayals for a long time. God urges you to open your heart, forgive others, and let go of bitterness. View those who hurt you with empathy, and consider forgiveness a sign of strength.

You may even distrust yourself and your abilities. God sees your unique talents and urges you to have faith in yourself and boldly develop them. By facing your fears and overcoming self-limiting beliefs, your growth will be more than you have imagined.

God is calling you to harness your powerful passions into connections, art, charity work, and all endeavors that make a positive difference in the world. When channeled constructively, your gifts can transform lives.

Spiritual Growth Tips

✓ Realize that in your search for spiritual development and clarity you will experience intense emotions and personal transformations.

✓ Be open to transformation, but let God guide you through it.

✓ Remember that when you struggle with trust, God sees your heart, loves you, and is always true.

✓ When you forgive and let go of resentments you will experience true freedom.

✓ Facing your inner fears will accelerate your growth.

💡 Scorpio – Take-Aways from Your Deep Dives

Now that you have reflected, meditated, and received insight from the Spirit from your time of prayer, meditation, and meeting with the Spirit about all Areas of Your Life, journal the revelations, words, and directions that come to mind for the coming Year.

What have you learned about yourself?

What have you learned about God?

What have you learned about the direction and plan for your life?

Finally – Submit Your Plans to God

While we can meet with the Lord and get direction and set intentions for the New Year, we ultimately need to submit to His Will and timing. We may not understand how things play out, but we will recognize areas of our life that we can intentionally bring into alignment with His ways. While we are honing our gifts and abilities, He will open doors and close doors accordingly and we will flow along with Him on this Year's journey.

*Many are the plans in a person's heart, but it is the LORD's purpose that prevails.
Proverbs 19:21*

*A man's heart plans his course, but the LORD determines his steps.
Proverbs 16:9 BSB*

And we know that in all things God works for the good of those who love him, who have been called according to his purpose. Romans 8:28

*To everything there is a season, and a time to every purpose under the heaven:
A time to be born, and a time to die; a time to plant,
and a time to pluck up that which is planted… Ecclesiastes 3:1-2 NKJV*

Biblical Affirmations to Declare Over Your Life

In addition to the specific traits you have been given to fulfill your God-given purpose, there are underlying truths about who God created you to be. These affirmations confirm the qualities you have been given for your underlying relationship and identity through Him.

Birthday affirmations, declarations, and prayers go beyond mere wishes; they are faith-filled expressions that align with God's Word that speak life, purpose, encouragement, and Divine blessing. The words we speak have power, and for those on a spiritual path, it is important to declare what God says about us. While the world may try to label us by our past, errors, or situations, we should instead rely on the truth found in God's Word.

Use these affirmations, supported by Scripture, to renew your mind, strengthen your faith and walk confidently in your God-given identity. Repeat them daily and let the truth of His promises transform your life!

Who Am I?

- I am a child of God and an heir to His promises. (Romans 8:17)
- I am fearfully and wonderfully made. (Psalm 139:14)
- I am God's masterpiece, created for good works. (Ephesians 2:10)
- I am chosen, holy, and dearly loved by God. (Colossians 3:12)
- I am bold because the Lord is my helper. (Hebrews 13:6)
- I am confident that God will finish the good work He started in me. (Philippians 1:6)

Promises of God

- This is the day the Lord has made; I will rejoice and be glad in it. (Psalm 118:24)
- Nothing can separate me from God's love. (Romans 8:38-39)
- God's plans for me are good, filled with hope and a future. (Jeremiah 29:11)
- God directs my steps and makes my paths straight. (Proverbs 3:5-6)
- God's power works in me to accomplish far more than I can imagine. (Ephesians 3:20)
- The Lord is faithful to keep His promises to me. (Deuteronomy 7:9)
- The Lord makes everything beautiful in His time. (Ecclesiastes 3:11)

I Am – Scorpio Personality Declarations

- ♥ I am an investigator.
- ♥ I am secretive.
- ♥ I am powerful and strong-willed.
- ♥ I am loyal and hard working.
- ♥ I am deep and intense.
- ♥ I am driven and competitive.
- ♥ I am powerful and self-controlled.
- ♥ I am drawn to the mysteries of life.
- ♥ I am interested in anything that might exist below the surface.
- ♥ I am a long-term true friend.
- ♥ I am attracted to wealth and power.
- ♥ I am being transformed by the renewing of my mind.

Scorpio – Reminders for Growth and Balance

- + I seek the truth beneath the surface.
- + I surrender what cannot be controlled.
- + I learn to forgive and not harbor grudges.
- + I forgive as I have been forgiven.
- + I seek total union.
- + I have a keen sense of purpose and will work hard to achieve my goals.
- + I struggle with trust and am learning to overcome.
- + I am learning that vulnerability can be strength.
- + I build healthy relationships based on mutual respect.
- + I find healthy outlets for emotions.

And there is more!

For more insight into the traits of Scorpio go to, "Nourishment from the Month of Scorpio," in Part Two, *Journey Around the Wheel of the Year*.

Happy Birthday, Sagittarius!

The Adventurer

The Transitional Last Month of Fall
November 22 – December 21

Sagittarius! You are always searching for truth, adventure, knowledge, and wisdom. Your curious and restless spirit drives you to explore the mysteries of life. These lead to new discoveries, understanding, beliefs and principles on which to live your life and share with others.

Your Birthday Promise - The Sagittarius Personality

With Your Birthday under the Month of Sagittarius you were born to explore, seek adventure, and inspire. You were born to discover the heights of spiritual, religious, and philosophical truth. You search out faraway places, whether it be material, physical or spiritual. You have strong faith, are forgiving, loving, and ethical.

Sagittarius is one of the most free-spirited, independent and curious of all the Months. You are always on the go and are often restless. You are hard to follow because your spirit and independent mind constantly lead you to go further and higher. You have the rare ability to see endless possibilities, think broadly, and make visions real where others see obstacles.

The Sagittarius nature is extroverted, independent, outgoing, and you love anything international. You are adventurous, spontaneous, and constantly seek new experiences. You like to play games. You explore new places through travel and learning about different cultures to further open your mind.

You are friendly, and cheerful, while also being overly trusting. You do not hold grudges. You have a sense of humor. You are charismatic and can be sensual and seductive but do not want to be tied down. You love to roam freely and become frustrated if a love interest is too clingy.

You have an open and ambitious approach to life. You are driven to be a good-natured leader. You make many contacts and share your ideas. You are an organizer of your life, but may also want to organize others. You can be brutally honest and say what you believe.

You are critical of your own behavior and take full responsibility for your actions. You are an expert at turning your mistakes, faults, and gaffes into hilarious stories that get the whole room laughing. You naturally radiate a warmth that puts others at ease. You are both clever and imaginative. You embody confidence yet humility.

Sagittarius needs open air and loves to be outdoors. You enjoy risky adventures. If you are not challenged, uncharacteristic depression can set in. You have big ideas and want your name to be associated with your concepts. You challenge yourself and succeed in accomplishing your goals.

Sagittarius is characterized by a continual pursuit of knowledge and understanding. You often recognize that your life encompasses diverse themes, truths, and evolving beliefs, which reflect the progression of your personal and spiritual development over time. Money may not be as important to you as spiritual principles and pursuits. You give things away thinking others need it more than you.

You are an avid reader with a remarkable combination of emotional and intellectual intelligence that is shown through exceptional wisdom and reasoning abilities. You truly enjoy the journey and always reach your destination because you are always learning new things along the way, which is part of your destination.

Each life experience over your lifetime will in some way be involved in fulfilling your need to explore and expand the horizons of your mind and world and be The Spontaneous Adventurer, The Traveler, and The Risk-Taker.

Why have you been given these traits? You carry these traits to equip you with what you need to fulfill your individual life's mission as well as the role you have in all of humanity.

Embracing the characteristics of Your Birthday Promise will help you navigate life with authenticity and purpose.

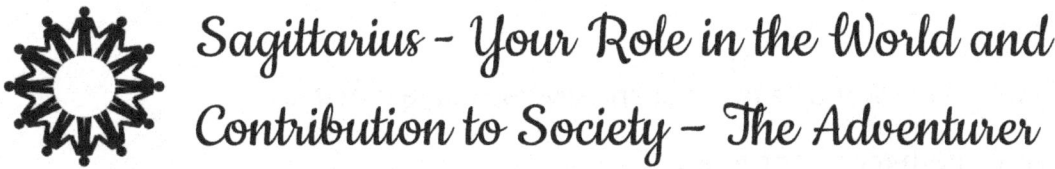 Sagittarius - Your Role in the World and Contribution to Society - The Adventurer

Each of you should use whatever gift you have received to serve others as faithful stewards of God's grace in its various forms. 1 Peter 4:10

We each have a role to fill for ourselves and for humanity. Born under the Month of Sagittarius your contribution to society is to be the philosopher and spiritual teacher of mankind. Your core purpose is to inspire and teach others with your unshakeable positivity, childlike curiosity, adventurous spirit, and philosophical insights.

You always encourage people to apply themselves more and live up to their potential. You want everyone around you to succeed by going after their goals. You are never satisfied with the status quo. You inspire future possibilities and varied potentials. You explore worldly beliefs and laws that invite or challenge ways of learning and knowing.

You lighten up the atmosphere with your humor. Your skill for turning embarrassing moments into funny stories is more than just a defense mechanism. It is also a beautiful gift to those around you. It makes space for others to share their own mishaps without fearing judgment, and this can help them move on from embarrassing episodes quickly instead of being defined by them.

You were born to make the world a better place with your abundance of optimism and idealism. You carry the wonder of God's creation *to the* world, sharing the enthusiasm of your discoveries with a joyful heart. Your true strength is not just about adventure – it is about leading others toward seeing what they have not seen before.

Sagittarius - What You are Here to Learn
Lessons to Learn to Excel at Your Role

Born under the Month of Sagittarius, throughout your life, you are here to learn:

...to open up to a variety of thoughts, opinions, and ideas without creating either divisiveness or judgment.

...a greater acceptance of differences, learning to detach from harsh judgments and rigid opinions.

...to begin to see the world as the vast and diverse place that it is.

...to consider another point of view.

...that you do not need to fix everyone else's reactions as well as your own.

...to be grounded in your concept of time, energy, and commitment.

...wisdom.

Sagittarius – Let Your Light Shine

Born under the Month of Sagittarius, the special light you shine is through your interest in spiritual and religious pursuits and the will to search the realms of higher education, law, and philosophy for truth and higher knowledge. You motivate others to see new opportunities and explore diverse possibilities. You engage with different beliefs and rules, encouraging exploration and questioning of how people learn and understand the world. These traits will be used and developed to fulfill your life's purpose.

> "You are the light of the world. A city set on a hill cannot be hidden. Nor do people light a lamp and put it under a basket, but on a stand, and it gives light to all in the house. In the same way, let your light shine before others, so that they may see your good works and give glory to your Father who is in heaven." Matthew 5:14-16 ESV

 Taking Inventory of the Qualities of Your Life

As you review your life during this time of Your Birthday Month, realize that you are already everything you need to be at this time in your journey. You are not broken or damaged. You are who you were created to be right now. We each have an opportunity to take stock and grow in the gifts and talents we have been given.

At this Yearly time of celebrating Your Birthday, you have an opportunity to get to know and love yourself more fully than you have before. It is a time to trust God in the unfolding and timing of your life and get a better sense of the meaning and purpose of your life.

Sagittarius – My Birthday Life Review

Do you recognize the Birthday Promise qualities in yourself?
If so, are they being used and developed? If you feel you are lacking in any of these, or are out of balance, you can ask the Spirit to help you make the most of them in this New Year. **Go to Page 190 for Your Birthday Life Review questions.**

The Fruit of the Tree of Life for Growth and Healing

Spiritual Fruit Tending - Reflect on These Virtues in Your Life and Rate Them

Fruit of the Spirit	👍 Growing Well?	➕ Needs Fertilizing?	👎 Needs Pruning
Love - A deep and abiding affection and concern for others.			
Joy – A state of happiness and delight, even in the midst of difficult circumstances.			
Peace – A state of tranquility and harmony, both internally and externally.			
Patience – The ability to endure challenges or agitation without becoming angry or upset.			
Kindness – A gentle and kind nature, showing compassion and care for others.			
Goodness – A moral excellence and uprightness of character.			
Faithfulness – Loyalty, trustworthiness, and steadfastness in commitments.			
Gentleness – A kind and considerate demeanor, avoiding harshness or aggression.			
Self-control – The ability to restrain impulses and appetites.			
Long-suffering - The capacity to endure hardship with patience and perseverance.			
Temperence - Moderation and self-restraint in all aspects of life.			
Wisdom - The ability to make sound judgments and decisions based on knowledge and experience.			

Sagittarius - Spiritual Fruit Tending
Questions and prompts for your quiet time
Go to Page 192 for a deep dive into your Fruit of the Tree of Life ratings.

Rate Your Life on the Wheel of Life

Think about the matters of your life shown in the Key Areas of Life Table from Page 13 and evaluate your current level of satisfaction in each Area on a scale from 1-8. The Wheel of Life segments correspond with the topics in this Table. Rate each Area and highlight the number you gave yourself in each Area on the blank Wheel below.

How is your life going? Be sure to rate yourself honestly. This is your reality check. Your honest evaluation will quickly help pinpoint any imbalance. The lower rated areas will show you where you need more focus. No more guessing!

Then, outline the highlighted Wheel of Life ratings with a marker to link them to each other to form a figure within the circle showing the degree of balance in your life, as in the following example.

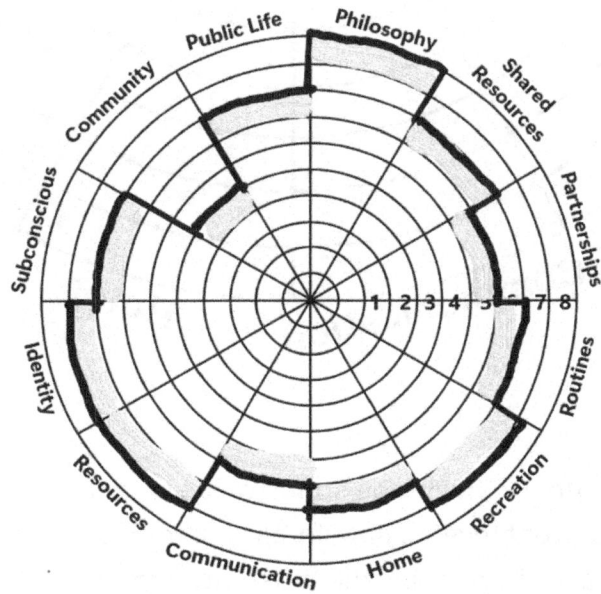

Example of the Wheel of Life with Evaluations

Wheel of Life

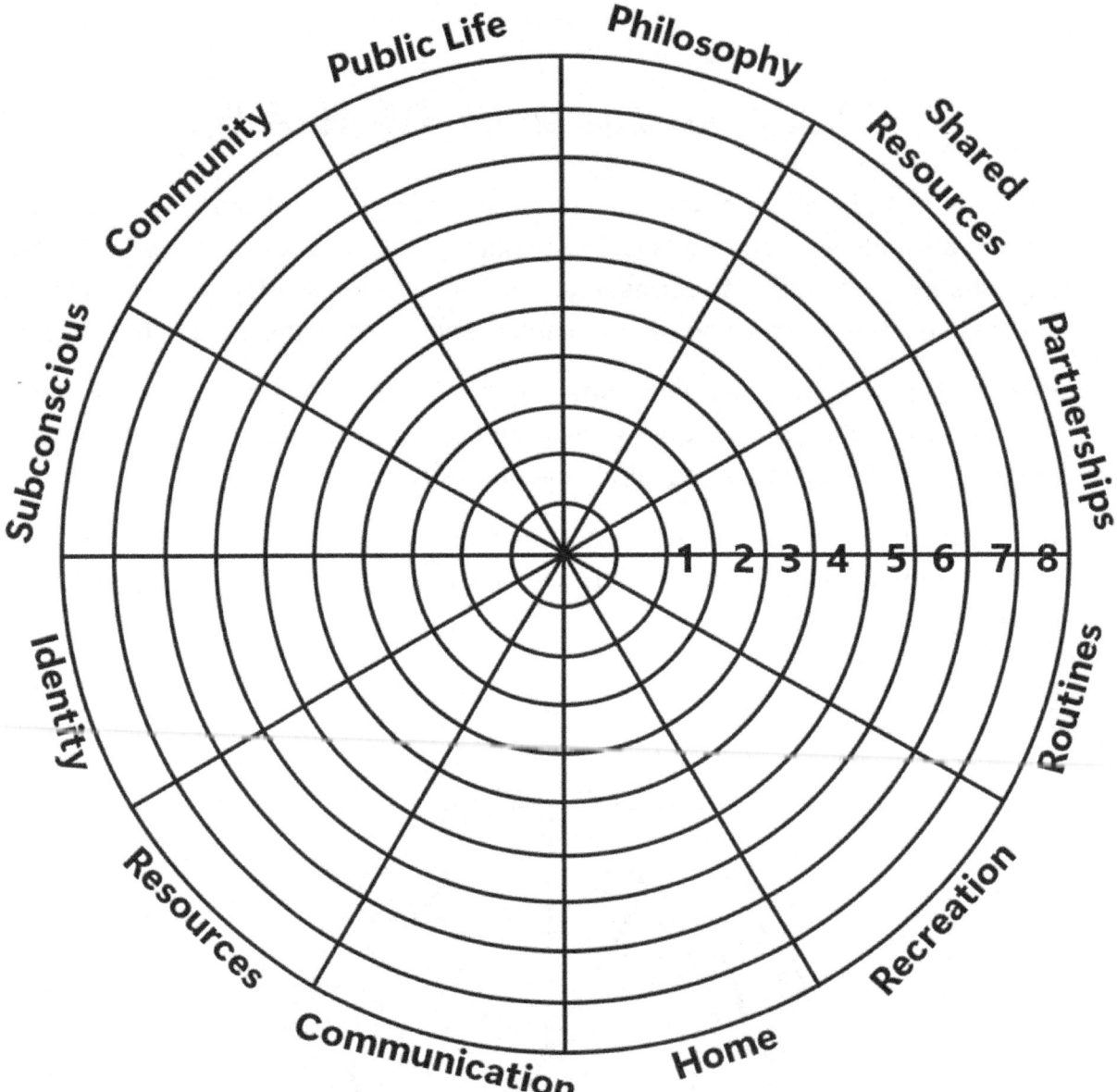

Filling in the Wheel of Life: Highlight the space on a scale from 1-8 under each Key Area that reflects your current level of satisfaction or imbalance in that area, with 8 being the most satisfying and 1 needing the most attention.

Next, interpret the results. How does the balance of your Key Areas of Life look? Analyze the resulting shape to identify the unbalanced areas that require attention and how to improve your satisfaction with them.

With a different color, mark the scores where you would like them to be in the future. Transfer your current and goal scores, as number of stars, to the table below to see where you stand in each category.

Fill in the stars for the Wheel of Life ratings you gave yourself for the current Year and then give yourself stars for next Year's goal.

Wheel of Life Area of Life	How many stars do you give yourself? 1-8 (from your Wheel of Life rating)	
	Current Wheel of Life	Goal for Next Year
Identity	☆☆☆☆☆☆☆☆	☆☆☆☆☆☆☆☆
Resources	☆☆☆☆☆☆☆☆	☆☆☆☆☆☆☆☆
Communication	☆☆☆☆☆☆☆☆	☆☆☆☆☆☆☆☆
Home	☆☆☆☆☆☆☆☆	☆☆☆☆☆☆☆☆
Recreation	☆☆☆☆☆☆☆☆	☆☆☆☆☆☆☆☆
Routines	☆☆☆☆☆☆☆☆	☆☆☆☆☆☆☆☆
Partnerships	☆☆☆☆☆☆☆☆	☆☆☆☆☆☆☆☆
Shared Resources	☆☆☆☆☆☆☆☆	☆☆☆☆☆☆☆☆
Philosophy	☆☆☆☆☆☆☆☆	☆☆☆☆☆☆☆☆
Public Life	☆☆☆☆☆☆☆☆	☆☆☆☆☆☆☆☆
Community	☆☆☆☆☆☆☆☆	☆☆☆☆☆☆☆☆
Subconscious	☆☆☆☆☆☆☆☆	☆☆☆☆☆☆☆☆

Good ratings in the different areas of your life have a major noticeable impact on your overall well-being and quality of life. A well-balanced life can reduce stress and anxiety, improve your mental wellbeing, and make you more productive, and will improve your self-esteem, family life, partnerships, career, and the other areas of

your life. On the other hand, a lack of balance in several areas of your life will cause instability in the other Areas of your life as well.

Make a conscious decision to take better care of your life and make it all that it can be. Start by giving some thought to each Area in the Wheel of Life. What is the status of each one? Reflect on what there is to learn about each one. Work on strengthening the various areas of your life to welcome more peace, purpose, and fulfillment.

Taking Inventory of the Qualities of Your Life

Sagittarius – Deep Dive on Your Wheel of Life Findings
Questions and prompts for your quiet time
Go to Page 194 for a deep dive into your Wheel of Life ratings.

Sagittarius – Your Birthday Promise Insights
Reflections on Last Year ✶ Intentions for the Year Ahead
Questions and prompts for your quiet time
Go to Page 197 for a deep dive into Your Birthday Promise Insights.

God's Birthday Message for Sagittarius...

Dear Sagittarius, as you review your life this Year, remember the unique individual that you have been created to be and the core qualities that you have been given to equip you for your role in life.

Born in Sagittarius, the third Month of Fall, you were given the qualities of optimism, philosophical insights, and the desire to travel. These equip you for your role of The Adventurer to fulfill your purpose of being an explorer and seeker of truth, leading you to profound insights about life and the universe.

Your philosophical nature and love for exploration make you an eternal student as well as teacher of the answers to life's big questions. God calls you to share the truths you have learned with others and help guide them on their spiritual journey.

You value independence but feel torn between adventure and committing yourself in relationships. God sees your struggle and wants to reassure you that with compromise, you can have the best of both worlds.

Sagittarius is the seeker of truth, and your spiritual gift is Wisdom. Your philosophical nature and love for exploration lead you to profound insights about life and the universe. You share your wisdom with others, guiding them on their spiritual journeys using your expansive perspective.

God encourages you to continue seeking truth and knowledge. To calm your restless spirit, feed your hunger through travel, even if only mentally through videos, books, study, research, and meaningful conversations. By expanding your perspective, you come closer to understanding the purpose of your life.

Spiritual Growth Tips

✓ Seek wisdom in God's Word, not just worldly experiences in your continuous quest for truth and significance.

✓ Remember that the ultimate truth lies in God's Word which brings clarity and freedom.

✓ Cultivate joy and trust in positive outcomes to strengthen your faith.

✓ Let faith guide your adventures and decisions.

💡 Sagittarius – Take-Aways from Your Deep Dives

Now that you have reflected, meditated, and received insight from the Spirit from your time of prayer, meditation, and meeting with the Spirit about all Areas of Your Life, journal the revelations, words, and directions that come to mind for the coming Year.

What have you learned about yourself?

What have you learned about God?

What have you learned about the direction and plan for your life?

Finally – Submit Your Plans to God

While we can meet with the Lord and get direction and set intentions for the New Year, we ultimately need to submit to His Will and timing. We may not understand how things play out, but we will recognize areas of our life that we can intentionally bring into alignment with His ways. While we are honing our gifts and abilities, He will open doors and close doors accordingly and we will flow along with Him on this Year's journey.

> *Many are the plans in a person's heart, but it is the LORD's purpose that prevails.*
> *Proverbs 19:21*

> *A man's heart plans his course, but the LORD determines his steps.*
> *Proverbs 16:9 BSB*

> *And we know that in all things God works for the good of those who love him, who have been called according to his purpose. Romans 8:28*

> *To everything there is a season, and a time to every purpose under the heaven: A time to be born, and a time to die; a time to plant, and a time to pluck up that which is planted... Ecclesiastes 3:1-2 NKJV*

Biblical Affirmations to Declare Over Your Life

In addition to the specific traits you have been given to fulfill your God-given purpose, there are underlying truths about who God created you to be. These affirmations confirm the qualities you have been given for your underlying relationship and identity through Him.

Birthday affirmations, declarations, and prayers go beyond mere wishes; they are faith-filled expressions that align with God's Word that speak life, purpose, encouragement, and Divine blessing. The words we speak have power, and for those on a spiritual path, it is important to declare what God says about us. While the world may try to label us by our past, errors, or situations, we should instead rely on the truth found in God's Word.

Use these affirmations, supported by Scripture, to renew your mind, strengthen your faith and walk confidently in your God-given identity. Repeat them daily and let the truth of His promises transform your life!

Who Am I?

- I am a child of God and an heir to His promises. (Romans 8:17)
- I am fearfully and wonderfully made. (Psalm 139:14)
- I am God's masterpiece, created for good works. (Ephesians 2:10)
- I am chosen, holy, and dearly loved by God. (Colossians 3:12)
- I am bold because the Lord is my helper. (Hebrews 13:6)
- I am confident that God will finish the good work He started in me. (Philippians 1:6)

Promises of God

- This is the day the Lord has made; I will rejoice and be glad in it. (Psalm 118:24)
- Nothing can separate me from God's love. (Romans 8:38-39)
- God's plans for me are good, filled with hope and a future. (Jeremiah 29:11)
- God directs my steps and makes my paths straight. (Proverbs 3:5-6)
- God's power works in me to accomplish far more than I can imagine. (Ephesians 3:20)
- The Lord is faithful to keep His promises to me. (Deuteronomy 7:9)
- The Lord makes everything beautiful in His time. (Ecclesiastes 3:11)

I Am – Sagittarius Personality Declarations

- ♥ I am an adventurer.
- ♥ I am a perpetual student, I am always searching for new subjects to explore.
- ♥ I am optimistic and pursue life on a grand scale.
- ♥ I am freedom loving.
- ♥ I am a straight-forward, truth seeker.
- ♥ I am jovial and optimistic.
- ♥ I am generous and honest.
- ♥ I am independent.
- ♥ I am broadminded and philosophical.
- ♥ I am curious and love to read.

Sagittarius – Reminders for Growth and Balance

- + I love learning about spirituality, culture, law, and philosophy.
- + I search for purpose and meaning.
- + I have a great sense of humor.
- + I accept commitment if and only if it fits in with my core ideals.
- + I do not to get so caught up in intellectual pursuits that I neglect emotional and spiritual growth.
- + I find a balance between my mind and heart.
- + I find meaning in the everyday journey.
- + I trust my path without needing all of the answers.
- + I practice patience.
- + I am thankful every day for the blessings in my life.
- + I look for the silver lining in every cloud.
- + I make time to explore because it brings me joy.

And there is more!

For more insight into the traits of Sagittarius go to, "Nourishment from the Month of Sagittarius," in Part Two, *Journey Around the Wheel of the Year*.

Happy Birthday, Capricorn!

The Achiever

The Initiating First Month of Winter
December 22 – January 19

Capricorn! You are hardworking, ambitious, and goal-oriented. You are someone who can achieve great success through your determination and practicality. Your discipline and dedication inspire others to trust in the process and remain committed to their paths.

Your Birthday Promise - The Capricorn Personality

With Your Birthday under the Month of Capricorn you were born to work hard, achieve, and leave a legacy. You are meant to be ambitious, disciplined, and career focused.

You are realistic and grounded, and are empowered by authority, structure, and tradition. You want an honorable life and your reputation is important to you. You seek status. You operate in a practical, ambitious way seeking reliable results through initiating efforts and putting comforts aside for the end goal.

You have a unique talent for creating lasting value that endures beyond your lifetime. You have the foresight to look beyond the immediate moment. You are self-disciplined and thrive on repetition and consistency. You understand that true mastery is achieved through refinement and perseverance. Unlike other individuals who may seek quick victories or transient success, you are committed to playing for future rewards.

Capricorn is the most mature and serious Month of the Seasonal Year. You are old for your age when you are young and young for your age when you get old. Capricorns struggle with numerous setbacks and delays in their early life. You are used to hardship and are not deterred by challenges. You have learned. You are self-directed and have a drive to succeed. Achievement is important to you. Sometimes referred to as The Ruthless Climber, you work hard until you reach your goals. You know how to work to accomplish your goals. Capricorn is one of the strongest and most enduring of the twelve Months in many ways.

Success is a requisite for your self-worth. You are dedicated and trustworthy and need approval from those in authority. You make and follow your own boundaries, come up with your own game plan and refine it until it works. You are hardworking and keep to the task until the goal is achieved. You take security driven measures that propel you toward greater heights, self-reliance, and mastery.

Capricorns are loners and are slow to make friends. You have a sense of realism about yourself and the material reality of the world. You speak the truth, reveal the truth, and therefore are often unfairly judged just for being the bearer of bad news. Instead of being valued for your sharp insights, you are more often castigated.

Capricorn is a difficult Month under which to be born, with a built-in sense of duty and obligation. Many Capricorn souls tend to feel responsible for more than just themselves starting at a young age taking on what needs to be done, especially in the family. You were not meant to just succeed. You were meant to create systems that others follow. Legacies that outlast your name.

Born under the Month of Capricorn, you often have an exterior that appears reserved and tough. However, your inner personality is generally charming and gentle, as though the armor protection developed during childhood has safely guarded the purity and warmth of your soul inside. You have a dry sense of humor and have figured out how to make people laugh.

Each life experience over your lifetime will in some way be involved in fulfilling your need for structure, organization, and social accomplishment and be The Achiever, The Planner, and The CEO.

Why have you been given these traits? You carry these traits to equip you with what you need to fulfill your individual life's mission as well as the role you have in all of humanity.

Embracing the characteristics of Your Birthday Promise will help you navigate life with authenticity and purpose.

For we are God's handiwork, created in Christ Jesus to do good works, which God prepared in advance for us to do. Ephesians 2:10 NIV

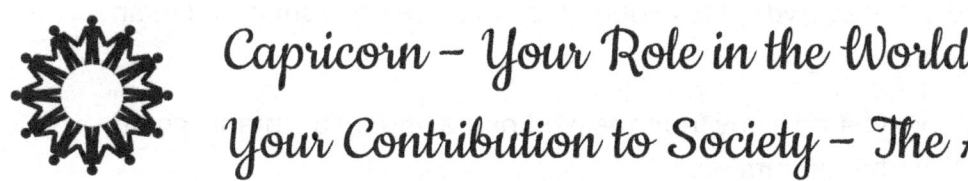

Capricorn – Your Role in the World
Your Contribution to Society – The Achiever

Each of you should use whatever gift you have received to serve others as faithful stewards of God's grace in its various forms. 1 Peter 4:10

We each have a role to fill for ourselves and for humanity. Born under the Month of Capricorn, your contribution to society is to be a leader, executive, and authority in whatever occupation you choose.

Your purpose is to teach how to overcome challenges, endure training, take on responsibilities, and achieve respect and authority. You have a deep sense of responsibility and duty to provide guidance and support and are here to lend a helping hand to those who are lost.

Your Capricorn attributes are needed in the world to provide continuing direction, endurance, staying power, and achievement in all areas. You are known for being able to handle a lot at once, especially when you are called to take on major responsibilities like running a company or the family.

You are determined to make the most of your time and make a worth-while contribution to the world. You may be the person in your family who is driven to build a family legacy. You demonstrate how life rewards individuals over time, showing that determination and consistency are essential for long-term success.

Your unwavering dedication to loved ones and your ability to create a sense of safety make you invaluable to those you are close to. You are an old soul who creates a stable foundation for others.

Your journey is a testament to hard work, resilience, and personal achievement. You are well-positioned to guide others with a realistic understanding of what is required to reach a goal or destination.

Capricorn – What You are Here to Learn

Lessons to Learn to Excel at Your Role

Born under the Month of Capricorn, throughout your life, you are here to learn:

...to open up to quality connections.

...to take pleasure in the everyday life experiences that are not connected to an achievement or goal.

...that it is acceptable to step away from the workplace and take a break, go on vacation, or a walk in the mountains.

...to master your impatience and excessive ambition.

...to settle down to an appreciation of reasonable and simple things.

...empathy and how to care for others.

...not to always compete with others in order to get ahead in life.

...true success comes from creating a meaningful impact in the world.

Capricorn - Let Your Light Shine

Born under the Month of Capricorn, the special light you shine is through your desire to attain positions of power, responsibility, and authority. You must establish yourself out in the world. You pursue goals with a practical and ambitious approach, setting aside comfort in order to achieve reliable outcomes. Focusing on concrete facts, you prefer direct, security-oriented strategies that drive you toward greater success, independence, and expertise. Your profession and public persona will be used as a vehicle to develop and fulfill your life's purpose.

> *"You are the light of the world. A city set on a hill cannot be hidden. Nor do people light a lamp and put it under a basket, but on a stand, and it gives light to all in the house. In the same way, let your light shine before others, so that they may see your good works and give glory to your Father who is in heaven." Matthew 5:14-16 ESV*

 Taking Inventory of the Qualities of Your Life

As you review your life during this time of Your Birthday Month, realize that you are already everything you need to be at this time in your journey. You are not broken or damaged. You are who you were created to be right now. We each have an opportunity to take stock and grow in the gifts and talents we have been given.

At this Yearly time of celebrating Your Birthday, you have an opportunity to get to know and love yourself more fully than you have before. It is a time to trust God in the unfolding and timing of your life and get a better sense of the meaning and purpose of your life.

Capricorn – My Birthday Life Review

Do you recognize the Birthday Promise qualities in yourself?
If so, are they being used and developed? If you feel you are lacking in any of these, or are out of balance, you can ask the Spirit to help you make the most of them in this New Year. **Go to Page 190 for Your Birthday Life Review questions.**

The Fruit of the Tree of Life for Growth and Healing

Spiritual Fruit Tending - Reflect on These Virtues in Your Life and Rate Them

Fruit of the Spirit	👍 Growing Well?	➕ Needs Fertilizing?	👎 Needs Pruning
Love - A deep and abiding affection and concern for others.			
Joy – A state of happiness and delight, even in the midst of difficult circumstances.			
Peace – A state of tranquility and harmony, both internally and externally.			
Patience – The ability to endure challenges or agitation without becoming angry or upset.			
Kindness – A gentle and kind nature, showing compassion and care for others.			
Goodness – A moral excellence and uprightness of character.			
Faithfulness – Loyalty, trustworthiness, and steadfastness in commitments.			
Gentleness – A kind and considerate demeanor, avoiding harshness or aggression.			
Self-control – The ability to restrain impulses and appetites.			
Long-suffering - The capacity to endure hardship with patience and perseverance.			
Temperance - Moderation and self-restraint in all aspects of life.			
Wisdom - The ability to make sound judgments and decisions based on knowledge and experience.			

Capricorn - Spiritual Fruit Tending
Questions and prompts for your quiet time
Go to Page 192 for a deep dive into your Fruit of the Tree of Life ratings.

Rate Your Life on the Wheel of Life

Think about the matters of your life shown in the Key Areas of Life Table from Page 13 and evaluate your current level of satisfaction in each Area on a scale from 1-8. The Wheel of Life segments correspond with the topics in this Table. Rate each Area and highlight the number you gave yourself in each Area on the blank Wheel below.

How is your life going? Be sure to rate yourself honestly. This is your reality check. Your honest evaluation will quickly help pinpoint any imbalance. The lower rated areas will show you where you need more focus. No more guessing!

Then, outline the highlighted Wheel of Life ratings with a marker to link them to each other to form a figure within the circle showing the degree of balance in your life, as in the following example.

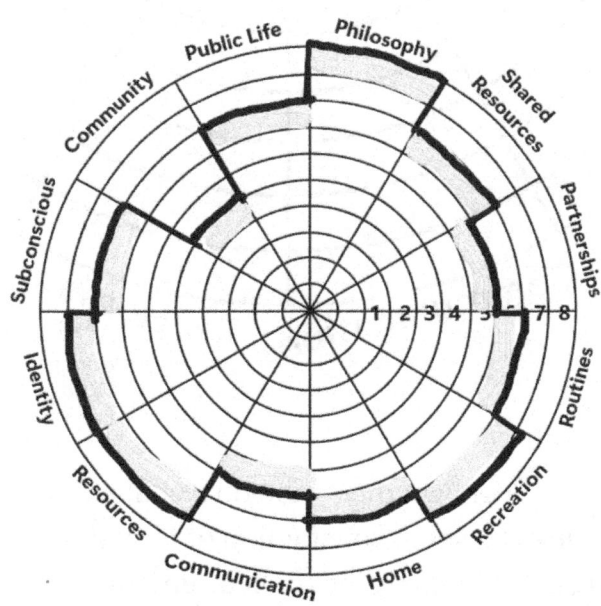

Example of the Wheel of Life with Evaluations

Wheel of Life

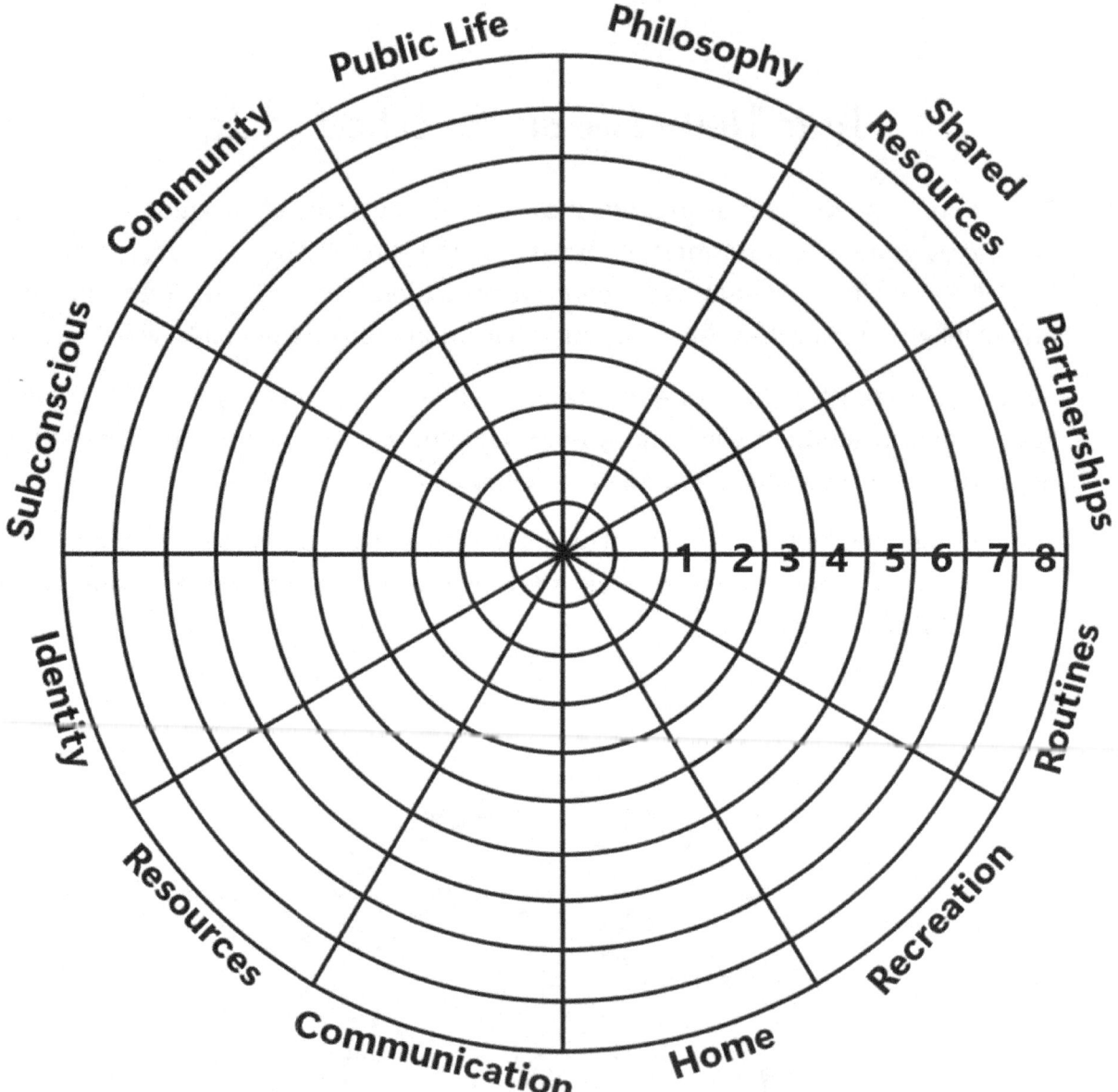

Filling in the Wheel of Life: Highlight the space on a scale from 1-8 under each Key Area that reflects your current level of satisfaction or imbalance in that area, with 8 being the most satisfying and 1 needing the most attention.

Next, interpret the results. How does the balance of your Key Areas of Life look? Analyze the resulting shape to identify the unbalanced areas that require attention and how to improve your satisfaction with them.

With a different color, mark the scores where you would like them to be in the future. Transfer your current and goal scores, as number of stars, to the table below to see where you stand in each category.

Fill in the stars for the Wheel of Life ratings you gave yourself for the current Year and then give yourself stars for next Year's goal.

Wheel of Life Area of Life	How many stars do you give yourself? 1-8 (from your Wheel of Life rating)	
	Current Wheel of Life	Goal for Next Year
Identity	☆☆☆☆☆☆☆☆	☆☆☆☆☆☆☆☆
Resources	☆☆☆☆☆☆☆☆	☆☆☆☆☆☆☆☆
Communication	☆☆☆☆☆☆☆☆	☆☆☆☆☆☆☆☆
Home	☆☆☆☆☆☆☆☆	☆☆☆☆☆☆☆☆
Recreation	☆☆☆☆☆☆☆☆	☆☆☆☆☆☆☆☆
Routines	☆☆☆☆☆☆☆☆	☆☆☆☆☆☆☆☆
Partnerships	☆☆☆☆☆☆☆☆	☆☆☆☆☆☆☆☆
Shared Resources	☆☆☆☆☆☆☆☆	☆☆☆☆☆☆☆☆
Philosophy	☆☆☆☆☆☆☆☆	☆☆☆☆☆☆☆☆
Public Life	☆☆☆☆☆☆☆☆	☆☆☆☆☆☆☆☆
Community	☆☆☆☆☆☆☆☆	☆☆☆☆☆☆☆☆
Subconscious	☆☆☆☆☆☆☆☆	☆☆☆☆☆☆☆☆

Good ratings in the different areas of your life have a major noticeable impact on your overall well-being and quality of life. A well-balanced life can reduce stress and anxiety, improve your mental wellbeing, and make you more productive, and will improve your self-esteem, family life, partnerships, career, and the other areas of

your life. On the other hand, a lack of balance in several areas of your life will cause instability in the other Areas of your life as well.

Make a conscious decision to take better care of your life and make it all that it can be. Start by giving some thought to each Area in the Wheel of Life. What is the status of each one? Reflect on what there is to learn about each one. Work on strengthening the various areas of your life to welcome more peace, purpose, and fulfillment.

 *Taking Inventory of the Qualities of Your Life*

Capricorn – Deep Dive on Your Wheel of Life Findings
Questions and prompts for your quiet time
Go to Page 194 for a deep dive into your Wheel of Life ratings.

Capricorn – Your Birthday Promise Insights
Reflections on Last Year ✶ Intentions for the Year Ahead
Questions and prompts for your quiet time
Go to Page 197 for a deep dive into Your Birthday Promise Insights.

God's Birthday Message for Capricorn...

Dear Capricorn, as you review your life this Year, remember the unique individual that you have been created to be and the core qualities that you have been given to equip you for your role in life.

Born in Capricorn, the first Month of Winter, you were given the qualities of initiative, wisdom, ambition, and endurance. These equip you for your role as The Achiever to fulfill your purpose of climbing to success in both worldly and spiritual pursuits. You were born to work hard, carry responsibilities, and earn respect.

God encourages you to continue pursuing your ambitions with dedication and perseverance. Although challenges may arise, your determination to achieve your goals is admirable, and consistent effort will be rewarded if you remain committed to the tasks before you.

While your sense of responsibility and commitment to achievement are virtues to be celebrated, God also cautions you about the dangers of being driven only by work and worldly success. Do not sacrifice rest, family, relationships, or your spiritual life at the altar of achievement. While career honors are possible, lasting fulfilment and purpose come from more than just status or achievements.

God is calling you to faithfully nurture the gifts and talents He has given you and to purposely make time for adventure, laughter, and go after the activities that light up your soul. Develop your gifts while making room for connection, spiritual growth, and joy.

Spiritual Growth Tips

✓ Embrace challenges with patience in order to develop discipline.

✓ Trust that God's plan is greater than your own.

✓ Do not let ambition and working hard pull you away from spiritual peace.

✓ Surrender your worries and allow God to guide your path.

✓ Set long-term spiritual goals in addition to career goals.

💡 Capricorn – Take-Aways from Your Deep Dives

Now that you have reflected, meditated, and received insight from the Spirit from your time of prayer, meditation, and meeting with the Spirit about all Areas of Your Life, journal the revelations, words, and directions that come to mind for the coming Year.

What have you learned about yourself?

What have you learned about God?

What have you learned about the direction and plan for your life?

Finally – Submit Your Plans to God

While we can meet with the Lord and get direction and set intentions for the New Year, we ultimately need to submit to His Will and timing. We may not understand how things play out, but we will recognize areas of our life that we can intentionally bring into alignment with His ways. While we are honing our gifts and abilities, He will open doors and close doors accordingly and we will flow along with Him on this Year's journey.

Many are the plans in a person's heart, but it is the LORD's purpose that prevails.
Proverbs 19:21

A man's heart plans his course, but the LORD determines his steps.
Proverbs 16:9 BSB

And we know that in all things God works for the good of those who love him, who have been called according to his purpose. Romans 8:28

To everything there is a season, and a time to every purpose under the heaven: A time to be born, and a time to die; a time to plant, and a time to pluck up that which is planted... Ecclesiastes 3:1-2 NKJV

Biblical Affirmations to Declare Over Your Life

In addition to the specific traits you have been given to fulfill your God-given purpose, there are underlying truths about who God created you to be. These affirmations confirm the qualities you have been given for your underlying relationship and identity through Him.

Birthday affirmations, declarations, and prayers go beyond mere wishes; they are faith-filled expressions that align with God's Word that speak life, purpose, encouragement, and Divine blessing. The words we speak have power, and for those on a spiritual path, it is important to declare what God says about us. While the world may try to label us by our past, errors, or situations, we should instead rely on the truth found in God's Word.

Use these affirmations, supported by Scripture, to renew your mind, strengthen your faith and walk confidently in your God-given identity. Repeat them daily and let the truth of His promises transform your life!

Who Am I?

- I am a child of God and an heir to His promises. (Romans 8:17)
- I am fearfully and wonderfully made. (Psalm 139:14)
- I am God's masterpiece, created for good works. (Ephesians 2:10)
- I am chosen, holy, and dearly loved by God. (Colossians 3:12)
- I am bold because the Lord is my helper. (Hebrews 13:6)
- I am confident that God will finish the good work He started in me. (Philippians 1:6)

Promises of God

- This is the day the Lord has made; I will rejoice and be glad in it. (Psalm 118:24)
- Nothing can separate me from God's love. (Romans 8:38-39)
- God's plans for me are good, filled with hope and a future. (Jeremiah 29:11)
- God directs my steps and makes my paths straight. (Proverbs 3:5-6)
- God's power works in me to accomplish far more than I can imagine. (Ephesians 3:20)
- The Lord is faithful to keep His promises to me. (Deuteronomy 7:9)
- The Lord makes everything beautiful in His time. (Ecclesiastes 3:11)

I Am – Capricorn Personality Declarations

- ♥ I am an achiever.
- ♥ I am disciplined and driven.
- ♥ I am ambitious and productive.
- ♥ I am mature, wise, and reserved.
- ♥ I am hard working and reliable.
- ♥ I am stern and willful.
- ♥ I am self-controlled and realistic.
- ♥ I am practical and focus on goals.
- ♥ I am a master of responsibility, commitment, and determination.
- ♥ I am driven, determined, and focused on success and achievements.
- ♥ I am concerned with status.

Capricorn – Reminders for Growth and Balance

- + I organize, plan, and execute tasks with precision.
- + I focus on rules and like structure and order.
- + I set long-term goals.
- + I make time for loved ones.
- + I trust that I am something beyond success.
- + I open my heart and form meaningful connections with others.
- + I accept the support and care of others.
- + I nurture my softness along with my strength.
- + I release outdated expectations of myself and others.
- + I schedule regular downtime.
- + I develop my whole being in the world.
- + I make time for social activities to balance work-life.

And there is more!

For more insight into the traits of Capricorn go to, "Nourishment from the Month of Capricorn," in Part Two, *Journey Around the Wheel of the Year*.

Happy Birthday, Aquarius!

The Humanitarian

The Fixed Middle Month of Winter
January 20 – February 18

Aquarius! You think differently from everyone else.
You challenge the status quo and dream of a better future.
You are forward-thinking and have a strong sense of social justice
and want to make a positive impact on the world.

Your Birthday Promise – The Aquarius Personality

With Your Birthday under the Month of Aquarius you were born to disrupt, innovate, and reform. You are meant to see the future before others and challenge outdated ways of thinking. You are a champion for causes that improve society.

You were born with a unique ability to identify inefficiencies and outdated systems, propose enhancements, and implement changes for improvement. You notice what is lacking and can anticipate potential improvements. From social reform to healthy living you are likely to be found pointing out the advantages of something new, and the hopeless disadvantage of things as they are.

You are inspired by systems that are defined by collective intention and a unified purpose. Driven by sharp thinking and a natural tendency to question standards, you pursue new ideas through original approaches and creative vision, often going against the grain and generating conflict along the way. You are rebellious, eccentric, and detached. You set yourself apart from the crowd by your originality. You are friendly and freedom-oriented, yet are very private and aloof. You tend to be optimistic and are able to see the bright side of every situation.

You try to surround yourself with people and circumstances that are in alignment with the positive changes you want to make. This involves collaborating with groups of people to work towards breaking down existing structures. You frequently provide a unique perspective at work. You excel in scenarios that call for originality, distinctiveness, and creativity. You are receptive to new ideas and approaches. You are able to think outside the box. You are often unwilling to follow any preset path. You can easily free yourself from social constructs and do something new. You are more likely to take the path less traveled than a safer option.

Aquarians are highly attuned to the importance of friendship, viewing themselves as a unique part of a larger group rather than seeking to boost their own ego or stand out individually. You demonstrate a commitment to building positive relationships and actively engaging in collaborative initiatives that benefit the global community while maintaining independence. You also exhibit genuine concern for humanitarian matters.

You are deeply concerned with the betterment of mankind as a whole and have a futuristic understanding about life. You are socially aware of the latest trends. You are known for your progressive ideas and humanitarian perspective and envision a better life for all. You embody tenacity while constantly rebelling against conservatism and institutions. You bring ancient wisdom from the past up to date.

You have a deep understanding that is the result of a consistent thought process. You may overthink matters. You are detached, objective and are a good observer of people and life. You like to know what makes other people tick. You also enjoy learning about yourself.

You come across as distant and hard to feel close to, even though you are really friendly, outgoing, and generally upbeat. You secretly long for a sense of belonging to a group, but are destined to stand apart. You are on an independent journey of self-discovery as you decide which path to follow to fulfil your mission.

Each life experience over your lifetime will in some way be involved in fulfilling your need to be innovative, original, and create social change and be The Humanitarian, The Innovator, The Rebel Genius.

Why have you been given these traits? You carry these traits to equip you with what you need to fulfill your individual life's mission as well as the role you have in all of humanity.

Embracing the characteristics of Your Birthday Promise will help you navigate life with authenticity and purpose.

 Aquarius – Your Role in the World and Contribution to Society – The Humanitarian

Each of you should use whatever gift you have received to serve others as faithful stewards of God's grace in its various forms. 1 Peter 4:10

We each have a role to fill for ourselves and for humanity. Born under the Month of Aquarius you were born to think outside the box, tear up the rulebook, and overturn traditions, stereotypes, and hierarchies. You see opportunities that others cannot and bring people together to achieve a greater goal. You are one of the originals that make the world go round. You are a rebel with a cause.

Your role is to mix things up, creating some sort of turmoil, with the intent of getting people to think, debate, and understand an issue from various viewpoints, even if others are offended. You appear rebellious, radical, or offbeat to those who think you should follow a more conventional path. You offer new insights, wisdom, and a higher understanding of what you perceive of the world around you. Unlike others that stick to tradition or wait for approval, you challenge conventional norms by introducing innovative ideas before they are widely accepted. Your revolutionary insights inspire mindsets, industries, and entire movements.

Your purpose in life is to make this world a better place. You boost the confidence of people around you and help them to reach their dreams and desires. Your positive attitude brings a burst of fresh air wherever you go. Embracing your uniqueness can lead to innovations for all.

You are born to work for humanitarian causes with the goal of changing the world in a big way, whether by making advancement in any technology or by volunteering for social causes. Your ability to see the bigger picture helps guide humanity toward progress and innovation.

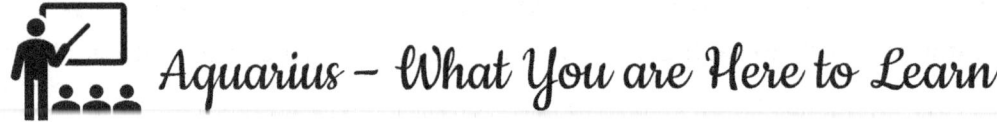

Aquarius – What You are Here to Learn

Lessons to Learn to Excel at Your Role

Born under the Month of Aquarius, throughout your life, you are here to learn:

...you cannot fit in when you stand out.

...to accept your unique spark, ideas, and vision as a needed contribution to the whole.

...to do something different and fascinating in this lifetime that allows for independence, creativity, freedom, and self-expression on your own terms.

...to participate in the world in a significant way.

...to combine your many talents into something you can offer.

...new ways of living and then pass the information along to others.

Aquarius - Let Your Light Shine

Born under the Month of Aquarius, the special light you shine is through your friends, associates, and groups. You focus on innovative ideas, challenging norms with intellectual curiosity and inventiveness, often sparking conflict as a result. Your group associations and friendships will be used and developed to fulfill your purpose.

> *"You are the light of the world. A city set on a hill cannot be hidden. Nor do people light a lamp and put it under a basket, but on a stand, and it gives light to all in the house. In the same way, let your light shine before others, so that they may see your good works and give glory to your Father who is in heaven." Matthew 5:14-16 ESV*

 ## Taking Inventory of the Qualities of Your Life

As you review your life during this time of Your Birthday Month, realize that you are already everything you need to be at this time in your journey. You are not broken or damaged. You are who you were created to be right now. We each have an opportunity to take stock and grow in the gifts and talents we have been given.

At this Yearly time of celebrating Your Birthday, you have an opportunity to get to know and love yourself more fully than you have before. It is a time to trust God in the unfolding and timing of your life and get a better sense of the meaning and purpose of your life.

❓ Aquarius – My Birthday Life Review

Do you recognize the Birthday Promise qualities in yourself?
If so, are they being used and developed? If you feel you are lacking in any of these, or are out of balance, you can ask the Spirit to help you make the most of them in this New Year. **Go to Page 190 for Your Birthday Life Review questions.**

The Fruit of the Tree of Life for Growth and Healing

Spiritual Fruit Tending - Reflect on These Virtues in Your Life and Rate Them

Fruit of the Spirit	👍 Growing Well?	➕ Needs Fertilizing?	👎 Needs Pruning
Love - A deep and abiding affection and concern for others.			
Joy – A state of happiness and delight, even in the midst of difficult circumstances.			
Peace – A state of tranquility and harmony, both internally and externally.			
Patience – The ability to endure challenges or agitation without becoming angry or upset.			
Kindness – A gentle and kind nature, showing compassion and care for others.			
Goodness – A moral excellence and uprightness of character.			
Faithfulness – Loyalty, trustworthiness, and steadfastness in commitments.			
Gentleness – A kind and considerate demeanor, avoiding harshness or aggression.			
Self-control – The ability to restrain impulses and appetites.			
Long-suffering - The capacity to endure hardship with patience and perseverance.			
Temperance - Moderation and self-restraint in all aspects of life.			
Wisdom - The ability to make sound judgments and decisions based on knowledge and experience.			

Aquarius - Spiritual Fruit Tending
Questions and prompts for your quiet time
Go to Page 192 for a deep dive into your Fruit of the Tree of Life ratings.

Rate Your Life on the Wheel of Life

Think about the matters of your life shown in the Key Areas of Life Table from Page 13 and evaluate your current level of satisfaction in each Area on a scale from 1-8. The Wheel of Life segments correspond with the topics in this Table. Rate each Area and highlight the number you gave yourself in each Area on the blank Wheel below.

How is your life going? Be sure to rate yourself honestly. This is your reality check. Your honest evaluation will quickly help pinpoint any imbalance. The lower rated areas will show you where you need more focus. No more guessing!

Then, outline the highlighted Wheel of Life ratings with a marker to link them to each other to form a figure within the circle showing the degree of balance in your life, as in the following example.

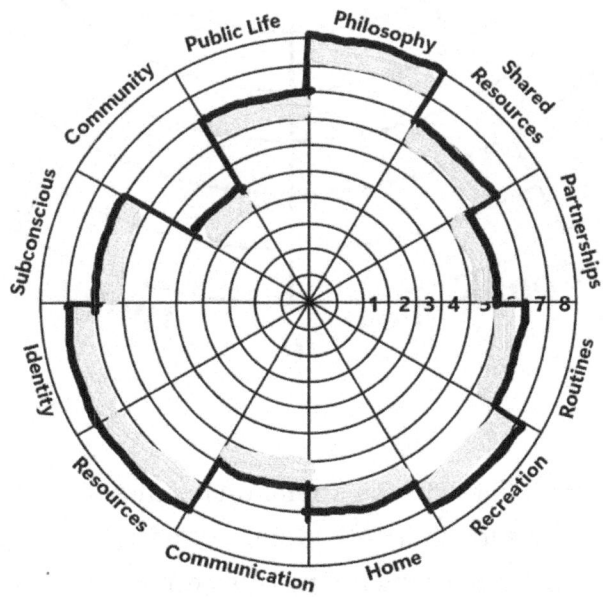

Example of the Wheel of Life with Evaluations

167

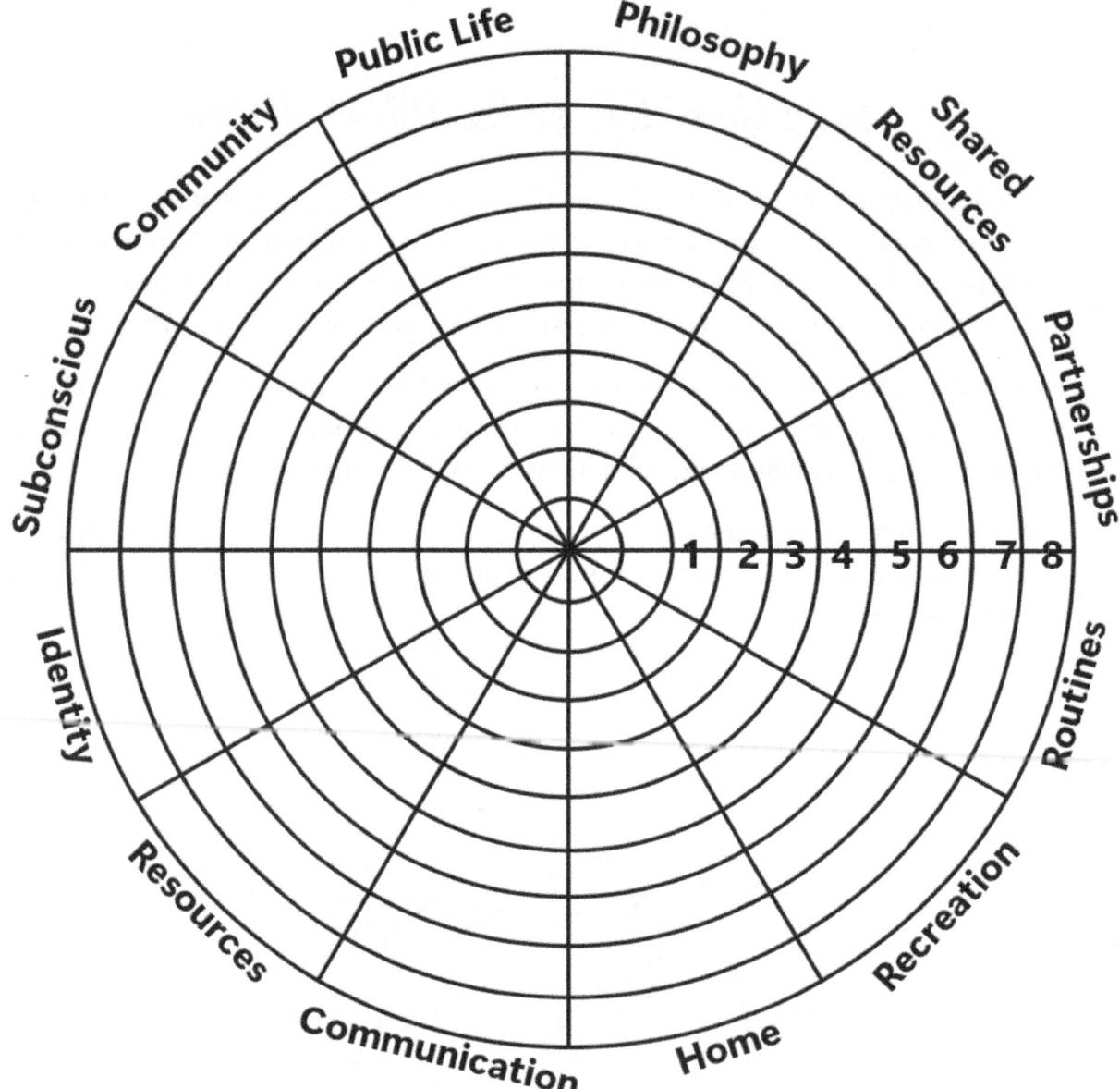

Filling in the Wheel of Life: Highlight the space on a scale from 1-8 under each Key Area that reflects your current level of satisfaction or imbalance in that area, with 8 being the most satisfying and 1 needing the most attention.

Next, interpret the results. How does the balance of your Key Areas of Life look? Analyze the resulting shape to identify the unbalanced areas that require attention and how to improve your satisfaction with them.

With a different color, mark the scores where you would like them to be in the future. Transfer your current and goal scores, as number of stars, to the table below to see where you stand in each category.

Fill in the stars for the Wheel of Life ratings you gave yourself for the current Year and then give yourself stars for next Year's goal.

Wheel of Life Area of Life	How many stars do you give yourself? 1-8 (from your Wheel of Life rating)	
	Current Wheel of Life	Goal for Next Year
Identity	☆☆☆☆☆☆☆☆	☆☆☆☆☆☆☆☆
Resources	☆☆☆☆☆☆☆☆	☆☆☆☆☆☆☆☆
Communication	☆☆☆☆☆☆☆☆	☆☆☆☆☆☆☆☆
Home	☆☆☆☆☆☆☆☆	☆☆☆☆☆☆☆☆
Recreation	☆☆☆☆☆☆☆☆	☆☆☆☆☆☆☆☆
Routines	☆☆☆☆☆☆☆☆	☆☆☆☆☆☆☆☆
Partnerships	☆☆☆☆☆☆☆☆	☆☆☆☆☆☆☆☆
Shared Resources	☆☆☆☆☆☆☆☆	☆☆☆☆☆☆☆☆
Philosophy	☆☆☆☆☆☆☆☆	☆☆☆☆☆☆☆☆
Public Life	☆☆☆☆☆☆☆☆	☆☆☆☆☆☆☆☆
Community	☆☆☆☆☆☆☆☆	☆☆☆☆☆☆☆☆
Subconscious	☆☆☆☆☆☆☆☆	☆☆☆☆☆☆☆☆

Good ratings in the different areas of your life have a major noticeable impact on your overall well-being and quality of life. A well-balanced life can reduce stress and anxiety, improve your mental wellbeing, and make you more productive, and will improve your self-esteem, family life, partnerships, career, and the other areas of

your life. On the other hand, a lack of balance in several areas of your life will cause instability in the other Areas of your life as well.

Make a conscious decision to take better care of your life and make it all that it can be. Start by giving some thought to each Area in the Wheel of Life. What is the status of each one? Reflect on what there is to learn about each one. Work on strengthening the various areas of your life to welcome more peace, purpose, and fulfillment.

Taking Inventory of the Qualities of Your Life

Aquarius – Deep Dive on Your Wheel of Life Findings
Questions and prompts for your quiet time
Go to Page 194 for a deep dive into your Wheel of Life ratings.

Aquarius – Your Birthday Promise Insights
Reflections on Last Year ✶ Intentions for the Year Ahead
Questions and prompts for your quiet time
Go to Page 197 for a deep dive into Your Birthday Promise Insights.

God's Birthday Message for Aquarius...

Dear Aquarius, as you review your life this Year, remember the unique individual that you have been created to be and the core qualities that you have been given to equip you for your role in life.

Born in Aquarius, the second Month of Winter, you were given the qualities of originality, humanitarianism, and detachment. These equip you for your role of The Humanitarian to fulfill your purpose of breaking up old systems and inspiring change for the collective.

God sees your futuristic thinking, brilliant mind, philanthropic spirit, and passion for making the world a better place. Your compassion for humanity as a whole is a gift. He calls you to continue working for change, justice, equality, and human rights for all people.

Though the world needs your innovative thinking, don't forget to live in the day to day too. Do not let yourself become too detached or isolated. God cautions you not to become independent from friends and family in your need for individuality.

Though the road may be difficult and lonely at times, God walks with you and encourages you to keep your hope alive. With faith, love and persistence, your dreams of the unity of all mankind can become reality. You have the ability to make the world a little bit better step by step, one day at a time.

Spiritual Growth Tips

✓ Focus on changing not only the world, but also on transforming your own heart and beliefs.

✓ Be assured that your efforts to influence the planet will pay off.

✓ Remember that your rebellious nature can make you feel like an outsider.

✓ Recall that part of your role is to stand out.

✓ Realize that your unique mind is a strength, not a weakness, and is something to celebrate.

 Aquarius – Take-Aways from Your Deep Dives

Now that you have reflected, meditated, and received insight from the Spirit from your time of prayer, meditation, and meeting with the Spirit about all Areas of Your Life, journal the revelations, words, and directions that come to mind for the coming Year.

What have you learned about yourself?

What have you learned about God?

What have you learned about the direction and plan for your life?

Finally – Submit Your Plans to God

While we can meet with the Lord and get direction and set intentions for the New Year, we ultimately need to submit to His Will and timing. We may not understand how things play out, but we will recognize areas of our life that we can intentionally bring into alignment with His ways. While we are honing our gifts and abilities, He will open doors and close doors accordingly and we will flow along with Him on this Year's journey.

> *Many are the plans in a person's heart, but it is the LORD's purpose that prevails.*
> *Proverbs 19:21*

> *A man's heart plans his course, but the LORD determines his steps.*
> *Proverbs 16:9 BSB*

> *And we know that in all things God works for the good of those who love him, who have been called according to his purpose. Romans 8:28*

> *To everything there is a season, and a time to every purpose under the heaven: A time to be born, and a time to die; a time to plant, and a time to pluck up that which is planted... Ecclesiastes 3:1-2 NKJV*

Biblical Affirmations to Declare Over Your Life

In addition to the specific traits you have been given to fulfill your God-given purpose, there are underlying truths about who God created you to be. These affirmations confirm the qualities you have been given for your underlying relationship and identity through Him.

Birthday affirmations, declarations, and prayers go beyond mere wishes; they are faith-filled expressions that align with God's Word that speak life, purpose, encouragement, and Divine blessing. The words we speak have power, and for those on a spiritual path, it is important to declare what God says about us. While the world may try to label us by our past, errors, or situations, we should instead rely on the truth found in God's Word.

Use these affirmations, supported by Scripture, to renew your mind, strengthen your faith and walk confidently in your God-given identity. Repeat them daily and let the truth of His promises transform your life!

Who Am I?

- I am a child of God and an heir to His promises. (Romans 8:17)
- I am fearfully and wonderfully made. (Psalm 139:14)
- I am God's masterpiece, created for good works. (Ephesians 2:10)
- I am chosen, holy, and dearly loved by God. (Colossians 3:12)
- I am bold because the Lord is my helper. (Hebrews 13:6)
- I am confident that God will finish the good work He started in me. (Philippians 1:6)

Promises of God

- This is the day the Lord has made; I will rejoice and be glad in it. (Psalm 118:24)
- Nothing can separate me from God's love. (Romans 8:38-39)
- God's plans for me are good, filled with hope and a future. (Jeremiah 29:11)
- God directs my steps and makes my paths straight. (Proverbs 3:5-6)
- God's power works in me to accomplish far more than I can imagine. (Ephesians 3:20)
- The Lord is faithful to keep His promises to me. (Deuteronomy 7:9)
- The Lord makes everything beautiful in His time. (Ecclesiastes 3:11)

I Am – Aquarius Personality Declarations

- ♥ I am a humanitarian.
- ♥ I am independent and detached.
- ♥ I am rebellious and contradictory.
- ♥ I am mindful of my rebellious nature.
- ♥ I am friendly and compassionate.
- ♥ I am humanistic and charitable.
- ♥ I am intelligent and curious.
- ♥ I am original and authentic.
- ♥ I am driven by a desire to pursue progressive ideas and collective efforts.
- ♥ I am focused on societal issues and systems.
- ♥ I am happy to be unconventional.
- ♥ I am a good listener.
- ♥ I am comfortable with computers and other technical equipment.

Aquarius – Reminders for Growth and Balance

- + I cannot stand any kind of constraint.
- + I enjoy stirring the pot.
- + I may sacrifice a permanent relationship for my independence.
- + I search for a group with whom to connect.
- + I embrace connections with others without losing my individuality.
- + I honor both my head and my heart.
- + I follow my passion and interests .
- + I come to terms with the fact that I am often ahead of the crowds and may feel as if I do not belong anywhere.
- + I embrace what makes me different and special in the world.
- + I discover better ways of living with others.

And there is more!

For more insight into the traits of Aquarius go to, "Nourishment from the Month of Aquarius," in Part Two, *Journey Around the Wheel of the Year*.

Happy Birthday, Pisces!

The Dreamer
The Transitional Last Month of Winter
February 19 – March 20

Pisces! You are emotional, intuitive, and feel things more deeply than others and often carry the burdens of those around you. You possess a strong spiritual connection and have a natural ability to understand and empathize with others.

Your Birthday Promise - The Pisces Personality

With Your Birthday under the Month of Pisces you were born to dream, create, and show a higher form of love. You were born with an amazing ability to get along with others and give unconditional love.

You are able to identify with people from all over the world, as well as with people whose lives are altogether different than yours. You can be the best of all friends and people feel comfortable confiding in you. Even so, you are introverted and private.

Pisces is known to have the smallest of all egos of all the Months. You do not like to worry about yourself, instead you care for others. It is one of your strongest attributes. However, you can be so busy doing things for others that you do not reach for your own highest potential. You are a humanitarian who finds fulfillment in devoting your life to others.

Pisces is one of the most sensitive Months of the Year. You are deeply emotional and intuitive, as well as compassionate and trustworthy. You connect with others through your sympathetic, supportive, and caring nature.

Pisces is recognized for their sensitivity to others' pain, often absorbing much of the world's sorrow themselves. You are deeply empathetic and often feel compelled to help others, but it is crucial for you to set boundaries and practice self-care. When you focus your empathy on thoughtful acts of service, you can enjoy a fulfilling exchange of giving and receiving, instead becoming the lone martyr.

Those born under the Month of Pisces are spiritually and intuitively sensitive and reach beyond what is tangible. Unlike others that rely on logic or external validation, you can explore unseen realms and possibilities before they materialize. You have a strong imagination and can be prone to fantasies and escapism. You often believe in your ability to change reality through the power of belief.

Pisces souls are remarkable chameleons who can blend in and become what is needed wherever they may be. You often provide the backdrop to life events as you like to blend in with others and do not want to stand out in the crowd, so much so you may disappear into your surroundings. However, you would be sorely missed.

You are inspired by emotional depths. Feelings and emotions take precedence over intellect and reason. You wander through the world driven by inspiration and indirect motivation, shifting quickly from feeling to belief. Your restless search often leads you to overlook the emotions you create in yourself.

You can feel and even mirror other people's emotional values. You are easily affected by your environment. You can be more prone to anxiety. You need some time each day to get away from it all and be alone to recharge.

Each life experience over your lifetime will in some way be involved in fulfilling your need to commit yourself to a dream or ideal and work toward its realization and be The Dreamer, The Imaginator, The Mystic.

Why have you been given these traits? You carry these traits to equip you with what you need to fulfill your individual life's mission as well as the role you have in all of humanity.

Embracing the characteristics of Your Birthday Promise will help you navigate life with authenticity and purpose.

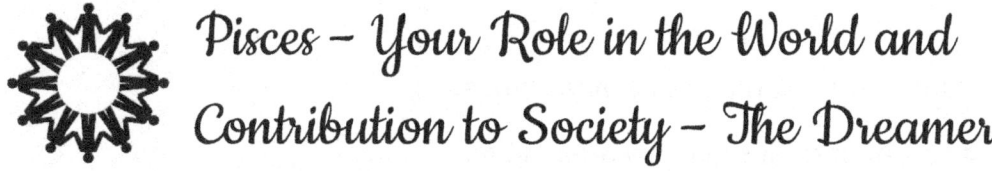

Pisces – Your Role in the World and Contribution to Society – The Dreamer

Each of you should use whatever gift you have received to serve others as faithful stewards of God's grace in its various forms. 1 Peter 4:10

We each have a role to fill for ourselves and for humanity. Born under the Month of Pisces, your contribution to society is to offer a kind relief from the harshness of the everyday world. Your Pisces energy brings in beauty, harmony, and a gentle trust in life that can be reassuring on stressful days. Your deep spirituality and unwavering faith inspires others.

You are here to connect to souls on the deepest levels. You were born with the ability to understand what is being felt or left unspoken. You make a wonderful friend and are a great listener to anyone who seeks your presence.

You can provide others with a glance into the world of spirit, and remind them that we are all in need of empathy, kindness, and support. You help them to believe, keep the faith, and find strength in difficult times.

Your purpose is to convey wise counsel and guide others. Your insight, innovativeness, and helpful nature are respected by others.

Your creative and spiritual energy inspires people to see how beautifully all life is intertwined. Your artistic, spiritual or poetic energy allows others to see the connection of all life. You encourage people to emphasize the importance of their relationships with others.

You are a natural healer and are to use your intuitive gifts to bring healing and love to those in need. You understand others' emotions intuitively. Your work is of real value to your community.

 *Pisces - What You are Here to Learn*

Lessons to Learn to Excel at Your Role

Born under the Month of Pisces, throughout your life, you are here to learn:

...what it means to have a strong sense of self while separating from the ego's desires.

...to trust your intuition while practicing boundaries.

...to develop strong boundaries in every area of life.

...to be detached and remain in your spiritual power. It will be one of your greatest strengths.

...to take care of your own needs, emotions, and energies on a regular basis, without avoiding your daily tasks.

...to build your tolerance for uncomfortable feelings, versus denying or avoiding.

... how to balance deep emotions with spiritual clarity.

...to honor your emotional messages and trust that what you feel is correct for you.

...to take the responsibility to uncover your individuality instead of blending in.

...to not let your empathetic emotions control your life.

...to develop trust in your intuition while maintaining appropriate boundaries.

Pisces - Let Your Light Shine

Born under the Month of Pisces, the special light you shine is through service and sacrifice to others. You are kind-hearted and dependable and will never let others down. You are open-minded and non-judgmental and place other people's wants, needs, and feelings before you own. Because of your imagination and creativity, you can come up with a unique solution for any problem. Your spiritual sensitivity and self-sacrifice will be used and developed to fulfill your life's purpose.

"You are the light of the world. A city set on a hill cannot be hidden. Nor do people light a lamp and put it under a basket, but on a stand, and it gives light to all in the house. In the same way, let your light shine before others, so that they may see your good works and give glory to your Father who is in heaven." Matthew 5:14-16 ESV

 ## Taking Inventory of the Qualities of Your Life

As you review your life during this time of Your Birthday Month, realize that you are already everything you need to be at this time in your journey. You are not broken or damaged. You are who you were created to be right now. We each have an opportunity to take stock and grow in the gifts and talents we have been given.

At this Yearly time of celebrating Your Birthday, you have an opportunity to get to know and love yourself more fully than you have before. It is a time to trust God in the unfolding and timing of your life and get a better sense of the meaning and purpose of your life.

 ### Pisces – My Birthday Life Review

Do you recognize the Birthday Promise qualities in yourself?
If so, are they being used and developed? If you feel you are lacking in any of these, or are out of balance, you can ask the Spirit to help you make the most of them in this New Year. **Go to Page 190 for Your Birthday Life Review questions.**

The Fruit of the Tree of Life for Growth and Healing

Spiritual Fruit Tending - Reflect on These Virtues in Your Life and Rate Them

Fruit of the Spirit	👍 Growing Well?	➕ Needs Fertilizing?	👎 Needs Pruning
Love - A deep and abiding affection and concern for others.			
Joy – A state of happiness and delight, even in the midst of difficult circumstances.			
Peace – A state of tranquility and harmony, both internally and externally.			
Patience – The ability to endure challenges or agitation without becoming angry or upset.			
Kindness – A gentle and kind nature, showing compassion and care for others.			
Goodness – A moral excellence and uprightness of character.			
Faithfulness – Loyalty, trustworthiness, and steadfastness in commitments.			
Gentleness – A kind and considerate demeanor, avoiding harshness or aggression.			
Self-control – The ability to restrain impulses and appetites.			
Long-suffering - The capacity to endure hardship with patience and perseverance.			
Temperance - Moderation and self-restraint in all aspects of life.			
Wisdom - The ability to make sound judgments and decisions based on knowledge and experience.			

Pisces - Spiritual Fruit Tending
Questions and prompts for your quiet time
Go to Page 192 for a deep dive into your Fruit of the Tree of Life ratings.

Rate Your Life on the Wheel of Life

Think about the matters of your life shown in the Key Areas of Life Table from Page 13 and evaluate your current level of satisfaction in each Area on a scale from 1-8. The Wheel of Life segments correspond with the topics in this Table. Rate each Area and highlight the number you gave yourself in each Area on the blank Wheel below.

How is your life going? Be sure to rate yourself honestly. This is your reality check. Your honest evaluation will quickly help pinpoint any imbalance. The lower rated areas will show you where you need more focus. No more guessing!

Then, outline the highlighted Wheel of Life ratings with a marker to link them to each other to form a figure within the circle showing the degree of balance in your life, as in the following example.

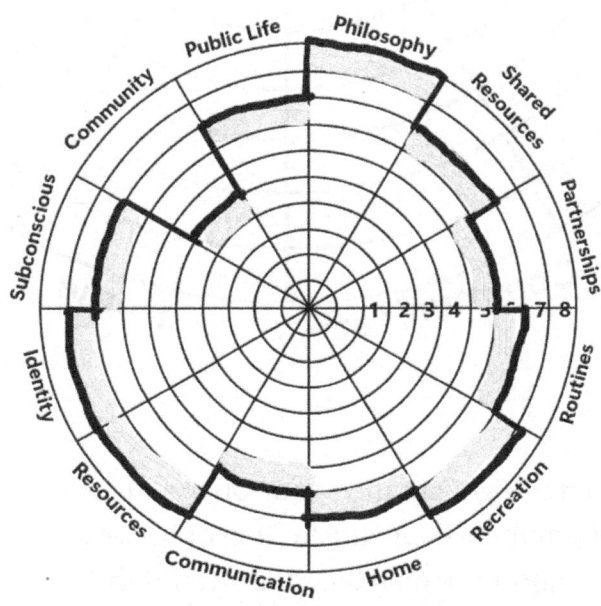

Example of the Wheel of Life with Evaluations

181

Wheel of Life

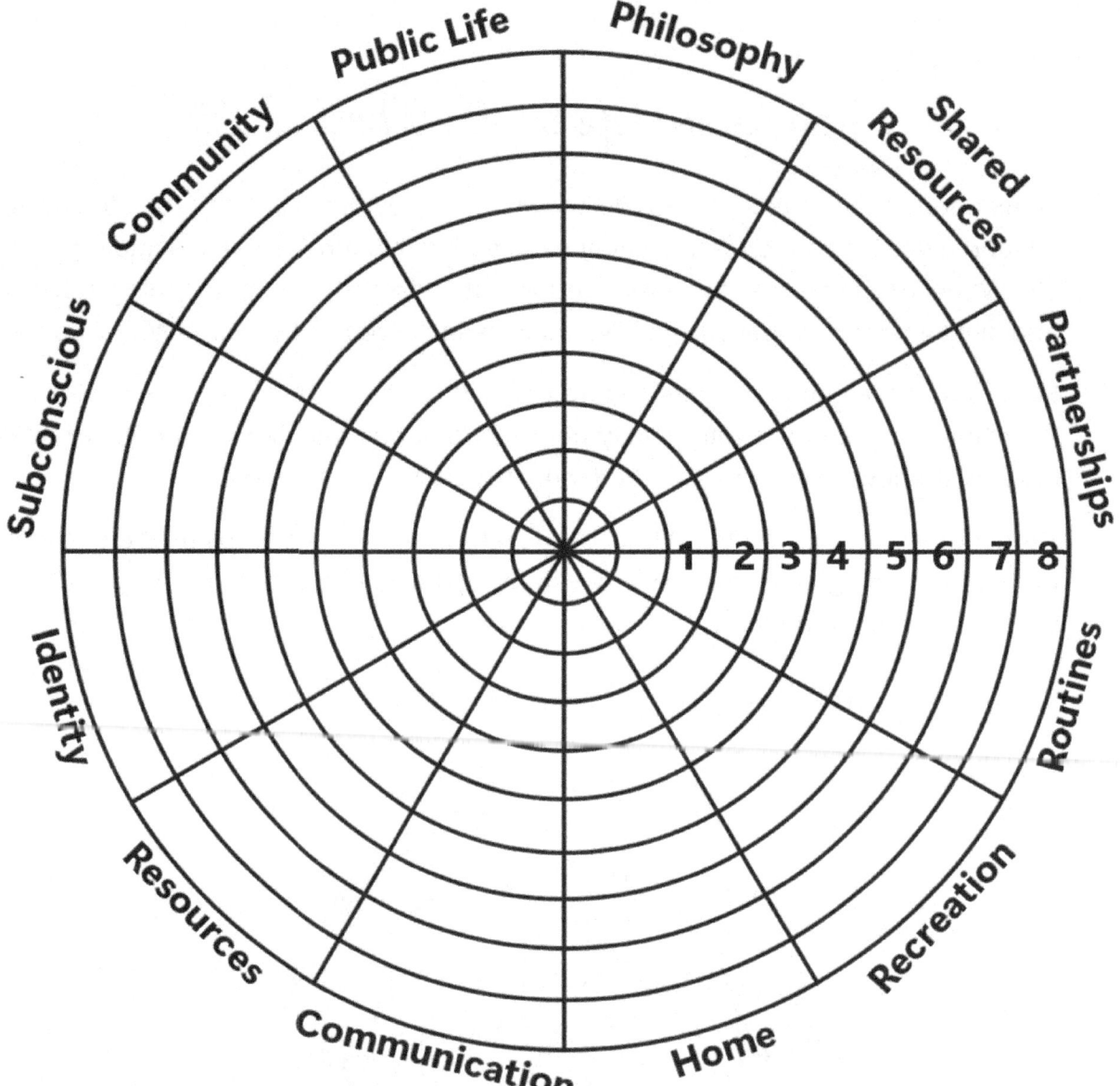

Filling in the Wheel of Life: Highlight the space on a scale from 1-8 under each Key Area that reflects your current level of satisfaction or imbalance in that area, with 8 being the most satisfying and 1 needing the most attention.

Next, interpret the results. How does the balance of your Key Areas of Life look? Analyze the resulting shape to identify the unbalanced areas that require attention and how to improve your satisfaction with them.

With a different color, mark the scores where you would like them to be in the future. Transfer your current and goal scores, as number of stars, to the table below to see where you stand in each category.

Fill in the stars for the Wheel of Life ratings you gave yourself for the current Year and then give yourself stars for next Year's goal.

Wheel of Life Area of Life	How many stars do you give yourself? 1-8 (from your Wheel of Life rating)	
	Current Wheel of Life	Goal for Next Year
Identity	☆☆☆☆☆☆☆☆	☆☆☆☆☆☆☆☆
Resources	☆☆☆☆☆☆☆☆	☆☆☆☆☆☆☆☆
Communication	☆☆☆☆☆☆☆☆	☆☆☆☆☆☆☆☆
Home	☆☆☆☆☆☆☆☆	☆☆☆☆☆☆☆☆
Recreation	☆☆☆☆☆☆☆☆	☆☆☆☆☆☆☆☆
Routines	☆☆☆☆☆☆☆☆	☆☆☆☆☆☆☆☆
Partnerships	☆☆☆☆☆☆☆☆	☆☆☆☆☆☆☆☆
Shared Resources	☆☆☆☆☆☆☆☆	☆☆☆☆☆☆☆☆
Philosophy	☆☆☆☆☆☆☆☆	☆☆☆☆☆☆☆☆
Public Life	☆☆☆☆☆☆☆☆	☆☆☆☆☆☆☆☆
Community	☆☆☆☆☆☆☆☆	☆☆☆☆☆☆☆☆
Subconscious	☆☆☆☆☆☆☆☆	☆☆☆☆☆☆☆☆

Good ratings in the different areas of your life have a major noticeable impact on your overall well-being and quality of life. A well-balanced life can reduce stress and anxiety, improve your mental wellbeing, and make you more productive, and will improve your self-esteem, family life, partnerships, career, and the other areas of

your life. On the other hand, a lack of balance in several areas of your life will cause instability in the other Areas of your life as well.

Make a conscious decision to take better care of your life and make it all that it can be. Start by giving some thought to each Area in the Wheel of Life. What is the status of each one? Reflect on what there is to learn about each one. Work on strengthening the various areas of your life to welcome more peace, purpose, and fulfillment.

 *Taking Inventory of the Qualities of Your Life*

Pisces – Deep Dive on Your Wheel of Life Findings
Questions and prompts for your quiet time
Go to Page 194 for a deep dive into your Wheel of Life ratings.

Pisces – Your Birthday Promise Insights
Reflections on Last Year ✳ Intentions for the Year Ahead
Questions and prompts for your quiet time
Go to Page 197 for a deep dive into Your Birthday Promise Insights.

God's Birthday Message for Pisces...

Dear Pisces, as you review your life this Year, remember the unique individual that you have been created to be and the core qualities that you have been given to equip you for your role in life.

Born in Pisces, the last Month of Winter, you were given the qualities of creativity, compassion, and spiritual gifts. These equip you for your role as The Dreamer to fulfill your purpose of embracing peace, spreading compassion, dissolving boundaries, and merging with the Divine.

As the last, most matured sign of the Year, you are known for your kindness, empathy, and selflessness. Dealing with the suffering of others may feel overwhelming, but God wants you to know that every act of compassion makes a difference. You have great inner resilience. Draw from your deep strength during trials.

God sees your tender heart and reminds you must gently care for yourself before pouring love into the world. You may feel the weight of the pain of the world, so it is important that you learn to set boundaries and withdraw often to renew your spirit.

God calls you to use your gift of sensitivity to connect with others on a deeper level to help bring the world together. Continue to develop your natural ability to receive messages through dreams, visions, and your intuition to help others find spiritual clarity and direction.

Have faith in your abilities. Learn to rely on your intuition when making decisions. When you fall short, forgive yourself. You are wonderfully human. God knows your struggles and encourages you to trust in a promising future.

Spiritual Growth Tips

- ✓ Remember that laughter and faith can shift even the darkest situations - happiness is a powerful spiritual tool.
- ✓ Learn to let go of excessive worry and fear and embrace life's unexpected turns.
- ✓ Consider God's unbounded love to find peace and comfort.
- ✓ Write down your emotions and prayers in a journal to bring clarity and comfort when you feel overwhelmed.

 Pisces – Take-Aways from Your Deep Dives

Now that you have reflected, meditated, and received insight from the Spirit from your time of prayer, meditation, and meeting with the Spirit about all Areas of Your Life, journal the revelations, words, and directions that come to mind for the coming Year.

What have you learned about yourself?

What have you learned about God?

What have you learned about the direction and plan for your life?

Finally – Submit Your Plans to God

While we can meet with the Lord and get direction and set intentions for the New Year, we ultimately need to submit to His Will and timing. We may not understand how things play out, but we will recognize areas of our life that we can Intentionally bring into alignment with His ways. While we are honing our gifts and abilities, He will open doors and close doors accordingly and we will flow along with Him on this Year's journey.

Many are the plans in a person's heart, but it is the LORD's purpose that prevails.
Proverbs 19:21

A man's heart plans his course, but the LORD determines his steps.
Proverbs 16:9 BSB

And we know that in all things God works for the good of those who love him, who have been called according to his purpose. Romans 8:28

To everything there is a season, and a time to every purpose under the heaven: A time to be born, and a time to die; a time to plant, and a time to pluck up that which is planted... Ecclesiastes 3:1-2 NKJV

Biblical Affirmations to Declare Over Your Life

In addition to the specific traits you have been given to fulfill your God-given purpose, there are underlying truths about who God created you to be. These affirmations confirm the qualities you have been given for your underlying relationship and identity through Him.

Birthday affirmations, declarations, and prayers go beyond mere wishes; they are faith-filled expressions that align with God's Word that speak life, purpose, encouragement, and Divine blessing. The words we speak have power, and for those on a spiritual path, it is important to declare what God says about us. While the world may try to label us by our past, errors, or situations, we should instead rely on the truth found in God's Word.

Use these affirmations, supported by Scripture, to renew your mind, strengthen your faith and walk confidently in your God-given identity. Repeat them daily and let the truth of His promises transform your life!

Who Am I?

- I am a child of God and an heir to His promises. (Romans 8:17)
- I am fearfully and wonderfully made. (Psalm 139:14)
- I am God's masterpiece, created for good works. (Ephesians 2:10)
- I am chosen, holy, and dearly loved by God. (Colossians 3:12)
- I am bold because the Lord is my helper. (Hebrews 13:6)
- I am confident that God will finish the good work He started in me. (Philippians 1:6)

Promises of God

- This is the day the Lord has made; I will rejoice and be glad in it. (Psalm 118:24)
- Nothing can separate me from God's love. (Romans 8:38-39)
- God's plans for me are good, filled with hope and a future. (Jeremiah 29:11)
- God directs my steps and makes my paths straight. (Proverbs 3:5-6)
- God's power works in me to accomplish far more than I can imagine. (Ephesians 3:20)
- The Lord is faithful to keep His promises to me. (Deuteronomy 7:9)
- The Lord makes everything beautiful in His time. (Ecclesiastes 3:11)

I Am – Pisces Personality Declarations

- ♥ I am a dreamer.
- ♥ I am spiritual and faith-filled.
- ♥ I am understanding and sacrificial.
- ♥ I am a storyteller.
- ♥ I am flexible.
- ♥ I am creative and intuitive.
- ♥ I am caring and nurturing.
- ♥ I am loving, empathic, and understanding.
- ♥ I am worthy of love.

Pisces – Reminders for Growth and Balance

- + I forget myself.
- + I work selflessly in the background.
- + I need privacy and time alone to regenerate.
- + I ground my dreams in reality.
- + I engage in self-reflection to tackle underlying difficulties.
- + I balance giving to others and giving to myself.
- + I look for deeper truths and not just illusions.
- + I enjoy whole and full living on earth.
- + I set goals to minimize daydreaming.
- + I find focus and purpose by creating specific measurable goals.
- + I enjoy helping and healing others.
- + I learn to set balanced physical and emotional boundaries.

And there is more!

For more insight into the traits of Pisces go to, "Nourishment from the Month of Pisces," in Part Two, *Journey Around the Wheel of the Year*.

Yearly Birthday Life Review Questions

❓ My Birthday Life Review

Do you recognize qualities of Your Birthday Month Promise in yourself? If so, are they being used and developed? If you feel you are lacking in any of these, or are out of balance, ask the Spirit to help you make the most of them in this New Year.

What traits in the description of My Birthday Promise can I relate to?

Which traits of My Birthday Promise do not describe me?

What personality traits do I like the best in myself?

Are there traits that seem weak and need to be strengthened?

Are there traits that are too strong and need to be modified?

What are some traits that I recognize in myself that are not included in this Month's description?

What lessons did I learn last Year?

Which of the lessons did I struggle with the most?

What learning experience gave me the most growth during the past Year?

What aspects of my role do I express in a productive and healthy way?

What is the most fulfilling contribution I have made in the lives of those around me?

In what ways can I strengthen the role I have been given?

What did I learn about myself this Year?

In what ways can I use my role to contribute to my family or community?

What doors of opportunity do I privately long for God to open for me, even if I have not told anyone?

Spiritual Fruit Tending
Questions and prompts for your quiet time

Note: These questions serve as a guide for your time of reflection on the Spiritual Fruit in your life. Not every question needs a written answer, only your consideration.

What Fruits of the Spirit, or virtues, are evident in your life?

What Fruits are not as evident in your life?

Which Fruits do you want more of?

Are there inner conflicts that are blocking your Fruit?

Are the conflicts harming other areas of your life?

What insights have you received from the Spirit regarding these areas?

In what ways can you begin expressing the positive aspects of your personality to balance and heal the conflicts?

What acts of kindness can you show to encourage others?

In what ways can you help others more?

How can you display more of the Fruit of the Tree of Life in your daily life?

Journaling the Reflections on the Key Areas of Life

Key Life Area	My reflections and Insights into these Areas of my Life
Identity	Who am I?
Resources	What do I value?
Communication	How do I communicate?
Home	My foundation?
Recreation	My creative self-expression?
Routines	My daily routines?
Partnerships	How do I relate?
Shared Resources	How do I protect my resources?
Philosophy	My spiritual path?
Public Life	My social standing?
Community	How do I connect with like-minded people?
Subconscious	My hidden matters?

Deep Dive on Your Wheel of Life Findings
Questions and prompts for your quiet time

Note: The following questions serve as a guide to help you think deeply about your Wheel of Life findings and the ratings you gave yourself for each Area. They will help you set your course for the New Year. Not every question needs a written answer, only your awareness.

As you look at your completed wheel, how do you feel about your life?

What surprised you about the results?

What did not surprise you?

If this was an actual wheel on your 'vehicle' of life, would it be a bumpy ride?

What are the highest rated areas of your life right now?

What area are you the most satisfied with?

Is this an area you have already been specifically trying to grow in? If so, notice that you have improved!

What area of life did you give yourself the lowest rating?

Were you surprised by the low score?

What troubles you the most in this Area of your Life?

Have you already tried ways to grow in this Area?

What Areas of your Life do you focus on the most?

Which Area of Life needs more attention?

What is an obvious change to make first?

What lifestyle change would help you to improve this Area?

What is the 'opposite' Area of Life to this area (see page XXX)?

Which of the traits of the 'opposite' Area of Life could help balance or improve this low scored Area? Consider studying those traits to see how they can be beneficial in your life.

How can you begin to grow those 'opposite' traits into your life?

What challenges seem to repeat over and over?

How can you break this cycle?

Notice the things that you think about. Do you notice any thoughts that could be hindering your progress?

What are some positive thoughts you can start thinking about this Area?

Which of the Wheel of Life Areas would you be most excited to work on?

Which Area of Your Life do you feel you can make the most significant improvements?

What is one key action that could bring more change for the better?

What ideas do you already have that would raise your rating in this Wheel of Life Area?

What is the smallest step you could take to get started this Year?

How will improving the results in the challenging Area positively affect the results in another Area?

Which Months contain the traits you want to grow in?

Connecting the Results

When you connect the insights from the Wheel of Life results above with the following Your Birthday Promise Insights, you will gain a more meaningful understanding of the Key Areas of Your Life which will help you learn how to use and develop them to help fulfill your role and purpose in life.

Your Birthday Promise Insights
Reflections on Last Year + Intentions for the Year Ahead
Questions and prompts for your quiet time

Note: These questions serve as a guide for your time of reflection on last Year as well as your intentions for the Year ahead. Not every question needs a written answer, only your awareness.

Reflect on the past Year --- what stands out to you?

How is your life different on this birthday than it was on your last birthday?

What brings you the most satisfactions from last Year?

What personal goals did you accomplish this past Year?

What accomplishment in the past Year are you most proud of?

What was the most fun last Year?

What challenges did you overcome last Year?

Is there anything you need to let go of from last Year? If so, what is it and why?

What surprises you about being your age?

What is the best thing about being your age?

Which Areas of your Life do you feel is working the best right now?

What do you really enjoy doing?

What is the best relationship you currently have?

In what ways can your activities help you grow the Fruit of the Tree of Life?

What are ways that can you grow in your relationship with the Spirit?

In what ways can you implement more of the traits of your role into your everyday life?

How can you contribute to something bigger than yourself?

How does your daily life reflect the legacy you wish to leave?

What gets you most excited about this New Year?

What would you most like to accomplish this coming Year?

What is something you are looking forward to in the coming Year?

What Area do you want to learn to be the best you can be in this New Year?

What are 3 personal goals to set for this Year?

What can you do now to start any new goals or activities for this Year?

May this New Year of your life be filled with blessings, success, and unforgettable memories!

Now, let's get ready to grow the rest of the Year!

Journey Around the Wheel of the Year

Part Two

Your Journey Around the Wheel of the Year

Follow along throughout the Year to continue your spiritual and personal growth. Learn and glean from the unique attributes of the Month under which you were born, plus the other Months of the Year for insight and understanding. You will discover that each Month has its own positive attributes to download for your empowerment. See what the traits of each Month are that will enrich you and help align you to your role.

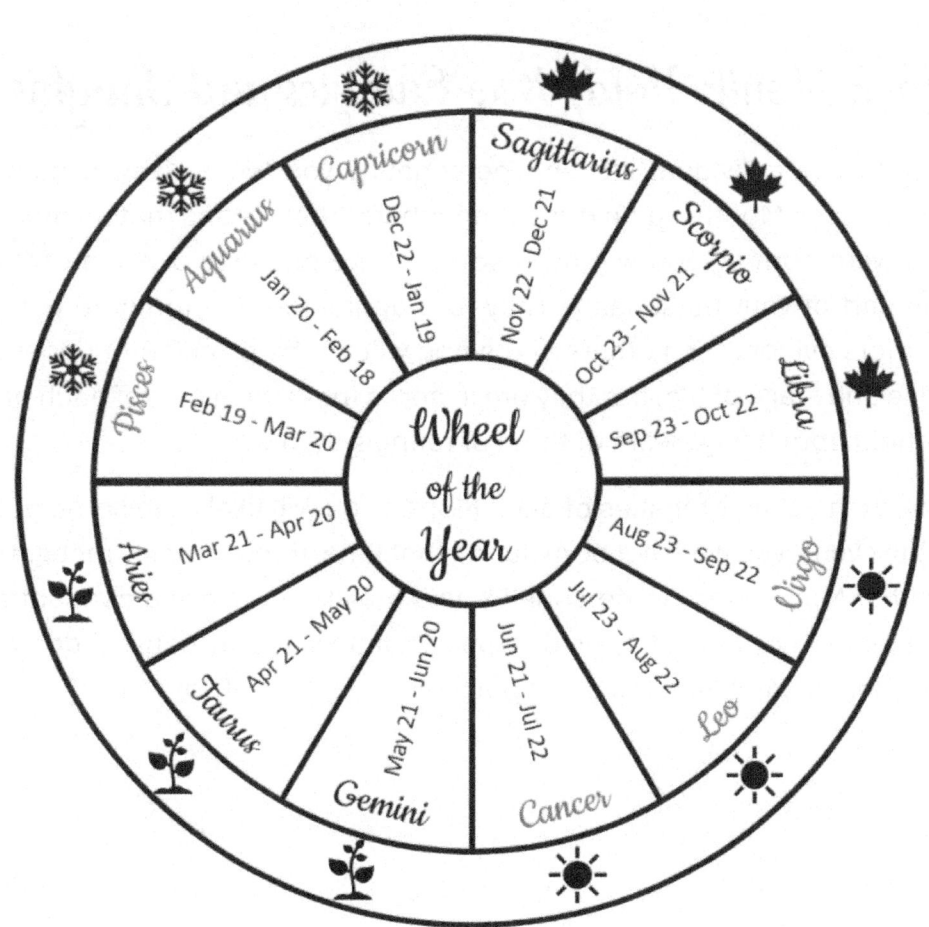

Nourishment from Each Month

Each Month of the Seasonal Year provides physical, spiritual, and developmental nourishment. Each has a specific role and purpose in the growth cycle of nature and humankind.

As with physical fruits, each of the Months' fruits, or characteristics, have their own distinctive 'taste', 'texture', and 'quality'. Each Month has its own attributes that provide nourishment and guidance for your life and growth. Their unique 'flavor' are the traits and characteristics. These Fruits are available for everyone throughout the Year.

This Part, *Journey Around the Wheel of the Year*, describes energies that flow from Heaven each Month when a portal, or heavenly gate, is opened and the gifts, talents, abilities, wisdoms, understandings, and timings are poured down. They are there every Month, according to the Month. It is up to us if we want to purposefully receive them into our lives for our personal and spiritual growth.

Each Month Holds New Energies and Insights

According to your individual life and personality, you were given a measure of qualities from each Month, some more than others. That means that no matter what Month you were born in, you will have some of the qualities of each of the other Months as part of your personality. They are appointed differently to each of us. Some are more evident than others and some will not be prominent, depending on our purpose and stage of life, but they are in some measure a part of each of us and we can benefit from being aware of them or refining them.

As you look at the characteristics of each Month, you will likely see some of them in your own life even if you were not born during that time. If you strongly recognize traits from the other Months in your personality, you are likely to have a concentration of that energy in some area of Your Birthday Promise, which can be documented through further research into the exact place and moment of Your Birth.

Balance and Grow from Each Month's Traits, Qualities, and Challenges

Each Year it is possible to glean from every Month and learn to grow in traits we may be lacking. They can be used to balance our negative traits or give us ideas on new ways to approach life.

Each Month has characteristics that are available for all. Take time to review these characteristics to see if you recognize them in yourself. Are they traits you want to grow in, or are they needed to help balance other traits you already have? It will add a new dimension to your walk and help you live a happier, balanced, more fulfilled life.

As you journey through the Year and observe the qualities of each Month, note if there are traits you see at work in your life.

Are they helpful to you or do they need some refining?

Learn More about Your Friends, Family, Children, and Co-Workers

In addition to discovering more about yourself, you will get to know your friends, family, and your children better through learning the qualities of the other Birth Months.

For example, you will be able to identify the qualities of your child's Birth Month, recognize them in your child, then give guidance on how to educate them according to their core role, personality and abilities. Throughout our lives, we are teaching and learning from each other, just by being ourselves.

Train up a child in the way he should go, And when he is old he will not depart from it. Proverbs 22:6 NKJV

Therefore encourage one another and build each other up, just as in fact you are doing. 1 Thessalonians 5:11 NIV

And let us consider how to stir up one another to love and good works. Hebrews 10:24

Love your neighbor as yourself. Mark 12:31

Self-awareness and Development Over Time

In addition to the positive traits, each Month is also associated with some negative characteristics. If you recognize some of these in your personality, you can learn to overcome them over time through self-awareness and development.

Embrace the unique characteristics that are associated with each Month, and make it a point to improve the Areas in which you struggle. Keep in mind that self-awareness and a willingness to change are important skills that will help you on the journey toward personal and spiritual development and healthier relationships.

Months That Will Help You Balance

Reflecting on the characteristics of each new Month is an effective way of rounding out your personality. In this Part of the Journal you will find the Wheel of the Year, where you can follow the Months and Seasons throughout the Year. Getting to know the characteristics of each Month will help you to realize how they support each other in carrying out the roles and the activities of the Wheel of Life.

When you understand the traits of all of the Months you will be able to use them to develop your life throughout the Year. Pay special attention to the Months that contain the traits associated with the Areas of Life that you need help with. Often developing the opposite Wheel of Life qualities will balance and grow the one that needs attention. Through this Monthly Review you can glean the insights and opportunities that are provided each Month.

The Date Range of each Month and the Months associated with each Area of Life are shown in the following tables.

The Seasonal Months and their Calendar Date Ranges

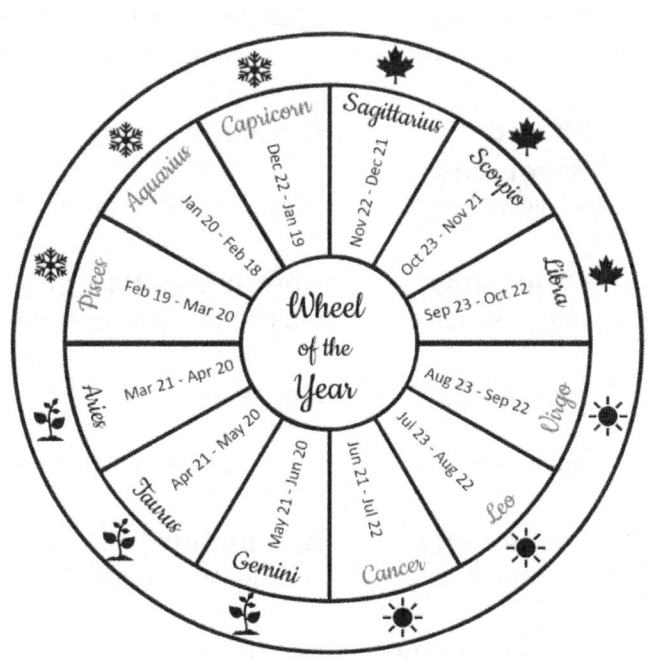

The Area of Life, its Month, its Traits, and its Opposite

The Month, Motto, Traits, Emphasis	Area of Life	Opposite Area of Life	The Month that Emphasizes the Opposite Traits
1 – Aries, I Am Assertive and pioneering nature	**Identity - Self**	**Partnerships**	7 – Libra, I Balance Desire for harmony, fairness in relationships
2 – Taurus, I Have Appreciation for material wealth and stability	**Resources**	**Shared Resources**	8 – Scorpio, I Desire Passion and intensity in all interests
3 – Gemini, I Think Intellectual curiosity and communication skills	**Communication**	**Philosophy**	9 – Sagittarius, I See Love for exploration and adventure
4. Cancer, I Feel Emotional depth and sensitivity	**Home**	**Public Life**	10 – Capricorn, I Achieve Pragmatic and goal-oriented mindset
5 – Leo, I Will Confidence and determination to lead	**Recreation**	**Community**	11 – Aquarius, I Know Innovative and forward-thinking nature
6 – Virgo, I Analyze Detail-oriented and practical approach to life	**Routines**	**Subconscious**	12 – Pisces, I Believe Faith and connection to the spiritual realm
7 – Libra, I Balance Desire for harmony, fairness in relationships	**Partnerships**	**Identity - Self**	1 – Aries, I Am Assertive and pioneering nature
8 – Scorpio, I Desire Passion and intensity in all interests	**Shared Resources**	**Resources**	2 – Taurus, I Have Appreciation for material wealth and stability
9 – Sagittarius, I See Love for exploration and adventure	**Philosophy**	**Communication**	3 – Gemini, I Think Intellectual curiosity and communication skills
10 – Capricorn, I Achieve Pragmatic and goal-oriented mindset	**Public Life**	**Home**	4 – Cancer, I Feel Emotional depth and sensitivity
11 – Aquarius, I Know Innovative and forward-thinking nature	**Community**	**Recreation**	5 – Leo, I Will Confidence and determination to lead
12 – Pisces, I Believe Faith and connection to the spiritual realm	**Subconscious**	**Routines**	6 – Virgo, I Analyze Detail-oriented and practical approach to life

It's a Learning Process

This is not a quick solution but a process of learning the traits that can build each Area of Your Life. For example, during the Month of Aries, you would reflect on Your Personal Identity, which would help in your self-development; during the Month of Taurus you would focus on Your Resources, which would help with your earning ability and spending; during the Month of Gemini you would reflect on your Communication Skills which would help with your interaction with others, and so on. You can note the attributes you want to grow in and write affirmations. Post sticky notes in conspicuous places around your home, office, or school. Add a special wallpaper or reminder on your device that will highlight the traits of the Month as helpful reminders of the traits you want to recognize.

Growing Fruit All Throughout the Year

We start each New Year with a heart full of hope and a mind brimming with possibilities for what is to come. As times goes by, seasons change, and so do we. Each Month holds new energies and insights that bring direction and hope through answers to questions, solutions to challenges, strength to overcome, encouragement for the future, and celebration when success is achieved. As you travel through the Yearly cycle, each Month serves as a guide to help you to grow on your life's path and provides the experiences, opportunities, lessons, and qualities that feed your purpose.

Imagine your Year as a book and each Month is a new chapter filled with stories of triumph, learning, and growth. Turn the page and let's begin the new story!

Tools and Insights

For helpful tools and insights you can use for development and growth on Your Birthday as well as throughout the Year, see Part Three, *Personal Development and Spiritual Growth Tools*.

"The purpose of becoming aware of yourself, your role, your purpose, your gifts and talents, is not to take anything away from God's glory. Instead, it is to acknowledge Him in every part of the life you have been given. It is to make the most of the opportunities and life lessons that God has provided for you. It is to connect you to the reality of who you were created to be." Page 9

March 21 – April 20

Nourishment
from the Month of
Aries

Aries is associated with the qualities of pioneering, leadership, courage, determination, and being first.

The Month of Aries

Natural Features of the Month of Aries

Aries is the first! Aries itself is the first Month of God's Seasonal Year, the first Month of the Yearly growth cycle, and the first Month of Spring. It is the beginning of the Spiritual growth cycle with the significance of Passover and Resurrection Sunday being observed at this time.

"This month shall be your beginning of months; it shall be the first month of the Year to you." Exodus 12:2 NKJV

Aries Ushers in the Spring Season. Spring begins on or about March 20th in the Northern Hemisphere, under the Month of Aries. On the first day, the Vernal Equinox, both day and night are of equal length. The Year starts in balance.

But soon the balance shifts. Through the three Months of Spring, the days grow longer and the nights grow shorter. It is the most youthful time of the Year. Then, when daytime becomes its longest, Spring is over.

Aries begins the Seasonal and Spiritual Year with a ray of hope and renewal after the long Winter. It marks a period of enthusiasm for new life and new beginnings. It provides the energy of the Sun bursting forth out of the Winter into new life starting in the Spring.

Aries is known for its energetic and dynamic nature. It brings about a time of renewal, awakening, setting goals, initiating projects, and embracing fresh opportunities. It is the time for fresh starts, vibrant growth, and great energy that urges preparation and planting for the New Year.

This describes the natural energy pattern associated with the Month of Aries.

The Personality of the Month of Aries
What Can We Learn From the Aries Nature?

Aries energy is reflected in the Aries traits of being an initiator, starter, filled with new ideas and many new beginnings. Aries energy is fearless and inspires boldness, courage, and action.

Aries individuals are The Pioneers of the Year, known for their trailblazing spirit and energetic leadership. Their fiery energy represents their courage and initiative. They have a forceful personality that drives them to initiate projects and activities.

Aries prefers to lead rather than follow. Their energy and determination make them natural leaders, and their bravery and drive inspires those around them. Aries are eager to improve themselves, to set bold goals, and to take risks to achieve them.

Aries like taking on leadership roles, physical challenges, and individual sports. They dislike inactivity, delays, and meaningless tasks.

Physical activity, athletics, and movement are key factors in the Aries' lifestyle.

Aries – Keyword Qualities

Self-Aware Seeds to Plant		Unaware Weeds to Uproot	
leader	instigator	naïve	daring
initiator	courageous	domineering	primitive
ambitious	confident	self-centered	impulsive
passionate	quick-witted	impatient	hot-tempered
wants to be first	bold	rash	aggressive
headstrong	enthusiastic	thoughtless	too passionate
willful	optimistic	blundering	possessive
indomitable spirit	dynamic	childish	reckless
unwavering	pioneering	quick-tempered	
determined	active		
takes risks	athletic		

Aries Identifiers – Positive Qualities
Aries' positive energy that can be of benefit to all

- ☺ The need for speed!
- ☺ Self-assured and capability.
- ☺ Not afraid to go after what they want.
- ☺ Stand up for what they believe.
- ☺ Pioneers, mavericks, independent.
- ☺ Frank, fast, bold, expansive, impulsive, heroic, competitive.
- ☺ Determined to succeed.
- ☺ Enthusiastic.
- ☺ Spontaneous, dynamic.
- ☺ Take the lead.
- ☺ Act on their own ideas.
- ☺ Ability to recoup after disasters.

Aries Identifiers – Challenging Qualities
Aries' challenging traits to recognize and balance

- ☹ Aries, known for their fiery passion and determination, can sometimes find themselves caught in the trap of impulsiveness.
- ☹ Their hot temper and relentless pursuit of success can lead to conflicts and strained relationships.
- ☹ They do not like to take advice from others and often start but do not finish projects.
- ☹ People who possess many of the Aries' traits are notorious for their hasty decisions and short tempers.

How to Refine Challenging Personality Traits

If you read this list of challenging personality traits and recognized yourself in some of them, don't worry—they are not etched in stone.

In fact, you've already taken the first and most difficult step - becoming aware of them.

Self-aware people reflect on their lives, recognize their emotions, consider their impact on others, and adapt based on feedback.

People who lack self-awareness are often blind to their own faults, struggle with personal and spiritual growth, and may find self-reflection challenging. They repeatedly make the same mistakes and then blame others for their outcome.

By acknowledging that you have unwanted traits, you can now start the process of refining or even eliminating them.

Aries - Modifying Challenging Traits

Those born under the Month of Aries, are gifted with a strong independence and will learn to work with others through the give and take of their close partnerships and relationships.

They have a tendency to want to be the star of their own personal movie which must be tempered with intentional curiosity and empathy for others.

Aries enjoys the chase and the next adventure. Each new experience provides fresh ways to assert themselves. However, part of the Aries soul growth journey is to recognize that many of the finest things in life can only be experienced at a slower pace – including friendships and relationships with those who possess less speedy souls.

Aries' high self-sufficiency might intimidate others, leading them to think they do not need or want them. It may be necessary for Aries to actively and deliberately invite others into their life, even when they don't have to.

Taming Impulsivity - Tips to Refine the Aries Nature

Cultivating these life skills over time will bring the Aries Nature into alignment with the positive traits of their role and provide more inner peace and fulfillment.

- Practice patience.
- Practice slowing down.
- Learn to pause before reacting.
- Take several deep breaths before reacting as a way to deal with a challenge.
- Learn anger management skills.
- Think carefully about the consequences of decisions.
- Cultivate empathy and self-awareness.
- Learn to pause, consider the perspectives of others, and control impulses.
- Reconsider before burning bridges.
- Channel energy into constructive action.
- Balance self-focus with consideration for others.
- Invest in leadership development to support and lead others in a broader capacity.
- Balance the enthusiastic nature with thoughtful deliberation.

Activities, Actions, Attitudes to Contemplate During the Month of Aries

Try out new Aries-type experiences, as led, to round out your personality!

- Contemplate the life question: "Who am I?"
- Identify the Month of Aries traits you notice in your life.
- Find opportunities to apply the lessons of Aries – leadership, courage, determination, initiation, action, and passion - to your life.
- Start something new in your life – a new beginning.
- Exercise leadership even in minor situations.
- Be alert for any situations that give you the opportunity to take the lead.
- Wear red more often.
- Search for clues to your identity.
- Write one sentence that can describe your identity.
- Focus on others.
- Overcome self-centeredness by sacrificing something you want for someone else.
- Make time for a workout routine.
- Practice being guided by your gut instincts.
- Find a challenging and exciting new hobby.

Reflections on this Month's Aries Traits
Growing in Understanding Aries

Are there Aries traits that you can identify in your life?

If so, which are positive and which ones need to be refined?

Do you recognize these traits in someone that was born under the Month of Aries?

Does recognizing these traits in them help you to better understand them?

Are there any experiences you need or want to heal regarding these traits?

What Aries traits can help you to lead by initiating and directing new endeavors?

Which of this Month's 'Activities, Actions, Attitudes' growth opportunities are you looking forward to trying?

 **Reflections for the Aries Personality**
For Those Born Under the Month of Aries

- ? Are you grateful for all that you have accomplished?

- ? Are you thankful for all you will achieve?

- ? Would it benefit you to include someone else in a few activities that you normally do by yourself?

- ? How would it benefit you? How would it benefit them?

- ? What has helped you to calm down when you were angry?

- ? In what ways can you learn to be more patient?

- ? What lessons have you learned from any recent setbacks?

- ? In what ways have you taken responsibility for yourself and your life?

Ask to be Filled

Ask the Spirit to fill your life with the fresh Fruit of this Month of Aries for nourishment and healing. (Revelation 22:1-2).

Pray, to receive the nourishment you need that the Month of Aries provides; to receive revelation and insight into your life and the life of others; to receive the Heavenly blessings of the Month.

> *"Holy Spirit, You know the plan for my life, you know my heart and what is needed for the New Year. Fill me with the energies, the gifts and abilities of Aries that I need, to use for the best and highest good..."*

April 21 – May 20

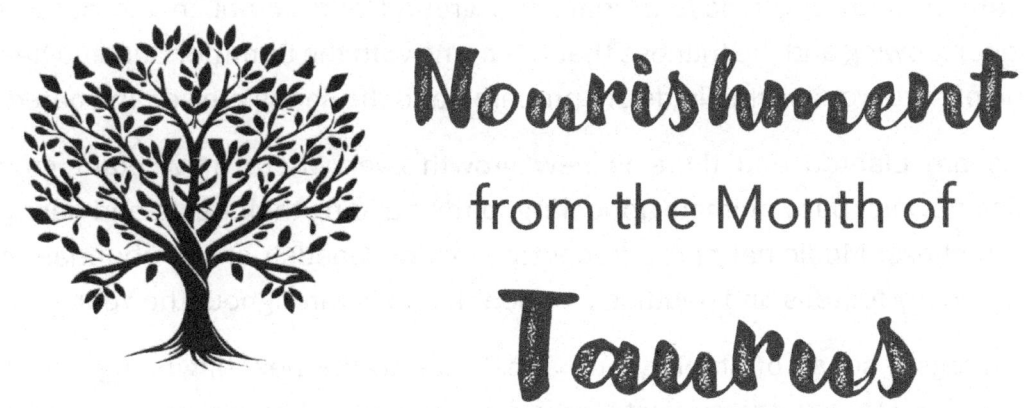

Nourishment from the Month of Taurus

Taurus teaches the importance of patience, loyalty, and savoring life's simple pleasures.

The Month of Taurus

Natural Features of the Month of Taurus

Taurus is a fixed Month locked in the middle of the Spring Months. Taurus brings forth and stabilizes what was started at the first initiations of Spring in Aries.

Taurus establishes the Spring Season. Taurus is the second month of God's Seasonal Year, the second Month in the Yearly growth cycle, and the second Month of the Spring Season.

Spring continues when the Sun reaches Taurus in late April. The warming temperatures and longer days prepare the ground and establish the seed time needed for growing and the fullness that will come with the Summer Sun and heat. It is a time of hard work as the fields are prepared and the seeds are set and cared for.

Gardens are planted and there is new growth everywhere; new plant growth, blooming flowers, baby animals appearing, birds building their nests and caring for their hatchlings. Medicinal herbs (recently labeled 'weeds') are in abundance, to harvest and dry for teas and poultices for health needs throughout the Year.

Taurus brings a sense of stability and substance to the new beginnings of Aries. Taurus is about learning to cultivate patience, build foundations, and nurture what has been started. The hard work that needs to be done at this time of the Year gives the foundation for growth. It aligns with the growing season of nature, emphasizing the importance of persistence and hard work which leads to an enjoyment of life's pleasures.

This describes the natural energy pattern associated with the Month of Taurus.

The Personality of the Month of Taurus
What Can We Learn From the Taurus Nature?

Taurus energy is characterized by the Taurus nature of being steady and productive. Taurus values comfort and financial stability, often focusing on practical and sustainable habits.

Taurus energy symbolizes constancy, sensuality, and a deep connection to the earth. They enjoy the finer things in life, such as massages, long baths, and delicious desserts. Their sensual nature appreciates the natural comforts and pleasures of the material world.

Taurus needs security and is determined to be grounded and safe. They build up their resources, possessions, and values in a practical steadfast way.

Taurus likes beauty and working with their hands through gardening and cooking. They also enjoy music and romance. They dislike sudden changes, complications, and insecurity of any kind.

Taurus' are known for their loyalty and form deep and enduring connections, sometimes to an extreme. Their practical approach to life and strong sense of loyalty make them dependable partners and friends.

Taurus – Keyword Qualities

Self-Aware Seeds to Plant		Unaware Weeds to Uproot
productive	focused	stubborn
slow to anger	sensual	inflexible
self-reliant	stable	reactive
steadfast	concrete	greedy
grounded	realistic	self-indulgent
faithful	steady	stubborn
constant	constructive	possessive
sturdy	tenacious	uncompromising
patient	persistent	slow to let it go
tough	reliable	untrusting
persevering	practical	fear of change
strong	natural	attachment
routine		

Taurus Identifiers – Positive Qualities
Taurus' positive energy that can be of benefit to all

- ☺ Taurus represents beauty and love.
- ☺ An appreciation for the sensual things in life.
- ☺ Enjoys a connection to Mother Nature.
- ☺ Responsible, stable, and devoted.
- ☺ Have a sense of value and expect respect from others.
- ☺ Have an eye for quality; they don't cut corners.
- ☺ Frugal but will splurge for their favorite luxuries.
- ☺ Excellent cooks and gardeners.
- ☺ Desire to be the foundation of any project.
- ☺ Cannot be rushed into anything.
- ☺ 'Slow and steady wins the race' mindset.

Taurus Identifiers – Challenging Qualities
Taurus' challenging traits to recognize and balance

- ☹ Taurus, known for their great will power, can be slow to move and resistant to change. They can be notoriously determined and obstinate.
- ☹ Taurus can be materialistic and too fearful of change or losing their possessions. They also cannot trust what they cannot see.
- ☹ Taurus can struggle with stubbornness and possessiveness. Their strong attachment to material possessions and routines can hinder their adaptability and growth.

How to Refine Challenging Personality Traits

If you read this list of challenging personality traits and recognized yourself in some of them, don't worry—they are not etched in stone.

In fact, you've already taken the first and most difficult step - becoming aware of them.

Self-aware people reflect on their lives, recognize their emotions, consider their impact on others, and adapt based on feedback.

People who lack self-awareness are often blind to their own faults, struggle with personal and spiritual growth, and may find self-reflection challenging. They repeatedly make the same mistakes and then blame others for their outcome.

By acknowledging that you have unwanted traits, you can now start the process of refining or even eliminating them.

Taurus – Modifying Challenging Traits

Those born with strong Taurus traits have a fixed stability and will learn how to transform, change, and share through interactions in their close relationships.

Taurus would do well by realizing that stability does not come from staying the same but from bringing into line what truly is meant for them. To break free from stubbornness and possessiveness, Taurus needs to embrace flexibility and open-mindedness. Embracing change, being willing to let go, and fostering a growth mindset will allow them to adapt to life's ever-changing circumstances and unlock new possibilities.

Activities that nourish their soul, not just their bank account, will help them align. They should gain stability in themselves first, and then in all areas of life that support a meaningful existence. This balanced, appreciative approach will lead to sustained joy.

Taurus needs to feel communion with the natural elements. Quiet time alone in nature, growing a garden, walking in a forest, or listening to the birds all nourish and replenish them. Their inner desire is to experience the best of the five senses. Connecting to anything that makes the physical world become more alive and raises personal awareness of what is satisfying and important is beneficial.

Self-care is important to prioritize as well. Recharge through enjoyable activities such as gardening, cooking, or spending. Ensure that balance between diligent work, adequate rest, and recreational activities is maintained.

Breaking Free from Stubbornness – Tips to Refine the Taurus Nature

Cultivating these life skills over time will bring the Taurus Nature into alignment with the positive traits of their role and provide more inner peace and fulfillment.

- Develop flexibility by taking on new challenges.
- Learn about the world from a variety of viewpoints to break free from extreme stubbornness.
- Accept change as a chance for personal development.
- Lessen the attachment to comfort and certainty.
- Embrace change as a path to growth.
- Honor their worth without proving it through possessions.
- Stay open to new possibilities.
- Embracing flexibility.
- Learn to appreciate life's simple pleasures.
- Create a stable work environment where there are few changes and those that happen are ideally under your guidance.

Activities, Actions, Attitudes to Contemplate During the Month of Taurus

Try out new Taurus-type experiences, as led, to round out your personality!

- Contemplate the life question: "What do I value?"
- Identify the Month of Taurus traits you notice in your life.
- Find opportunities to apply the lessons of Taurus – patience, loyalty, enjoying life's simple pleasures - to your life.
- Spend some time outdoors enjoying nature, the forest, or the beach.
- Enjoy gardening.
- Lie on the ground and feel the earth.
- Listen to soothing music.
- Express your creative side.
- Cook your favorite meal.
- Take an inventory of your talents.
- List how much time and money you have invested in your talents.
- Strive to appreciate your talents.
- Write your mission statement.
- Indulge and pamper yourself. Buy yourself a gift.
- Eat delicious desserts.
- Visit art galleries, museums, and go to concerts.
- Connect to your five senses.
- Play background music when you work.
- Reflect on what gives you self-worth.

Reflections on this Month's Taurus Traits
Growing in Understanding Taurus

Are there Taurus traits that you can identify in your life?

If so, which are positive and which ones need to be refined?

Do you recognize these traits in someone that was born under the Month of Taurus?

Does recognizing these traits in them help you to better understand them?

Are there any experiences you need or want to heal regarding these traits?

What Taurus traits can help you to accumulate and manage money and other resources?

Which of this Month's 'Activities, Actions, Attitudes' growth opportunities are you looking forward to trying?

 **Reflections for the Taurus Personality**

? What does success and abundance mean to you personally, not what society or family expects?

? Do you feel you are worthy of success and financial security?

? What makes you feel secure in life?

? How can you learn to embrace change?

? Are your accomplishments bringing you peace and fulfillment or just comfort?

? What would your dream life feel like without chasing external measures?

? In what ways do you take charge of providing resources for your life?

Ask to be Filled

Ask the Spirit to fill your life with the fresh Fruit of this Month of Taurus for nourishment and healing. (Revelation 22:1-2).

Pray, to receive the nourishment you need that the Month of Taurus provides; to receive revelation and insight into your life and the life of others; to receive the Heavenly blessings of the Month.

> *"Holy Spirit, You know the plan for my life, you know my heart and what is needed for the New Year. Fill me with the energies, the gifts and abilities of Taurus that I need, to use for the best and highest good..."*

May 21 – June 20

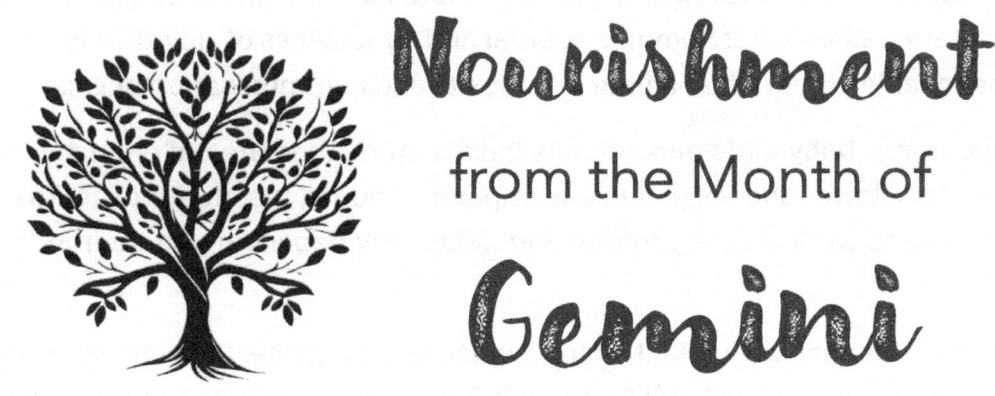

Nourishment
from the Month of
Gemini

Gemini embodies the duality of human nature and emphasizes the power of curiosity, adaptability, and effective communication.

The Month of Gemini

Natural Features of the Month of Gemini

Gemini is the third Month of God's Seasonal Year, the third Month of the Yearly growth cycle, and the third and last Month of the Spring season.

Gemini transitions Spring to the Summer Season. The ending of the Spring season is signaled by the Sun moving into Gemini in late May. It is the final transition from cold Winter weather to hot Summer weather and its activities of growth. It is a flexible and changeable Month when a time of curiosity and communication begins.

In nature, many baby birds and animals have matured and are old enough to leave the nest. The flower and vegetable seeds planted during the Month of Taurus have taken root, and work on the gardens and fields vary depending on their individual needs.

The Month of Gemini is a jubilant, inspirational, engaging time that sets the stage for the ray of hope and renewal that Summer brings. It hands over to Summer what has been birthed and grounded in Aries and Taurus, where afterwards the Month of Cancer officially initiates the Summer Months.

This describes the natural energy pattern associated with the Month of Gemini.

The Personality of the Month of Gemini

What Can We Learn From the Gemini Nature?

As a changeable Month, Gemini has acquired the ability to be versatile and smart in their ways. Geminis are spontaneous and curious, characterized by their dual nature and playfulness. Gemini likes to debate, share ideas, and connect with people.

Gemini energy is intellectual and adaptable, encouraging social gatherings and learning. They enjoy sharing, whether through feelings, words, or the gift of writing. They bring lively conversations and a thirst for knowledge.

Gemini enjoys exploring varied ideas and perspectives and is constantly looking for new experiences to expand their minds. They thrive in environments that stimulate their intellect and seek knowledge through connection with others.

Gemini has a sense of wisdom and is proficient at handing many energies at once. Their active mind and body lead to many places and experiences. They have a restlessness that keeps them moving on. Gemini experiences self-improvement through learning and exploration. Gemini likes music, books, media, talking with nearly anyone, and short travels. They do not like to focus or spend a lot of time on any one endeavor for very long.

In relationships, Gemini connects well with energetic people and many times forms stimulating and dynamic partnerships. Their adaptability and curiosity make them engaging companions who are always eager to share their latest discoveries.

Gemini – Keyword Qualities

Self-Aware Seeds to Plant		Unaware Weeds to Uproot	
expressive	flexible	nervous	moody
lively	ingenious	inconsistent	shallow
adaptable	imaginative	lose focus	opportunistic
quick-witted	charming	scattered	unconcerned
humorous	fanciful	indecisive	selfish
sparkling	intelligent	shallow minded	sarcastic
playful	fast-moving	superficial	changeable
sociable	communicative	capricious	distractable
clever	logical		
curious	rational		
independent	dualistic		
multi-valued	versatile		
brainy	inquisitive		
talkative	seeker of knowledge		

Gemini Identifiers – Positive Qualities
Gemini's positive energy that can be of benefit to all

- ☺ The social butterflies of the Months.
- ☺ The connector of resources for the community.
- ☺ Known for their humor, curiosity, and adaptability.
- ☺ The ability to communicate effortlessly.
- ☺ Excellent at networking, problem-solving, and engaging in long conversations with those around them.
- ☺ Ability to handle multiple tasks at the same time.
- ☺ They have a special kind of dexterity.
- ☺ Represent the power of clear thought and wisdom.
- ☺ Jack-of-all trades, yet master of none.
- ☺ Prefer short-term activities with numerous ongoing options.

Gemini Identifiers – Challenging Qualities
Gemini's Challenging Traits to recognize and balance

- ☹ Gemini, the versatile and communicative sign, can face challenges due to their dual nature. This can hold them back from long-term commitments and personal growth.
- ☹ Due to their versatility they can change according to their circumstances. This also applies to their truths. Gemini does not mind bending the truth if the circumstances call for it.
- ☹ They can often be scattered and unfocused.
- ☹ They can struggle with indecision because of their need to analyze every option before committing to a decision.
- ☹ When Gemini's intelligence is misused, it can manifest in deceit or manipulation.
- ☹ They always want to have the last word.
- ☹ Their words can sometimes be reckless and stinging.

How to Refine Challenging Personality Traits

If you read this list of challenging personality traits and recognized yourself in some of them, don't worry—they are not etched in stone.

In fact, you've already taken the first and most difficult step - becoming aware of them.

Self-aware people reflect on their lives, recognize their emotions, consider their impact on others, and adapt based on feedback.

People who lack self-awareness are often blind to their own faults, struggle with personal and spiritual growth, and may find self-reflection challenging. They repeatedly make the same mistakes and then blame others for their outcome.

By acknowledging that you have unwanted traits, you can now start the process of refining or even eliminating them.

Gemini - Modifying Challenging Traits

Those with strong Gemini traits need diversity and will learn the value of consistency through their partnerships. By interacting with varied viewpoints, Geminis can foster personal growth and develop empathy.

If Gemini is feeling confined by their current job, relationship, or lifestyle, it may indicate a need for greater variety and stimulation. To be able to honor their need for more interesting projects and pursuits, engaging in work that offers dynamic challenges rather than excessive routine or responsibility can be beneficial.

For these individuals who thrive on curiosity and adaptability, an ideal work environment is one that provides ongoing interest and the flexibility to operate independently will help them overcome attention-based obstacles.

They can harness their versatility and create a fulfilling life by cultivating discipline, focus, and deeper emotional connections.

Reducing the Distractions – Tips to Refine the Gemini Nature

Cultivating these life skills over time will bring the Gemini Nature into alignment with the positive traits of their role and provide more inner peace and fulfillment.

- Embrace their dual nature.
- Learn to communicate effectively by listening deeply.
- Focus on maintaining organization and keeping commitments.
- Create a routine to better focus their attention.
- Practice depth over surface attention.
- Hone decision-making skills.
- Develop a sense of purpose.
- Strengthen emotional bonds.
- Focus on concentration.
- Engage in reading, puzzles, or other solo effort tasks to minimize scattered thoughts.

Activities, Actions, Attitudes to Contemplate During the Month of Gemini

Try out new Gemini-type experiences, as led, to round out your personality!

- Contemplate the life question: "How do I communicate?"
- Identify the Month of Gemini traits you notice in your life.
- Find opportunities to apply the lessons of Gemini – curiosity, adaptability, effective communication - to your life.
- Focus on your communication skills.
- Work on your writing skills.
- Take time for your siblings and neighbors.
- Pay attention to the words you speak.
- Keep negative talk about people at a minimum.
- Omit slander and gossip.
- Observe and improve how you greet people on the phone.
- Improve your voicemail and emails content.
- Share information with others.
- Notice the message you are sharing.
- Talk less, listen more.
- Find your dual natures and try to bring them together.
- Try a new challenging mental activity.
- Spend time playing games or puzzles.
- Socialize with others.
- Look for common interest activities to do with others.

Reflections on this Month's Gemini Traits
Growing in Understanding Gemini

Are there Gemini traits that you can identify in your life?

If so, which are positive and which ones need to be refined?

Do you recognize these traits in someone that was born under the Month of Gemini?

Does recognizing these traits in them help you to better understand them?

Are there any experiences you need or want to heal regarding these traits?

What Gemini traits can help you to acquire, use, and communicate factual information?

Which of this Month's 'Activities, Actions, Attitudes' growth opportunities are you looking forward to trying?

 Reflections for the Gemini Personality

- ? Are you too interested in thinking or being and not actually doing?

- ? What helps you when you have restless thoughts?

- ? In what ways can you learn to take time to relax and slow down?

- ? Do you feel you take the time to listen, instead of talking?

- ? Do you study ways to change and keep up to date?

Ask to be Filled

Ask the Spirit to fill your life with the fresh Fruit of this Month of Gemini for nourishment and healing. (Revelation 22:1-2).

Pray, to receive the nourishment you need that the Month of Gemini provides; to receive revelation and insight into your life and the life of others; to receive the Heavenly blessings of the Month.

Holy Spirit, You know the plan for my life, you know my heart and what is needed for the New Year. Fill me with the energies, the gifts and abilities of Gemini that I need, to use for the best and highest good...

June 21 – July 22

Nourishment from the Month of Cancer

Cancer highlights the value of emotional connection and the strength found in protecting those they love.

The Month of Cancer

Natural Features of the Month of Cancer

Cancer is the initiating Month of the three-Month Summer season. It is the fourth Month of God's Seasonal Year, the fourth Month of the Yearly growth cycle, and the first Month of Summer.

Cancer Ushers in the Summer Season. After longer and longer days of sunshine, Summer arrives on or about June 20th-21st at the Summer solstice, the longest day of the Year. The Sun rises to its maximum height on that day and afterwards daylight begins to dwindle down, gradually becoming shorter as the nights grow longer. When day and night are roughly equal in length, Summer is over and Fall begins. But while it lasts, Summer is the most exciting Season of the Year.

Blooming flowers and lush plants are abundant. The long days, plenty of sunlight, and the hottest temperatures promote full plant growth, ripe fruits, and vegetables. Some of the food from the gardens are ready to eat.

It is a time to protect the land, as the crops are growing and attract insects, deer, rabbits, squirrels, and groundhogs seeking to benefit from the hard work of the previous Months. In response to the threats instinctual and important triggers are activated to care for the growing life.

During this season, people often feel playful and in need of connection. There is a pull towards their emotional roots, seeking comfort and bonding with loved ones. It is a time for family reunions, picnics, and vacations. Care for home, family, heritage, foundations, and land are associated with this time.

This describes the natural energy pattern associated with the Month of Cancer.

The Personality of the Month of Cancer
What Can We Learn From the Cancer Nature?

Cancer energy is often characterized by its nurturing qualities and emotional depth. Home, family, and taking care of personal needs are important concerns of the Month of Cancer.

Cancer individuals are intuitive and protective. They are connected to their internal wisdom, and thrive from being in touch with their instincts. Their ability to connect both emotionally and materially makes them empathetic and supportive partners, always ready to offer a comforting presence and a listening ear.

Emotional development and nurturing relationships are important to Cancers who often journal their insights and feelings. Cancers look for relationships where their caring nature is valued, thereby establishing trust as a foundation for deep connections where they can share their deepest feelings.

Cancers like one-on-one conversations, home-based hobbies, relaxing near or in the water, helping loved ones, or a good meal with friends. They dislike strangers, any criticism of their mother, or revealing their personal life to others.

Cancer – Keyword Qualities

Self-Aware		Unaware	
Seeds to Plant		Weeds to Uproot	
emotional	motherly or	timid	clingy
sentimental	fatherly	unrealistic	greedy
peaceful	dreamy	evasive	idle
imaginative	devoted	passive	secretive
sensitive	tenacious	anxious	unwavering
faithful	protective	dependent	moody
resistant	loyal	lazy	possessive
vulnerable	sympathetic	touchy	suspicious
generous	persuasive	stay-at-home	manipulative
romantic	intuitive	inaccessible	insecure
nostalgic	patriotic		
tender			

Cancer Identifiers – Positive Qualities
Cancer's positive energy that can be of benefit to all

- ☺ Intuitive and emotional understanding.
- ☺ Caregivers, supportive presences, kind ally, empathetic ear.
- ☺ The mothers to all.
- ☺ Emotionally sensitive.
- ☺ Nurturing of self and others.
- ☺ Compassionate, and intuitive.
- ☺ Focus on home and family.
- ☺ Very protective of their family.
- ☺ Sensitive to the feelings of others.
- ☺ Can be touchy, needy.
- ☺ Introverted and moody.
- ☺ Closed inner circle.
- ☺ Prone to experiencing weariness.
- ☺ High intellect.
- ☺ Keen intuitive abilities.
- ☺ Intimidatingly perceptive.

Cancer Identifiers – Challenging Qualities
Cancer's challenging traits to recognize and balance

- ☹ Cancer can be overly concerned and overly motherly to those they love.
- ☹ The fear of being emotionally hurt can keep them immobilized.
- ☹ While Cancer energy provides emotional depth and spiritual insight, it can also bring moodiness if not balanced.
- ☹ They take on everyone else's burdens, forgetting that God is the true source of peace.
- ☹ Cancer is very selective on who they allow in their very closed inner circle.

How to Refine A Challenging Personality Trait

If you read this list of challenging personality traits and recognized yourself in some of them, don't worry—they are not etched in stone.

In fact, you've already taken the first and most difficult step - becoming aware of them.

Self-aware people reflect on their lives, recognize their emotions, consider their impact on others, and adapt based on feedback.

People who lack self-awareness are often blind to their own faults, struggle with personal and spiritual growth, and may find self-reflection challenging. They repeatedly make the same mistakes and then blame others for their outcome.

By acknowledging that you have unwanted traits, you can now start the process of refining or even eliminating them.

Cancer - Modifying Challenging Traits

Those with many Cancerian tendencies have deep emotions, and they will learn to balance their feelings through relationships that provide them with emotional discipline.

Cancers are encouraged to honor their feelings and use their intuition as a guiding force. By nurturing themselves and others, Cancers learn that true strength lies in vulnerability, allowing them to build authentic connections.

Cancers have a tendency to be extremely sensitive, making them susceptible to emotional wounds. Self-care and learning to regulate their emotions are two practices that can help them manage this attribute.

Self-care means being intentional about their physical, mental, and emotional health. It involves using all the tools and knowledge at their disposal to ensure that they are managing stress and their energy appropriately.

All too often Cancer gives and gives, and gives, only to realize that they have become severely depleted. Self-care may involve solitude.

Cancers need to realize that just because they are able to help, whether it be in time, money, energy, or other resources, does not mean that they automatically need to sacrifice all they have until they are empty. Having access to proper tools and support can turn sensitivity and strong emotions into valuable strengths that offer encouragement and resilience.

Unclinging the Clinger - Tips to Refine the Cancer Nature

Cultivating these life skills over time will bring the Cancer Nature into alignment with the positive traits of their role and provide more inner peace and fulfillment.

- Learn to set emotional boundaries.
- Allow themselves to be vulnerable without crossing boundaries.
- Nurture themselves as they nurture others.
- Trust that safety comes from within.
- Release the past to make space for the new.
- If necessary, seek professional help in the form of therapy or counseling in order to create more positive coping strategies.
- Be conscious and intentional about cultivating self-love and self-care.
- Do not try to sort out the problems of others or manage their emotions for them.
- Give friends or family members the space to work through their own emotions or find their own way out of a problem.
- Realize that someone else's solution may not look exactly like theirs and they found a way in the end.
- In their involvement with helping others, they need to ask themselves regularly – How much can I give without become depleted?
- Develop emotional regulation practices.
- Journal their feelings to promote emotional clarity.

Activities, Actions, Attitudes to Contemplate During the Month of Cancer

Try out new Cancer-type experiences, as led, to round out your personality!

- Contemplate the life question: "What is my foundation?"
- Identify the Month of Cancer traits you notice in your life.
- Find opportunities to apply the lessons of Cancer – home, family, nurturing, caring, emotional control - to your life.
- Stabilize your emotions.
- Identify the fears that keep you from feeling secure.
- Spend time doing something special for your home.
- Call your mother.
- Forgive your mother.
- Look up at the Moon when it is visible and contemplate.
- Commit yourself to showing compassion to others.
- Spend time with family.
- Prepare your favorite meal.
- Make time to express your creativity.
- Spend time journaling, listening to music, or creating art.
- Read a book that you have always wanted to read.

Reflections on this Month's Cancer Traits
Growing in Understanding Cancer

Are there Cancer traits that you can identify in your life?

If so, which are positive and which ones need to be refined?

Do you recognize these traits in someone that was born under the Month of Cancer?

Does recognizing these traits in them help you to better understand them?

Are there any experiences you need or want to heal regarding these traits?

What Cancer traits can help you to create strong emotional bonds with home and family?

Which of this Month's 'Activities, Actions, Attitudes' growth opportunities are you looking forward to trying?

 **Reflections for the Cancer Personality**

? What helps when you feel depressed or sad?

? How do you recover from feeling emotionally drained?

? Are there emotions that are keeping you trapped in the past?

? What can your emotions teach you?

? How do you react emotionally when you assert yourself?

? In what ways can you nurture yourself?

Ask to be Filled

Ask the Spirit to fill your life with the fresh Fruit of this Month of Cancer for nourishment and healing. (Revelation 22:1-2).

Pray, to receive the nourishment you need that the Month of Cancer provides; to receive revelation and insight into your life and the life of others; to receive the Heavenly blessings of the Month.

> *"Holy Spirit, You know the plan for my life, you know my heart and what is needed for the New Year. Fill me with the energies, the gifts and abilities of Cancer that I need, to use for the best and highest good…"*

July 23 – August 22

Nourishment

from the Month of

Leo

Leo reminds us to shine with confidence and generosity, inspiring others through leadership, self-expression, creativity, and passion.

The Month of Leo

Natural Features of the Month of Leo

Leo is the fifth month of God's Seasonal Year, the fifth Month of the Yearly growth cycle, the second Month of the Summer season. It is a fixed Month between Cancer and Virgo, in the middle of the beginning and end of Summer.

Leo stabilizes the Summer Season. The Summer is at its hottest under the Month of Leo which begins on July 23rd each Year. Leo Season features consistent hot temperatures, full plant growth, abundant sunlight, long days, ripe fruits, vegetables, and an active insect life. More food is available from the gardens. It is a time for picnics, parties, and recreation. People can play and relax and enjoy the rewards from the creations of the Summer.

Leo season brings warmth, self-expression, and creativity, mirroring the height of Summer. Leo's energy is vibrant and confident, inspiring self-discovery and leadership. This is a time to shine, pursue passions, and embrace individuality, as Leo emboldens people to take center stage and radiate their inner strength.

This describes the natural energy pattern associated with the Month of Leo.

The Personality of the Month of Leo
What Can We Learn From the Leo Nature?

Leos are charismatic and confident, often taking center stage with their natural leadership qualities. They thrive on recognition and feedback, using it to hone their skills and improve themselves. In group situations, Leos tend to take charge, earning respect and admiration through their decisive actions.

Leo loves being seen and is comfortable on stage. Their natural charismatic energy and zest for life draw people in. Combining confidence, leadership, and appeal, Leos create a powerful presence that inspires and motivates others.

Leo's individuality and self-expression mesmerize people around them. They are idealistic and never compromise with their values and principles. They live their life on their own terms and unapologetically motivate others to do the same.

Leos have a childlike nature that likes the theater, taking vacations, being admired, expensive items, bright colors, and fun with friends. They dislike being ignored, facing difficult realities, and not being treated like royalty.

Leo is confident and radiates personal authority and is one of the most driven and stubborn of all the Months. They demonstrate dedication and integrity, valuing decisive action and consistently fulfilling commitments and obligations.

Leo – Keyword Qualities

Self-Aware Seeds to Plant		Unaware Weeds to Uproot
proud	fiery	domineering
determined	majestic	vain
strong-willed	honest	susceptible
leader	noble	bossy
loyal	charismatic	stubborn
solemn	responsible	intolerant
generous	principled	self-centered
ambitious	dramatic	violent
courageous	passionate	quick-tempered
heroic	warm-hearted	nonchalant
conquering	cheerful	arrogant
creative	humorous	lazy
confident	loving	inflexible
seductive	ambitious	pompous
happy		pretentious
daring		interfering

Leo Identifiers – Positive Qualities
Leo's positive energy that can be of benefit to all

- ☺ Represents entertainment, joy, magnetism, and self-confidence.
- ☺ Embody charisma, creativity, and self-expression.
- ☺ Loved by almost everyone, and they know how to please a crowd.
- ☺ Know their value.
- ☺ Bold leadership.
- ☺ Require a lot of attention and praise.
- ☺ Make their voices heard.
- ☺ See themselves through their creations.
- ☺ When they are happy, angry, or sad, everyone knows it.
- ☺ Inspire others to follow their dreams.
- ☺ Want to prosper and do well for themselves and their family.
- ☺ Great at organizing.
- ☺ Make strong, dynamic leaders.
- ☺ Believe they know better than all others.
- ☺ Inspiring, intuitive, charming, and playful.
- ☺ Protective of those they love.
- ☺ Proud of their children.

Leo Identifiers – Challenging Qualities
Leo's challenging traits to recognize and balance

- ☹ Leo's confident nature can turn into arrogance.
- ☹ Their pride and ego can go to the extreme.
- ☹ They love the spotlight and do not want to share it with anyone.
- ☹ Always knowing what is best.
- ☹ Think the world revolves around them.
- ☹ Not giving praise and compliments to others.
- ☹ Anger is often triggered by a sense of unfairness to them.

How to Refine Challenging Personality Traits

If you read this list of challenging personality traits and recognized yourself in some of them, don't worry—they are not etched in stone.

In fact, you've already taken the first and most difficult step - becoming aware of them.

Self-aware people reflect on their lives, recognize their emotions, consider their impact on others, and adapt based on feedback.

People who lack self-awareness are often blind to their own faults, struggle with personal and spiritual growth, and may find self-reflection challenging. They repeatedly make the same mistakes and then blame others for their outcome.

By acknowledging that you have unwanted traits, you can now start the process of refining or even eliminating them.

Leo - Modifying Challenging Traits

Those born under the Month of Leo were born with great passion and will learn to temper it through the objectivity of those with whom they are in a relationship.

Leos tend to give off an air of superiority. To balance this, they need to develop a spirit of humility and attentiveness to others. They need to motivate other people to take the spotlight and be able to acknowledge their accomplishments.

Cultivating humility will help Leo to grow and be able to admit to their faults, acknowledge their mistakes, and apologize to others when appropriate. Having the strength to show their weak side can attract even more admiration over time.

Leo's anger can flare up over perceived unfairness. Learning to choose their battles wisely and to accept the small injustices of life will help focus their energy into fixing the wrongs that really matter.

Assessing how they appear at work, in relationships, in friendship, and in their family life can determine if they are merely playing a role in any of these areas. Increasing confidence in their abilities will lead to more authentic self-expression and creativity. Polishing up their sense of self from within will reduce the weight they give to what others think.

Refining the Leader - Tips to Refine the Leo Nature

Cultivating these life skills over time will bring the Leo Nature into alignment with the positive traits of their role and provide more inner peace and fulfillment.

- Realize that not all attention is good attention.
- Not to see themselves short or perform for the applause of others.
- Learn to take off any false mask worn for acceptance and love.
- Learn to acknowledge their authentic self.
- Shine without needing approval from anyone else.
- Remember that their worth is inside of them – they do not have to earn it.
- Celebrate other people's light as much as their own.
- Ask themselves what things in life are really worth getting angry about.
- Foster humility to minimize arrogance.
- Volunteer or give help regularly to develop a genuine concern for others.

Activities, Actions, Attitudes to Contemplate During the Month of Leo

Try out new Leo-type experiences, as led, to round out your personality!

- Contemplate the life question, "What is my creative expression?"
- Identify the Month of Leo traits you notice in your life.
- Find opportunities to apply the lessons of Leo – leadership, self-expression, responsibility, creativity - to your life.
- Spend time with children.
- Take a risk and go on an adventure.
- Step into the spotlight and act. Perform.
- Look for fun activities and play like a child.
- Try to create something new in your life.
- Look for ways to express yourself.
- Take creative classes.
- Write your motivation for life. What do you want?
- Call your father, your boss, or any other authoritative person you love.
- Be playful and happy. Leos like to have fun.
- Spend time entertaining and socializing.
- Have fun with friends and family.

Reflections on this Month's Leo Traits
Growing in Understanding Leo

Are there Leo traits that you can identify in your life?

If so, which are positive and which ones need to be refined?

Do you recognize these traits in someone that was born under the Month of Leo?

Does recognizing these traits in them help you to better understand them?

Are there any experiences you need or want to heal regarding these traits?

What Leo traits can help you to manage by stabilizing and strengthening groups?

Which of this Month's 'Activities, Actions, Attitudes' growth opportunities are you looking forward to trying?

 **Reflections for the Leo Personality**

? What creative and artistic talents do you have?

? Do you make time to do things that make you happy?

? Do you hold back because you fear judgment or imperfection?

? Do you find it hard to bond emotionally with others?

? How do you share your joy and love with all who surround you?

Ask to be Filled

Ask the Spirit to fill your life with the fresh Fruit of this Month of Leo for nourishment and healing. (Revelation 22:1-2).

Pray, to receive the nourishment you need that the Month of Leo provides; to receive revelation and insight into your life and the life of others; to receive the Heavenly blessings of the Month.

> *"Holy Spirit, You know the plan for my life, you know my heart and what is needed for the New Year. Fill me with the energies, the gifts and abilities of Leo that I need, to use for the best and highest good..."*

August 23 – September 22

Virgo encourages introspection and self-improvement, helping to find order in the chaos of life. It represents practicality, attention to detail, and service to others.

The Month of Virgo

Natural Features of the Month of Virgo

Virgo is the sixth Month of God's Seasonal Year, the sixth Month of the Yearly growth cycle, and the last month of the Summer Season.

Virgo transitions Summer to the Fall Season. It signals a time of preparation to make the changes necessary to move from Summer to Fall.

Under the Month of Virgo, the days start to get a little cooler. Even though it is still Summer, there is the realization that it will soon end. It is a time to begin the work of harvesting, storing and preparing food for the long cold Winter days and nights, as well as preparing the gardens and fields for their Winter rest. It is time to analyze and determine what has been completed and what still needs to be done to prepare for the next Season.

Virgo arrives with its practical, detail-oriented energy and brings Summer to an end. Virgo's season is about organization and self-improvement and is associated with health, work, and service. It's a time for analyzing plans, removing clutter, and focusing on health and wellness.

This describes the natural energy pattern associated with the Month of Virgo.

The Personality of the Month of Virgo
What Can We Learn From the Virgo Nature?

Virgos are logical and detail-oriented, known for their methodical approach to life. They thrive on structure and order, often creating detailed plans for self-improvement and personal growth. Virgos are health oriented and love order and cleanliness.

Virgo is a studious researcher with a thoughtful and contemplative nature, comprehensive and thorough in all aspects of life. Their logical tendencies drive them to continually refine their skills and habits, seeking to achieve the best possible outcomes in all they do.

Virgos are perfectionists. They want their work to reflect their professional attitudes. They are hard service-oriented workers. They take care of the small details and break down complex issues into manageable pieces that lead to greater efficiency and success.

Virgo is patient, kind, and willing to do whatever it takes to achieve their goals. They have many hobbies and look forward to retirement when they will be able to spend more time working on them.

Virgos like animals, healthy food, books, nature, order, and cleanliness. They dislike rudeness, asking for help, or taking center stage.

Their analytical nature and attention to detail make them excellent problem-solvers. This practical mindset helps Virgos navigate life's challenges with precision and clarity.

Virgo – Keyword Qualities

| Self-Aware
Seeds to Plant | | Unaware
Weeds to Uproot |
|---|---|---|
| service oriented | serious | narrow-minded |
| critical thinker | competent | calculating |
| intelligent | sensible | irritating |
| fact checker | modest | petty |
| problem solver | tidy | anxious |
| trustworthy | well-organized | cold |
| analytical | clean | repressed |
| health conscious | hard-working | caustic |
| healing abilities | provident | critical of themselves |
| selective | honest | critical of others |
| fastidious | faithful | correcting |
| efficient | reserved | controlling |
| responsible | helpful | too shy |
| detail oriented | perfectionist | introverted |
| logical | practical | |
| analytical | gentle | |
| modest | loyal | |
| humble | discerning | |

Virgo Identifiers – Positive Qualities
Virgo's positive energy that can be of benefit to all

- ☺ Virgos are kind, meticulous, fastidious, and detailed oriented.
- ☺ Analytical and discriminating.
- ☺ Good at organizing and perfecting techniques.
- ☺ Analytical fact-finders with meticulous attention to detail.
- ☺ Love to read, learn, and do detailed work.
- ☺ Need to examine every situation in detail.
- ☺ May come across as petty or fussy.
- ☺ Factual in communications.
- ☺ Hyper-aware of every detail.
- ☺ Attentive to detail and numbers.

Virgo Identifiers – Challenging Qualities
Virgo's challenging traits to recognize and balance

- ☹ Virgo's worst trait is being a chronic fault finder, finding fault in themselves and others.
- ☹ They do not like confrontation or being direct. This can lead to bottled up frustrations and emotions.
- ☹ They can be extreme perfectionists. Being too critical can keep them from 'seeing the forest for the trees.'
- ☹ Virgos can be excessively shy, overly worried, overly critical of themselves and others.
- ☹ They feel like they must always be helping with something. All work and no play.

How to Refine Challenging Personality Traits

If you read this list of challenging personality traits and recognized yourself in some of them, don't worry—they are not etched in stone.

In fact, you've already taken the first and most difficult step - becoming aware of them.

Self-aware people reflect on their lives, recognize their emotions, consider their impact on others, and adapt based on feedback.

People who lack self-awareness are often blind to their own faults, struggle with personal and spiritual growth, and may find self-reflection challenging. They repeatedly make the same mistakes and then blame others for their outcome.

By acknowledging that you have unwanted traits, you can now start the process of refining or even eliminating them.

Virgo - Modifying Challenging Traits

Those with strong Virgo traits have an overriding material practicality and they will learn spiritual sensitivity from those with which they are in relationship.

The Virgo tendency to be a perfectionist can cause them to experience worry and tension. To lessen the weight of this responsibility they can work on self-compassion, and acknowledge that attaining perfection is not always possible. They should put more emphasis on making progress rather than achieving perfection.

Virgos are encouraged to let go of unrealistic expectations, understanding that flaws are part of the human experience. By practicing self-acceptance and offering support without judgment, Virgos can foster healing within themselves and their communities.

Appreciate both the big picture and the details; learn to relax and worry less; have a more balanced outlook; see both the trees and the forest and enjoy life more.

Mellowing the Perfectionist – Tips to Refine the Virgo Nature

Cultivating these life skills over time will bring the Virgo Nature into alignment with the positive traits of their role and provide more inner peace and fulfillment.

- Monitor messages of guilt or imperfection.
- See imperfections as part of life.
- Offer their service without over doing it.
- Balance doing with being.
- Remind themselves that they are a human being and they are enough.
- Tune in to the detailed messages coming from their own body.
- Learn more healthier ways to care for themselves.
- Combine their physical perceptions with mental acuity.
- Analyze the way they express themselves.
- Trust that imperfect progress is still progress when done with a loving heart.
- Take a step back when feeling overwhelmed.
- Breathe, pray, and recenter in God's grace.
- Realize that perfection is impossible, but growth, learning and loving others are what life is about.
- Practice relaxation techniques to alleviate unnecessary stresses provoked by perfectionism.

Activities, Actions, Attitudes to Contemplate During the Month of Virgo

Try out new Virgo-type experiences, as led, to round out your personality!

- Contemplate the life question: "What are my daily routines?"
- Identify the Month of Virgo traits you notice in your life.
- Find opportunities to apply the lessons of Virgo – practicality, attention to detail, service to others - to your life.
- Focus on improving your diet and health.
- Detoxify from any substances, chemicals, or even people that you feel are depleting or abusing you.
- Purify yourself by omitting alcohol, fried foods, coffee, sweets, white foods such as bread, sugar, milk.
- Re-organize your life to get rid of any blockages that hold you back.
- Look for ways you can be of service to those close to you, your community, and the world as a whole.
- Practice setting healthy boundaries and saying 'no.'
- Do some behind the scenes service.
- Spend a day at the spa getting a massage and haircut.
- Make some quiet time to journal your thoughts and feelings.
- Spend time in nature, take a walk, or go hiking.

Reflections on this Month's Virgo Traits
Growing in Understanding Virgo

Are there Virgo traits that you can identify in your life?

If so, which are positive and which ones need to be refined?

Do you recognize these traits in someone that was born under the Month of Virgo?

Does recognizing these traits in them help you to better understand them?

Are there any experiences you need or want to heal regarding these traits?

What Virgo traits can help you to attain and maintain a healthy body?

Which of this Month's 'Activities, Actions, Attitudes' growth opportunities are you looking forward to trying?

 **Reflections for the Virgo Personality**

- ? What helps you control obsessive thoughts?

- ? Do you need to find ways to focus on and stick to your routine?

- ? Do you give yourself the same care that you give to others?

- ? How can you perfect your own internal growth, well-being, and happiness?

- ? How can you learn to make progress without doubting yourself, or asking if it is good enough?

- ? How can you release worry over things you cannot control?

- ? Do you seek the help you need?

Ask to be Filled

Ask the Spirit to fill your life with the fresh Fruit of this Month of Virgo for nourishment and healing. (Revelation 22:1-2).

Pray, to receive the nourishment you need that the Month of Virgo provides; to receive revelation and insight into your life and the life of others; to receive the Heavenly blessings of the Month.

> *"Holy Spirit, You know the plan for my life, you know my heart and what is needed for the New Year. Fill me with the energies, the gifts and abilities of Virgo that I need, to use for the best and highest good…"*

September 23 – October 22

Nourishment
from the Month of
Libra

Libra symbolizes balance, harmony,
and the quest for justice, reminding us of
the importance of relationships and fairness.

The Month of Libra

Natural Features of the Month of Libra

Libra is the seventh Month of God's Seasonal Year, the seventh Month of the Yearly growth cycle, and the first Month of the Fall season. In the Spiritual growth cycle it is the time for the Fall Feasts and ceremonial observations.

Libra Ushers in the Fall Season and begins on September 23rd at the Fall Equinox, when the day and night are again at equal lengths. The days begin to shorten, the weather changes from Summer heat to Winter chill. The temperature gets cooler and the leaves change colors. Life turns toward the indoors.

Changes for the new season are being made. It is a time to harvest the crops and store them for the winter when the land will produce no more food. It is a time to collect the seeds and make plans to sow them in the coming Spring.

Libra ushers in Autumn with a focus on balance, relationships, and harmony. It emphasizes the importance of fairness and partnership, as people work together to bring in the harvest. This time is viewed as one for evaluating relationships and aiming for balance in various areas of life. It is a time for unity (or for war). The Month of Libra brings a desire for collaboration and an interest in social justice.

This describes the natural energy pattern associated with the Month of Libra.

The Personality of the Month of Libra
What Can We Learn From the Libra Nature?

Libra loves companionship and enjoys being with one special person, a partner to share the dark time of the Year.

Libras are charming and relationship-focused, seeking balance and harmony in their interactions. They value partnerships and friendships, often striving to create equilibrium in their social and personal lives.

Libras are known for their fair-minded approach, aiming to establish justice and symmetry in all they do. They help others see both sides of the story.

In their quest for self-improvement, Libras often incorporate feedback from friends and family, using it to enhance their sense of balance and harmony. Their charm and focus on relationships make them natural peacemakers and diplomats.

Libras like companionship, commitment, harmony, sharing with others, and the outdoors. They dislike violence, injustice, loudmouths, and unconformity.

Libra is associated with harmony, balance, and relationships. The spiritual lesson for Libra revolves around seeking equilibrium in all areas of life.

Libra – Keyword Qualities

Self-Aware Seeds to Plant		Unaware Weeds to Uproot	
cooperative	charismatic	hesitant	insensitive
graceful	gifted mediator	weak	cutting words
charming	seeks balance	indecisive	competitive
diplomatic	polite	vacillating	partisan
easy going	refined	people pleasing	gullible
creative	loyal	carry a grudge	fear of making
idealistic	fair	fragile	bad choice
enjoy partnerships	learned	fearful	uncertain
sociable	considerate	indolent	
fashionable	sentimental	cool	
stylish	distinguished		

Libra Identifiers – Positive Qualities
Libra's positive energy that can be of benefit to all

- ☺ Natural peacemaker.
- ☺ Fair and equitable.
- ☺ Like balance and justice.
- ☺ Concerned with balance in all areas of life.
- ☺ Can see each side of the story.
- ☺ Are persuasive and will encourage others to see their point of view.
- ☺ Always good at teamwork.
- ☺ Shine when addressing imbalances of power.
- ☺ Friendly, compassionate, and gentle.
- ☺ Avoid conflict when possible.
- ☺ Will advocate for others if they sense injustice.
- ☺ Romantic, idealistic, and imaginative.
- ☺ Represents partnerships, justice, and social interaction.
- ☺ Analytically and intellectually inclined.
- ☺ Natural ability to talk with anyone about nearly anything.

Libra Identifiers – Challenging Qualities
Libra's challenging traits to recognize and balance

- ☹ Libra wants everyone to be happy. Their desire for harmony and balance can lead to indecision.
- ☹ Libras can easily ignore their personal problems.
- ☹ They can be vacillating, people pleasers, that avoid confrontations, carry a grudge, and have self-pity.
- ☹ They can be gullible, uncertain, and worry too much about what others think.
- ☹ Libra's can be paralyzingly indecisive for fear of making a bad choice.
- ☹ They may rush into commitments too quickly because of their strong need for relationships.
- ☹ They can follow the crowd against their own judgment.
- ☹ Libras have a hard time leaving well enough alone and can turn the simplest problems into a complicated mess.

How to Refine Challenging Personality Traits

If you read this list of challenging personality traits and recognized yourself in some of them, don't worry—they are not etched in stone.

In fact, you've already taken the first and most difficult step - becoming aware of them.

Self-aware people reflect on their lives, recognize their emotions, consider their impact on others, and adapt based on feedback.

People who lack self-awareness are often blind to their own faults, struggle with personal and spiritual growth, and may find self-reflection challenging. They repeatedly make the same mistakes and then blame others for their outcome.

By acknowledging that you have unwanted traits, you can now start the process of refining or even eliminating them.

Libra - Modifying Challenging Traits

Those born under the Month of Libra were born with a tendency to put their own thoughts aside to make peace with others. They will learn to define who they are through their close partnerships.

Because partnerships are important to Libra, they are often challenged to maintain their individuality while navigating the dynamics of their relationships. Libras can create harmonious relationships that enrich both their lives and the lives of others by nurturing fairness and open communication.

It is not always easy for Libras to decide what action to take. Trusting their gut instincts to know what is best for them and basing their decisions on what is important to them are two key steps in overcoming this challenge.

Libras may benefit from continuing purposeful development of their communication skills in areas that involve navigating meaningful connections such as negotiation, presentation, counseling, public speaking, group discussions, and moderation.

Libra develops through experiencing harmony, equality, and cooperation - their main life themes.

Balancing the Balancer – Tips to Refine the Libra Nature

Cultivating these life skills over time will bring the Libra Nature into alignment with the positive traits of their role and provide more inner peace and fulfillment.

- Develop assertiveness skills.
- Speak their needs without guilt and describe preferences clearly.
- Not hold themselves back and honor what they need.
- Realize they are not responsible for everyone else.
- Balance giving and receiving.
- Allow for differences without having to cut off the relationship.
- Grow their own inner sense of self-worth and not through external validation.
- Develop poise and grace within themselves.
- Pursue healthy connections.
- Pay more attention to their own needs in relationships, instead of always trying to make others comfortable at all costs.
- Resist people-pleasing and avoiding conflict.
- Practice self-assertiveness by frequently voicing their opinions and asserting boundaries.

Activities, Actions, Attitudes to Contemplate During the Month of Libra

Try out new Libra-type experiences, as led, to round out your personality!

- Contemplate the Life Question: "How do I relate?"
- Identify the Month of Libra traits you notice in your life.
- Find opportunities to apply the lessons of Libra – balance, harmony, justice, relationships - to your life.
- Notice the art and fashion around you.
- Go to an art or fashion show.
- Find beauty and surround yourself with it.
- Discover your creative side through painting, drawing, or crafts.
- Spend time with your partner.
- Take time to think about your relationships.
- Acknowledge oppositions in your life that require balance or harmony.
- Recognize if there is an area in which you are afraid to make a decision.
- Wear your nicer clothes when you go out.
- Practice compromising.
- Be a diplomat, avoid conflicts.
- Make time to spend alone to recharge.
- Look for something new to read or study.

Reflections on this Month's Libra Traits
Growing in Understanding Libra

Are there Libra traits that you can identify in your life?

If so, which are positive and which ones need to be refined?

Do you recognize these traits in someone that was born under the Month of Libra?

Does recognizing these traits in them help you to better understand them?

Are there any experiences you need or want to heal regarding these traits?

What Libra traits can help you to weigh and balance information and make fair comparisons?

Which of this Month's 'Activities, Actions, Attitudes' growth opportunities are you looking forward to trying?

Reflections for the Libra Personality

- ? How do you handle conflict?

- ? How can you consider what brings you balance instead of just smoothing out a situation?

- ? In what ways do you care more about making everyone else happy rather than considering what feels right for you?

- ? What type of relationship partner are you attracted to?

- ? In what ways do you generate peace and tranquility within your relationships?

- ? How do you get along with yourself and your internal thoughts?

Ask to be Filled

Ask the Spirit to fill your life with the fresh Fruit of this Month of Libra for nourishment and healing. (Revelation 22:1-2).

Pray, to receive the nourishment you need that the Month of Libra provides; to receive revelation and insight into your life and the life of others; to receive the Heavenly blessings of the Month.

"Holy Spirit, You know the plan for my life, you know my heart and what is needed for the New Year. Fill me with the energies, the gifts and abilities of Libra that I need, to use for the best and highest good..."

October 23 – November 21

Scorpio delves into the depths of
transformation and resilience, urging others
to embrace change and confront their shadows, too.

The Month of Scorpio

Natural Features of the Month of Scorpio

Scorpio is the eighth month of God's Seasonal Year, the eighth Month of the Yearly growth cycle, and the second Month of the Fall season.

Scorpio Stabilizes the Fall Season. It is the Month fixed in its position between the first and last Month of fall.

Over the next few weeks, plants appear to die as leaves fall and trees become bare. The Month of Scorpio emphasizes life and death, with the Year's plant life ending while at the same time focusing on new life by producing seeds for the next Year.

This is a critical and intense period for nature as the approaching Winter poses significant challenges. The window for Winter preparation for food and shelter is rapidly closing, yet Scorpio approaches this time without fear.

It is a secretive period, as others may attempt to steal the food supplies. Thus, Scorpio thrives in hiding and finding hidden things.

Scorpio season is marked by intensity and transformation. Its energy is associated with themes of death and rebirth, power, and mystery. This season frequently prompts individual transformation, reveals underlying truths, and supports the development of emotional resilience. It encourages the release of outdated patterns to facilitate progress and growth.

This describes the natural energy pattern associated with the Month of Scorpio.

The Personality of the Month of Scorpio
What Can We Learn From the Scorpio Nature?

Scorpios are known for the traits of transformation, intensity, and deep emotional insights. Scorpio is determined and penetrating, often displaying a mysterious quality that intrigues those around them. They are known for their obsessive nature and love for the chase, particularly in relationships.

Scorpio is focused on all of life's hidden aspects. Driven by a desire for personal transformation, Scorpios confront uncomfortable truths and emerge stronger from the challenges.

Their intense focus and determination make them powerful individuals capable of significant personal growth and profound impact on others. They possess strong spiritual abilities, fueling their deep emotional energy and introspective tendencies.

Scorpio is possessive. They control others' moods or are controlled by others' moods. They like to be right and having long-term friends. They dislike revealing their secrets, dishonesty, and passive people. They are fixed on the world of inner feeling.

Scorpio – Keyword Qualities

Self-Aware		Unaware	
Seeds to Plant		Weeds to Uproot	
secretive	intense	jealous	complex
investigative	competitive	suspicious	narrow-minded
powerful	driven	aggressive	calculating
resistant	focused	destructive	irritating
intuitive	deep	stubborn	petty
charismatic	intelligent	anxious	cold
magnetic	a survivor	tyrannical	repressed
strong-willed	clever	perverse	caustic
insightful	self-controlled	sadistic	domineering
passionate	penetrating	violent	possessive
creative	potent	self-centered	cunning
independent	resourceful	untamable	
vigorous	forceful		
loyal	brave		
hard-working	observant		
persevering	ambitious		
proud			

Scorpio Identifiers – Positive Qualities
Scorpio's positive energy that can be of benefit to all

- ☺ An intense curiosity.
- ☺ Love to dig into the heart of a matter.
- ☺ Drawn into the mysteries of life.
- ☺ Concerned with anything that might exist below the surface.
- ☺ Penetrates defenses.
- ☺ Reaches the core truth.
- ☺ Seeks total union.
- ☺ A long-term true friend.
- ☺ Attracted to wealth and power.
- ☺ One of the most misunderstood of the Months.
- ☺ A keen sense of purpose.
- ☺ Will work hard to achieve their goals.
- ☺ Detachment is important.
- ☺ Struggle with trust.

Scorpio Identifiers – Challenging Qualities
Scorpio's challenging traits to recognize and balance

- ☹ Can carry a grudge, be traumatic, unforgiving, and intimidating.
- ☹ Overly suspicious and revengeful to those who have betrayed them.
- ☹ Seek physical, mental, or emotional power over others through secretive methods.
- ☹ Extremely secretive, believing it is a form of control over others.
- ☹ Can be distrusting, jealous, angry, obsessive, compulsive, and possessive.

How to Refine Challenging Personality Traits

If you read this list of challenging personality traits and recognized yourself in some of If you read this list of challenging personality traits and recognized yourself in some of them, don't worry—they are not etched in stone.

In fact, you've already taken the first and most difficult step - becoming aware of them.

Self-aware people reflect on their lives, recognize their emotions, consider their impact on others, and adapt based on feedback.

People who lack self-awareness are often blind to their own faults, struggle with personal and spiritual growth, and may find self-reflection challenging. They repeatedly make the same mistakes and then blame others for their outcome.

By acknowledging that you have unwanted traits, you can now start the process of refining or even eliminating them.

Scorpio - Modifying Challenging Traits

Those born under the Month of Scorpio were born with a need to control others, but they will learn inner control and self-respect through their committed partnerships.

Jealousy and possessiveness are two of the most common traits associated with Scorpios. As they work on developing trust in themselves as well as their relationships they will be able to overcome these unfavorable features.

A main theme in Scorpio's life will be developing the ability to let go and release – personally, professionally, financially, spiritually, emotionally, and physically.

To overcome their intense attachments and challenges in letting go, Scorpio must develop trust, practice forgiveness, and focus their intensity into productive and positive endeavors. These can unlock their transformative power.

They must become aware of situations they hold on to or obsess over. Scorpios learn to let go through big professional changes, significant relationship shifts, financial upheavals or abundance, and ongoing turnover in life.

As they alchemize and transform, they will be called upon to open up to new energies and spaces by letting go of what is in the past. By harnessing this transformative power, they can come out stronger from challenges while helping others navigate their own journeys.

Releasing Control – Tips to Refine the Scorpio Nature

Cultivating these life skills over time will bring the Scorpio Nature into alignment with the positive traits of their role and provide more inner peace and fulfillment.

- Build healthy relationships based on mutual respect.
- Practice self-reflection.
- Find healthy outlets for emotions.
- Confront fears.
- Dive into emotions.
- Seek the truth beneath the surface.
- Surrender what cannot be controlled.
- Trust that vulnerability can be strength.
- Allow cycles of death and rebirth in life without fear.
- Focus intensity into creative outlets.
- Learn to forgive and not harbor grudges.
- Practice forgiveness to lead a less stressful and more empowering life.

Activities, Actions, Attitudes to Contemplate During the Month of Scorpio

Try out new Scorpio-type experiences, as led, to round out your personality!

- Contemplate the Life Question: "How do I overcome intense attachments?"
- Identify the Month of Scorpio traits you notice in your life.
- Find opportunities to apply the lessons of Scorpio – transformation, investigating, secrecy, resilience – to your life.
- Declutter what you do not need – things, relationships, and attitudes.
- Open up to new opportunities.
- Work on creating intimacy with the people in your life.
- Try to open up and reveal secrets.
- Create intimacy; be sexual with your partner.
- Allow whatever blocks the new growth to die.
- Focus on what needs to change.
- Allow the ending of whatever you don't need in your life.
- Make time to withdraw from others to recharge.
- Spend time reflecting and relaxing by a body of water or a water feature.

Reflections on this Month's Scorpio Traits
Growing in Understanding Scorpio

Are there Scorpio traits that you can identify in your life?

If so, which are positive and which ones need to be refined?

Do you recognize these traits in someone that was born under the Month of Scorpio?

Does recognizing these traits in them help you to better understand them?

Are there any experiences you need or want to heal regarding these traits?

What Scorpio traits can help you to uncover the deep secrets and mysteries of life?

Which of this Month's 'Activities, Actions, Attitudes' growth opportunities are you looking forward to trying?

 **Reflections for the Scorpio Personality**

? Is there anyone you need to forgive?

? How do you work on trusting others?

? Is the pain you are holding on to helping you to grow?

? Is it time to transform pent up anger into something beneficial?

? How can you use your intense emotions as fuel to transform?

? Do you make time to be on your own to recharge?

Ask to be Filled

Ask the Spirit to fill your life with the fresh Fruit of this Month of Scorpio for nourishment and healing. (Revelation 22:1-2).

Pray, to receive the nourishment you need that the Month of Scorpio provides; to receive revelation and insight into your life and the life of others; to receive the Heavenly blessings of the Month.

> *"Holy Spirit, You know the plan for my life, you know my heart and what is needed for the New Year. Fill me with the energies, the gifts and abilities of Scorpio that I need, to use for the best and highest good…"*

November 22 – December 21

Nourishment from the Month of Sagittarius

Sagittarius represents the eternal quest for knowledge, truth, and exploration, encouraging open-mindedness and optimism.

The Month of Sagittarius

Natural Features of the Month of Sagittarius

Sagittarius is the ninth month of God's Seasonal Year, the ninth Month of the Yearly growth cycle, and the third Month of the Fall season.

Sagittarius transitions the Fall to the Winter. It is the changeover period covering the ending of the Fall season to the beginning of Winter. The days are shorter and the temperatures change to the cooler days and nights that produce colorful Autumn leaves and begin the snow-covered chill of Winter.

Extra preparations are made as hunters and nomads travel great distances to secure extra food and game to make it through the Winter. The methods used to gather food are different than the earlier harvest season. Unlike the farmers who work in groups and follow strict rules, the hunter goes out alone, under only their own management. Knowledge and secrecy are essential to succcooful hunting.

Sagittarius season is adventurous, expansive and philosophical. It encourages a broadening of horizons, both mentally and physically, embracing the changes, and reflecting on them. It is an ideal time for seeking new experiences and understanding different perspectives through travel, exploration, and higher learning.

This describes the natural energy pattern associated with the Month of Sagittarius.

The Personality of the Month of Sagittarius
What Can We Learn From the Sagittarius Nature?

Sagittarius individuals are known for their love of adventure, hope, daring attitude, and philosophical nature. They possess a spirit of exploration and curiosity, always seeking new experiences and ideas.

They are seekers who pursue truth through exploration, both externally in the world around them and internally within themselves. They view self-improvement as a journey and are excited about getting fresh ideas and learning diverse philosophies and perspectives to grow. Sagittarians often travel or engage in activities that expand their horizons. Their outgoing and optimistic personality makes them inspiring companions, always ready to share their knowledge and enthusiasm with others.

Sagittarius likes freedom, exploration, and being outdoors. They would like to travel around the world. They dislike clingy people, being constrained, off-the-wall theories, and details.

Sagittarius likes to be with people on their own intellectual level. They are interested in the world around them and they enjoy higher learning and spirituality. Sagittarius is an energy of plentiful bounty and hope for the future. Its benevolence knows no bounds.

Sagittarius symbolizes expansion, generosity, and Divine justice. It brings blessings, success and abundance. They are often the ones who travel beyond where their family or friends have been – literally or figuratively. These qualities empower and motivate Sagittarians to pursue their dreams and achieve their ambitions. It fuels their wanderlust, ignites their curiosity, and helps them overcome obstacles on their path to success.

Sagittarius – Keyword Qualities

Self-Aware Seeds to Plant		Unaware Weeds to Uproot
freedom loving	fiery	authoritarian
truth-seeker	energetic	egotistical
straight-forward	pleasant	inconstant
broadminded	benevolent	unfaithful
philosophical	tidy	brutal
idealistic	jovial	unreliable
explorer	optimistic	unconscious
generous	extraverted	tactless
honest	amusing	derogatory
passionate	sense of humor	angry
flexible	demonstrative	short-tempered
adventurous	charming	
easy-going	independent	
likable	bold	
charismatic	exuberant	

Sagittarius Identifiers – Positive Qualities
Sagittarius' positive energy that can be of benefit to all

- ☺ Seeks broad understanding.
- ☺ The perpetual student.
- ☺ Always searching for new subjects to explore.
- ☺ Optimistic and pursue life on a grand scale.
- ☺ Love learning about spirituality, culture, law, and philosophy.
- ☺ Search for purpose and meaning.
- ☺ Truth seeker.
- ☺ Eager to explore the world.
- ☺ Eager to right any wrongs.
- ☺ Spiritual adventurer.
- ☺ Generous and prosperous.
- ☺ Curious and loves to travel.
- ☺ Outgoing, optimistic, and upwardly mobile.
- ☺ Have a great sense of humor.
- ☺ Always ready to get the party started.
- ☺ Has a grand time in life.
- ☺ Optimistic and future-oriented.
- ☺ Always looking toward future possibilities.
- ☺ Looks for happy endings.
- ☺ Typically has trouble sleeping.
- ☺ Insatiable appetite for trying new things.

Sagittarius Identifiers – Challenging Qualities
Sagittarius' challenging traits to recognize and balance

- ☹ Sagittarius can be tactless and awkward in their speech and mannerisms.
- ☹ They can have blind optimism, often promising more than they can deliver.
- ☹ They do not always see projects through.
- ☹ Sagittarius is impatient and will say what they think no matter how undiplomatic it may be.
- ☹ They sometimes struggle with finding deeper meaning and spiritual grounding.
- ☹ When Sagittarius' energy is misused it can lead to overindulgence or misplaced trust.

How to Refine Challenging Personality Traits

If you read this list of challenging personality traits and recognized yourself in some of them, don't worry—they are not etched in stone.

In fact, you've already taken the first and most difficult step - becoming aware of them.

Self-aware people reflect on their lives, recognize their emotions, consider their impact on others, and adapt based on feedback.

People who lack self-awareness are often blind to their own faults, struggle with personal and spiritual growth, and may find self-reflection challenging. They repeatedly make the same mistakes and then blame others for their outcome.

By acknowledging that you have unwanted traits, you can now start the process of refining or even eliminating them.

Sagittarius - Modifying Challenging Traits

Those born during the Month of Sagittarius were born with the ability to reach for higher truth and they will learn practical reality through their interaction with others.

Growing in their Sagittarian traits will help them to understand the significance of relationships so that they can get involved with larger groups and spread their ideas or learn from others.

Sagittarius is encouraged to remain open to new experiences while maintaining an awareness of their beliefs. By balancing wanderlust with reflection, Sagittarians can deepen their understanding of life's mysteries.

Sagittarians should be aware of the fact that they will always travel with themselves as they chase the next horizon. Their answers live inside of them. They need to set aside time for self-reflection to better understand their inner thoughts and feelings. While the external world offers its own attractions, personal insight can also be valuable.

Curbing the Wandererlust – Tips to Refine the Sagittarius Nature

Cultivating these life skills over time will bring the Sagittarius Nature into alignment with the positive traits of their role and provide more inner peace and fulfillment.

- Find equilibrium in life.
- Cultivate an attitude of conscious awareness and gratefulness for the here and now.
- Accept commitment if and only if it fits in with core ideals.
- Do not to get so caught up in intellectual pursuits that emotional and spiritual growth are neglected.
- Find a balance between the mind and heart.
- Find meaning in the everyday journey.
- Trust their path without needing all of the answers.
- To minimize recklessness, practice patience.
- Take up a hobby that needs attention to detail to develop concentration and endurance.

Activities, Actions, Attitudes to Contemplate During the Month of Sagittarius

Try out new Sagittarius-type experiences, as led, to round out your personality!

- Contemplate the Life Question: "What is my spiritual path?"
- Identify the Month of Sagittarius traits you notice in your life.
- Find opportunities to apply the lessons of Sagittarius – travel, exploring, adventure, truth seeking, studying - to your life.
- Spend time identifying what your truth is.
- Think about what the meaning of your life is.
- What is your doctrine, your belief system?
- Ask God to show you what you are to teach to the people around you.
- Cultivate an optimistic outlook on life.
- Explore your own hometown and look for other cultures and traditions that are there.
- Do not exaggerate.
- Speak optimistically.
- Watch a foreign movie or a documentary about a faraway land.
- Travel to a place you have always wanted to explore.
- Go to a seminar and learn something new.
- Find a new subject to study that inspires you.
- Take a class or read about different religions or spiritual traditions to increase understanding.
- Go into nature to hike and explore.

Reflections on this Month's Sagittarius Traits
Growing in Understanding Sagittarius

Are there Sagittarius traits that you can identify in your life?

If so, which are positive and which ones need to be refined?

Do you recognize these traits in someone that was born under the Month of Sagittarius?

Does recognizing these traits in them help you to better understand them?

Are there any experiences you need or want to heal regarding these traits?

What Sagittarius traits can help you to motivate others by inspiring them in the spiritual, legal, and religious arenas?

Which of this Month's 'Activities, Actions, Attitudes' growth opportunities are you looking forward to trying?

 **Reflections for the Sagittarius Personality**

- ? Do you make time for travel?

- ? Where do you want to go?

- ? How do you find ways to be spontaneous and adventurous?

- ? Are you chasing new experiences to run away from yourself?

- ? Are you building something meaningful inside yourself with your new discoveries?

- ? Do you trust God to provide you with all you need?

- ? Do you believe that everything happens for a reason?

- ? Do you make time to explore new philosophies ?

Ask to be Filled

Ask the Spirit to fill your life with the fresh Fruit of this Month of Sagittarius for nourishment and healing. (Revelation 22:1-2).

Pray, to receive the nourishment you need that the Month of Sagittarius provides; to receive revelation and insight into your life and the life of others; to receive the Heavenly blessings of the Month.

> *"Holy Spirit, You know the plan for my life, you know my heart and what is needed for the New Year. Fill me with the energies, the gifts and abilities of Sagittarius that I need, to use for the best and highest good..."*

December 22 – January 19

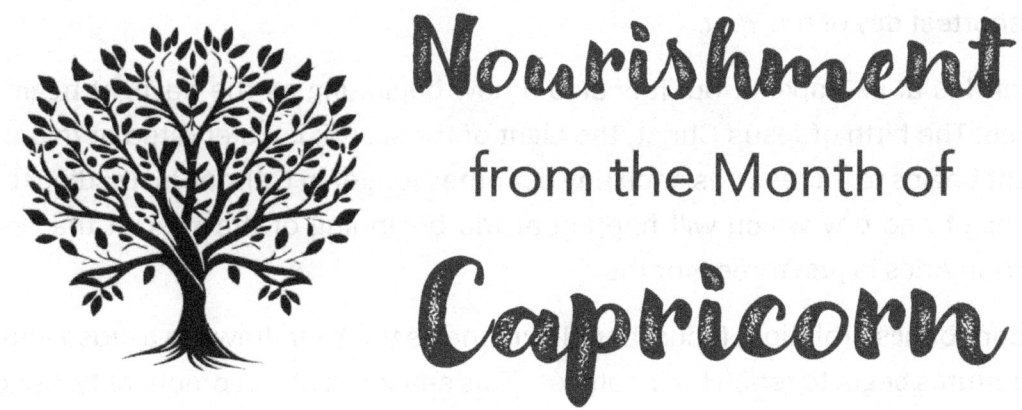

Capricorn is a beacon of discipline and ambition, showing us the value of hard work and perseverance.

The Month of Capricorn

Natural Features of the Month of Capricorn

Capricorn is the tenth month of God's Seasonal Year, the tenth Month of the Yearly growth cycle, and the first Month of Winter.

Capricorn Initiates the Winter Season. The first day of Capricorn occurs at the Winter Solstice on December 21st, in the northern hemisphere. It is the longest night/shortest day of the Year.

The world is at its darkest, but it is also a new beginning as the daylight begins to increase. The birth of Jesus Christ, the Light of the world, is celebrated at this time. The light begins to increase as each day becomes longer in Capricorn, leading to the equal night and day which will happen at the beginning of the Year at the Spring Equinox in Aries in just three Months.

Capricorn brings ambition, focus, and discipline as the Year draws to a close and the temperatures begin to reach their coldest. This season is about practicality, building structures, and achieving success through perseverance. This is a time to be frugal and wise in utilizing available resources. The strength of Capricorn comes from the hard effort needed to survive the darker colder days of this time of Year.

This describes the natural energy pattern associated with the Month of Capricorn.

The Personality of the Month of Capricorn
What Can We Learn From the Capricorn Nature?

Capricorns are grounded and responsible, set long-term goals and work diligently towards them. Capricorn energy is practical, responsible, and plans for the future.

Capricorns are ambitious and strive for success, even if it takes a while to figure out what that looks like for them. They are disciplined and consistently striving for high personal goals. Their goal-oriented mindset drives them to work tirelessly towards their aspirations, often exhibiting a strong sense of self-discipline and perseverance.

When they set their sights on anything, Capricorns often have a hard and fast approach. They apply their discipline rigorously, ensuring steady progress towards their objectives which include building a legacy through purposeful action. Their determination and hard work make them successful in their endeavors, inspiring others with their dedication and commitment.

Capricorns like status, quality craftsmanship, rank, and concrete results. They dislike just about everything at some point in their life.

Capricorn – Keyword Qualities

Self-Aware Seeds to Plant		Unaware Weeds to Uproot
achiever	cautious	calculating
reserved	persistent	curt
mature	provident	withdrawn
disciplined	steady	petty
conservative	stern	cruel
responsible	willful	unpleasant
determined	hard-working	cold
self-controlled	persevering	ruthless
grounded	honest	selfish
driven	realistic	dull
productive	loyal	rigid
ambitious	resolute	slow
wise	moralistic	introverted
serious	quiet	skeptical
long-suffering	reliable	fearful
focused	practical	materialistic
thoughtful	traditional	greedy
indomitable	goal-oriented	pessimistic

Capricorn Identifiers – Positive Qualities
Capricorn's positive energy that can be of benefit to all

- ☺ Practical and focused on goals.
- ☺ A master of responsibility, commitment, and determination.
- ☺ Driven, determined, and focused on success and achievements.
- ☺ Rarely stop to smell the flowers.
- ☺ Organize, plan, and execute tasks with precision.
- ☺ An old soul who creates a stable foundation for others.
- ☺ Focuses on rules and craves order and control.
- ☺ Looks to the past for security.
- ☺ Can come across as being rigid and self-controlled.
- ☺ Has a long to-do list.
- ☺ Prefers orderly environments.
- ☺ The CEOs of Humankind.
- ☺ Concerned with status.
- ☺ Takes life seriously.
- ☺ Interest in social and professional standing.

Capricorn Identifiers – Challenging Qualities
Capricorn's challenging traits to recognize and balance

- ☹ Capricorns can be too conservative, miserly, and gloomy.
- ☹ They can suffer from inhibition, lack of self-confidence, and pessimism.
- ☹ They can be cold, unforgiving, condescending, expect the worst, and avoid true connections with others.
- ☹ They can take too long to prepare before starting a project.

How to Refine Challenging Personality Traits

If you read this list of challenging personality traits and recognized yourself in some of them, don't worry—they are not etched in stone.

In fact, you've already taken the first and most difficult step - becoming aware of them.

Self-aware people reflect on their lives, recognize their emotions, consider their impact on others, and adapt based on feedback.

People who lack self-awareness are often blind to their own faults, struggle with personal and spiritual growth, and may find self-reflection challenging. They repeatedly make the same mistakes and then blame others for their outcome.

By acknowledging that you have unwanted traits, you can now start the process of refining or even eliminating them.

Capricorn - Modifying Challenging Traits

Those born under the Month of Capricorn were born with the drive to achieve, and they will learn about emotional nurturing through their committed partnerships.

Capricorns are encouraged to set long-term goals while remaining flexible in the face of obstacles. They should welcome providence and make room for creative exploration.

By aligning their ambitions with a sense of purpose that benefits not only themselves but also others, they can create a work-life balance that works for them.

Keep a loose grip when making plans and stay open and adaptable to shifting circumstances as unpredictability is inevitable.

Join friends and family in their challenges rather than standing apart as the person who always knows what to do. Even if Capricorns are reserved, close relationships can enrich their life and balance their work ethic.

Stay focused on where you want to go. Do not be discouraged by temporary setbacks or doubts from others.

Make small request of others on a regular basis to build your trust in them.

Grounding the Climber – Tips to Refine the Capricorn Nature

Cultivating these life skills over time will bring the Capricorn Nature into alignment with the positive traits of their role and provide more inner peace and fulfillment.

- Open their heart and form meaningful connections with others.
- Even with a busy schedule, make time for loved ones.
- Trust that they are something beyond success.
- Accept the support and care of others for encouragement during difficult seasons.
- Nurture softness along with strength.
- Lean into faith over fear to have more peace of mind along the journey.
- Do not cling tightly to control out of fear and self-reliance.
- Release outdated expectations of themselves and others.
- Schedule regular downtime.
- Make time for social activities to balance work-life.

Activities, Actions, Attitudes to Contemplate During the Month of Capricorn

Try out new Capricorn-type experiences, as led, to round out your personality!

- Contemplate the Life Question: "What is my social standing?"
- Identify the Month of Capricorn traits you notice in your life.
- Find opportunities to apply the lessons of Capricorn – discipline, ambition, hard work, legacy - to your life.
- Focus on your future.
- Focus on your career, your status in society.
- Make commitments to live up to your potential.
- Practice perseverance and discipline.
- Take note of any depressive issues that might develop so that you can begin to resolve them.
- Practice a discipline or commitment for the Month.
- Focus on a goal that you have wanted to complete and make a detailed plan of how you will accomplish it.
- Take your time. Do not rush.
- Practice doing things slowly – walking, eating, talking.
- Record all your expenses and income and see if you can reduce expenses.
- Get away from work and take time to relax.
- Plan a vacation.
- Do not take work home with you.
- Do not check your work email while you are at home.
- Take someone special out to a nice restaurant.

Reflections on this Month's Capricorn Traits
Growing in Understanding Capricorn

Are there Capricorn traits that you can identify in your life?

If so, which are positive and which ones need to be refined?

Do you recognize these traits in someone that was born under the Month of Capricorn?

Does recognizing these traits in them help you to better understand them?

Are there any experiences you need or want to heal regarding these traits?

What Capricorn traits can help you to build and manage business or governmental enterprises?

Which of this Month's 'Activities, Actions, Attitudes' growth opportunities are you looking forward to trying?

Reflections for the Capricorn Personality

? How do you achieve your goals and career ambitions?

? How do you balance work and family?

? Do you make time to spend on home and family activities?

? What is the ultimate bigger picture of what you are striving for?

? Where do you want to be in 10/20/50 Years?

? What do you truly want to build and why does it matter?

Ask to be Filled

Ask the Spirit to fill your life with the fresh Fruit of this Month of Capricorn for nourishment and healing. (Revelation 22:1-2).

Pray, to receive the nourishment you need that the Month of Capricorn provides; to receive revelation and insight into your life and the life of others; to receive the Heavenly blessings of the Month.

> *"Holy Spirit, You know the plan for my life, you know my heart and what is needed for the New Year. Fill me with the energies, the gifts and abilities of Capricorn that I need, to use for the best and highest good..."*

January 20 – February 18

Nourishment from the Month of Aquarius

Aquarius challenges conventions and advocates for progress and innovation. By combining individuality with philanthropy, they inspire others to work toward a better future.

The Month of Aquarius

Natural Features of the Month of Aquarius

Aquarius is the eleventh Month of God's Seasonal Year, the eleventh month of the Yearly growth cycle, and the second Month of the Winter season.

Aquarius stabilizes the Winter Season. It is a Month fixed in between the beginning and end of Winter. It is an implementer and builder of what the initiating Month of Capricorn began.

At this time in the Seasonal Year, we experience the coldest days of the Year. We may have to stay indoors most of the time and that leads to a time of thinking and reflecting on the New Year. There is time to invent new things and plan changes.

It is also a time of waiting as Spring is still far away, so it is a time of controlling the emotions. People become indifferent about most things as they await the Spring.

Aquarius season is all about invention, independence, and humanitarianism. This Month encourages us to think outside the box and embrace our individuality. It's a time to focus on everyone's well-being, community efforts, and progressive ideas.

This describes the natural energy pattern associated with the Month of Aquarius.

The Personality of the Month of Aquarius
What Can We Learn From the Aquarius Nature?

Aquarius energy is innovative, original, unique, and progressive. Aquarians display a spirit of independence, technological advancement, and are future oriented.

Aquarians are individualistic, contrary, futuristic, stubborn, and socially aware, yet somewhat traditional. Aquarius energy is known for its innovative spirit and humanitarian ideals. Those born under this Month are stirred to think outside traditional boundaries while championing causes that promote social justice and equality.

Their unique perspective and commitment to philanthropic causes make them inspiring leaders and visionaries, always looking for ways to make the world a better place.

Aquarians like to have fun with friends, helping others, fighting for worthwhile causes, and intellectual conversations. They dislike limitations, broken promises, being lonely, dull or boring situations, and people who disagree with them.

Aquarians are futuristic and compassionate, concerned with how to help their fellow man. They have a unique flair for connecting with people from all walks of life.

Aquarius energy is intuitive and often embraces unconventional methods for personal growth and improvement. Surprises and unexpected encounters are common occurrences.

Aquarius – Keyword Qualities

Self-Aware Seeds to Plant		Unaware Weeds to Uproot
rebellious*	friendly	distant
erratic*	self-confident	marginal
creative	quiet	stubborn
willful*	intuitive	resigned
contrary*	charitable	utopian
idealistic	elusive*	closed minded
altruistic	generous	maladjusted
detached*	tolerant	eccentric
independent	compassionate	cold
original	intelligent	
surprising	curios	
gifted	authentic	
contradictory*	humanistic	
innovative	likeable	

*Natural Aquarian traits that may seem negative, but are part of their makeup. Nevertheless they must be kept in balance.

Aquarius Identifiers – Positive Qualities
Aquarius' positive energy that can be of benefit to all

- ☺ Cannot stand any kind of constraint.
- ☺ Innovative and humanitarian.
- ☺ Driven by a desire to pursue progressive ideas and collective efforts.
- ☺ Focused on societal issues and systems.
- ☺ Aim to innovate and challenge the status quo.
- ☺ Happy to be unconventional.
- ☺ Quite independent.
- ☺ May sacrifice a permanent relationship for their independence.
- ☺ Comfortable with computers and other technical equipment.
- ☺ A good listener.
- ☺ Unconventional and can engage in activism.
- ☺ Energetic, strong mind.
- ☺ Enjoy stirring the pot.
- ☺ Does not like small talk.
- ☺ Does not like extended hugs.
- ☺ Seeks collective expression.

Aquarius Identifiers – Challenging Qualities
Aquarius' challenging traits to recognize and balance

- ☹ Aquarius energy can be detached, willful, and often agitated. They appear emotionally distant.
- ☹ Aquarius can be temperamental, contrary, unpredictable, uncompromising, egotistical, radical, unable to commit, and aloof.
- ☹ They fear the loss of their freedom.
- ☹ Aquarians may be unwilling to accept another's opinions.
- ☹ They can view others' opinions as a personal affront and an infringement of their sovereign rights.
- ☹ Cares more for the humanity as a whole than the individual.

How to Refine Challenging Personality Traits

If you read this list of challenging personality traits and recognized yourself in some of them, don't worry—they are not etched in stone.

In fact, you've already taken the first and most difficult step - becoming aware of them.

Self-aware people reflect on their lives, recognize their emotions, consider their impact on others, and adapt based on feedback.

People who lack self-awareness are often blind to their own faults, struggle with personal and spiritual growth, and may find self-reflection challenging. They repeatedly make the same mistakes and then blame others for their outcome.

By acknowledging that you have unwanted traits, you can now start the process of refining or even eliminating them.

Aquarius - Modifying Challenging Traits

Those born under the Month of Aquarius were born with a philanthropic, public oriented focus. They will learn about their own individuality through their interactions with others.

Aquarius enjoys what it means to be a part of something bigger than themselves without losing themself along the way. They can be a part and remain very strong in themselves without pushing others away or deciding they need to do everything their own way.

Aquarius must realize that stubbornness and being too rigid can create disorder. Instead, cooperation and community may lead to support from others in the long run. Discovering how to live their life in their unique way while staying within the limitations of the world at large will be one of their life quests and an important part of their personal development.

Aquarius may feel that everything needs to be handled intellectually, even when an emotional response may be more suitable. Developing the skills of empathy and attentive listening can help improve relationships. Whenever possible, they can look for ways to connect with others in a more emotional way.

While time alone refreshes their spirit, they must remember that they still need human ties and a sense of community no matter how hard it is. They cannot walk this path alone. It is important to make the effort to build connections, work together with others and share their gifts. The personal connections where they can come and go as they please will be the most comfortable for them. They will be able to trust that there is an accepting place for their unique self-expression.

Steadying the Rebel – Tips to Refine the Aquarius Nature

Cultivating these life skills over time will bring the Aquarius Nature into alignment with the positive traits of their role and provide more inner peace and fulfillment.

- Be mindful of their rebellious nature.
- Search for a group with whom to connect.
- Embrace connections with others without losing their individuality.
- Honor both their head and their heart.
- Follow their passion and interests to find their relationships.
- Try not to focus only on futuristic, big picture principles so as not to miss the simple joys that are right around them.
- Come to terms with the fact that they are often ahead of the crowds and may feel as if they do not belong anywhere.
- Embrace what makes them different and special in the world.
- Realize that they cannot stand out if they fit in to give them comfort and reassurance when they do not fit in somewhere.
- Practice grounding techniques to get out of their head
- Do hands-on activities such as gardening or cooking to help connect more with the physical world

Activities, Actions, Attitudes to Contemplate During the Month of Aquarius

Try out new Aquarius-type experiences, as led, to round out your personality!

- Contemplate the Life Question: "How do I connect with like-minded people?"
- Identify the Month of Aquarius traits you notice in your life.
- Find opportunities to apply the lessons of Aquarius – unconventional, trend setting, independent, humanitarian - to your life.
- Spend time with your friends to nurture and develop friendships.
- Consider getting involved in humanitarian or spiritual groups.
- Help out a nonprofit organization.
- Update or refresh your website.
- Buy a new device.
- Do something outside of the lines.
- Let yourself be a little wild and unconventional.
- Volunteer to host a group meeting at your house.
- Share creative ideas with your groups or friends.
- On a clear night, lie down on your back and try to identify the constellations.
- Remind yourself of your hopes, wishes, and dreams.
- Challenge your mind with games or puzzles.
- Read self-help books.

Reflections on this Month's Aquarius Traits
Growing in Understanding Aquarius

Are there Aquarius traits that you can identify in your life?

If so, which are positive and which ones need to be refined?

Do you recognize these traits in someone that was born under the Month of Aquarius?

Does recognizing these traits in them help you to better understand them?

Are there any experiences you need or want to heal regarding these traits?

What Aries traits can help you to understand universal principles to help the well-being of humanity?

Which of this Month's 'Activities, Actions, Attitudes' growth opportunities are you looking forward to trying?

Reflections for the Aquarius Personality

- ? How do you express your unconventional and original ideas?

- ? How do you handle your need for freedom and independence?

- ? In what ways do your own unique thoughts and personality show up?

- ? How do you find assurance when you are part of a group and feel like you do not fit in?

- ? How are you a lighthouse of awareness and hope to the rest of humanity?

- ? Do you have a strong support system of people who want the best for you?

Ask to be Filled

Ask the Spirit to fill your life with the fresh Fruit of this Month of Aquarius for nourishment and healing. (Revelation 22:1-2).

Pray, to receive the nourishment you need that the Month of Aquarius provides; to receive revelation and insight into your life and the life of others; to receive the Heavenly blessings of the Month.

> *"Holy Spirit, You know the plan for my life, you know my heart and what is needed for the New Year. Fill me with the energies, the gifts and abilities of Aquarius that I need, to use for the best and highest good..."*

February 19 – March 20

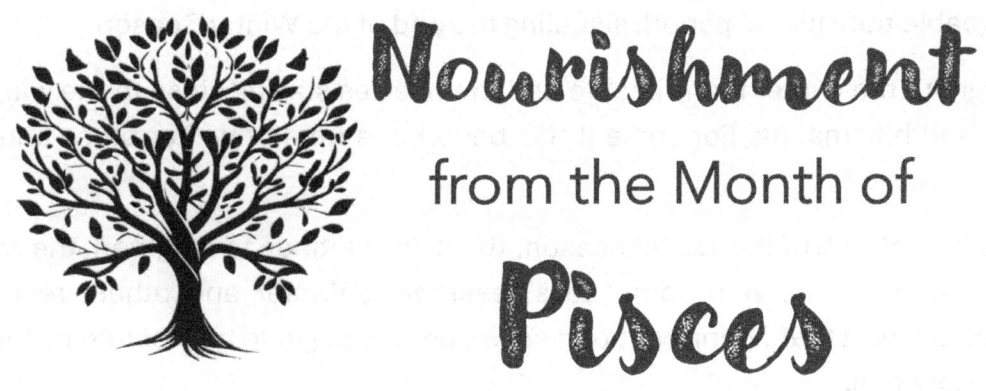

Nourishment from the Month of Pisces

Pisces highlights the power of compassion, imagination, intuition, creativity, and spiritual connection.

The Month of Pisces

Natural Features of the Month of Pisces

Pisces is the twelfth and last month of God's Seasonal Year, and the last Month of winter. Pisces ends the old Year in preparation for the new that begins with Aries.

Pisces transitions Winter to the Spring Season. The Month of Pisces is a changeable transitional period, signaling the end of the Winter Season.

Throughout the Winter many people find themselves staying close to the warmth of home and hibernating. For some it has become a time of winter blues and cabin fever.

In this final Month of the Winter season, the days continue to lengthen, the weather begins to fluctuate, with some days resembling Winter and others resembling Spring. Knowing that Spring will soon arrive, people begin to be inspired by thoughts of the New Year.

The Spiritual and Seasonal Year ends with Pisces, known for its empathy, intuition, and creativity. Pisces is dreamy and introspective time, encouraging spiritual growth and emotional healing. It is a time for reflection, letting go of the past, and embracing compassion. Pisces energy often connects people to their inner world, making it an ideal period for creative pursuits and meditation.

This describes the natural energy pattern associated with the Month of Pisces.

The Personality of the Month of Pisces
What Can We Learn From the Pisces Nature?

Pisces is characterized by empathy, sensitivity, and creativity. They possesses an imaginative soul. Their compassionate nature and intuitive abilities make them highly understanding and supportive on a deep emotional level of those around them. This blend of creativity and empathy allows them to connect with others in meaningful and transformative ways. Pisces has an enormous heart. They may feel connected to the whole world at times, and yet they are learning how to know themselves as a unique individual.

The Month of Pisces itself is associated with secrets, confinement, institutions, and creativity. For this reason, it is natural for Pisces to experience secret sorrows. They can empathize with individuals who may be mentally, emotionally, or physically challenged in some way.

Pisces likes being alone, sleeping, music, romance, fantasy, and spiritual themes. They dislike being criticized, cruelty of any kind, and being stuck in the past.

By finding balance between giving love freely while protecting their well-being, Pisceans learn how to nurture themselves as they nurture others.

Pisces – Keyword Qualities

Self-Aware Seeds to Plant		Unaware Weeds to Uproot	
flexible	faith-filled	indecisive	unstable emotions
spiritual	feeds the hungry	moody	a lack of reality
emotional	deeply intuitive	confused	overindulgence
empathetic	empathic	wavering	misplaced trust
gentle	sacrificial	lazy	hermit – isolating
hold space for others	understanding	scatterbrained	secretive
	wise	vulnerable	introverted
rescues the lost	devoted	unpredictable	ambiguous
forgets the self	creative	gullible	
dreamers	whimsical		
storytellers			

Pisces Identifiers – Positive Qualities
Pisces' positive energy that can be of benefit to all

- ☺ Works selflessly in the background.
- ☺ Highly creative and intuitive.
- ☺ Needs privacy and time alone to regenerate.
- ☺ Among the most caring and nurturing.
- ☺ Known for being introspective, emotional, and imaginative.
- ☺ A candidate for world savior.
- ☺ Loving, empathetic, a sense of understanding .

Pisces Identifiers - Challenging Qualities
Pisces' challenging traits to recognize and balance

- ☹ Can be idealistic, vague, weak-willed, aimless, lost, disillusioned, escapist, and elusive.
- ☹ Can become a victim or martyr or lose their identity as they naturally blend with others.
- ☹ Carries the burdens of those around them.
- ☹ Avoids facing harsh realities by withdrawing into their imaginations.
- ☹ They are challenged by their desire to escape.
- ☹ Being so sensitive, even small things often overwhelm them.
- ☺ Dreamers who can spend plenty of time in their heads, living in their fantasies.

How to Refine Challenging Personality Traits

If you read this list of challenging personality traits and recognized yourself in some of them, don't worry—they are not etched in stone.

In fact, you've already taken the first and most difficult step - becoming aware of them.

Self-aware people reflect on their lives, recognize their emotions, consider their impact on others, and adapt based on feedback.

People who lack self-awareness are often blind to their own faults, struggle with personal and spiritual growth, and may find self-reflection challenging. They repeatedly make the same mistakes and then blame others for their outcome.

By acknowledging that you have unwanted traits, you can now start the process of refining or even eliminating them.

Pisces – Modifying Challenging Traits

Those born under the Month of Pisces are born with natural spirituality and need the practicality of their partner to ground them.

Those born with significant Pisces qualities are encouraged to use their empathic abilities while at the same time to discern when it is necessary to protect their wellbeing from overwhelming emotional demands or external pressures.

Take time to unwind by being alone, sleeping, listening to music, enjoying romance, meditating, imagining, and spiritual themes.

Live life in new awareness, as if looking forward to the newness of Spring. Use this to build excitement and energy to begin operating on a higher level. Gain inspiration by looking forward to a goal that is still unseen. Develop a strong connection to God through the Spirit to bring comfort to your everyday experiences.

By finding balance between giving love freely while safeguarding their own wellbeing, Pisceans learn how to nurture themselves as they nurture others.

Grounding the Deamer – Tips to Refine the Pisces Nature

Cultivating these life skills over time will bring the Pisces Nature into alignment with the positive traits of their role and provide more inner peace and fulfillment.

- Honor their sensitivities as an empath, an intuitive, and a highly sensitive person.
- Ground dreams in reality.
- Engage in self-reflection to tackle underlying difficulties.
- Balance giving to others and giving to themselves.
- Look for deeper truths and not just illusions.
- Make plans to minimize daydreaming.
- Find focus and purpose by creating specific measurable goals.

Activities, Actions, Attitudes to Contemplate
During the Month of Pisces

Try out new Pisces-type experiences, as led, to round out your personality!

- Contemplate the Life Question: "What are my inner concerns?"
- Identify the Month of Pisces traits you notice in your life.
- Find opportunities to apply the lessons of Pisces – compassion, dreaming, imagination, spirituality, self-sacrifice - to your life.
- Identify when you need to set more boundaries.
- Work on creating boundaries in that area.
- Try to identify and eliminate an addiction.
- Recognize where you are showing empathy toward someone.
- Try an activity where you can use your imagination.
- Relax your mind and put aside your racing thoughts and anxieties.
- Learn to meditate; sit in silence, breathe, and focus on being still.
- Try creative activities: draw, paint, play music, go dancing.
- Begin a new spiritual activity.
- Use a Bible or any other spiritual texts for your studies.
- Visit a house of worship or a park where you can contemplate the positive energies of religion.
- Focus on The Creator God.
- Start a dream log.
- Join a dance class or go out dancing.
- Feed your imagination with some fantasy movies, musicals, biographies.
- Read about spiritual figures or religious stories.
- Practice seeing God in every person that you meet.
- Spend time in nature.
- Relax near water. Water is healing.
- Do water activities, swim, a boat ride, surf, or canoe.
- Take long salt water baths.

Reflections on this Month's Pisces Traits
Growing in Understanding Pisces

Are there Pisces traits that you can identify in your life?

If so, which are positive and which ones need to be refined?

Do you recognize these traits in someone that was born under the Month of Pisces?

Does recognizing these traits in them help you to better understand them?

Are there any experiences you need or want to heal regarding these traits?

What Pisces traits can help you to develop strong spiritual sensitivity and intimate feeling toward the Infinite??

Which of this Month's Activities, Actions, Attitudes growth opportunities are you looking forward to trying?

 **Reflections for the Pisces Personality**

- ? How can you develop stronger boundaries when helping others?
- ? Do you give yourself the same amount of love that you give to others?
- ? What signs of victimhood do you need to watch out for?
- ? What types of activities can help you when you are sad and depressed?
- ? Are there areas you need or want to heal?
- ? How can you handle stress and anxiety without withdrawing?
- ? What traits can help you become more self-reliant?
- ? Do you make time to be alone to recharge?

Ask to be Filled

Ask the Spirit to fill your life with the fresh Fruit of this Month of Pisces for nourishment and healing. (Revelation 22:1-2).

Pray, to receive the nourishment you need that the Month of Pisces provides; to receive revelation and insight into your life and the life of others; to receive the Heavenly blessings of the Month.

> *"Holy Spirit, You know the plan for my life, you know my heart and what is needed for the New Year. Fill me with the energies, the gifts and abilities of Pisces that I need, to use for the best and highest good..."*

Personal and Spiritual Growth Aides

Part Three

Personal and Spiritual Growth Aides

The following pages contain helpful tools and insights to support you during Your Birthday celebration and activation as well as throughout the Year.

Design Your Own Ritual – Suggestions for your personal celebration and activation. Page 306

My prayer to Father God for the Coming Year – A Prayer to pray and personalize for your New Year, *"Father God..."* Page 308

A Fresh Start Every Month! - Suggestions to stimulate growth. Every Month provides opportunities to plant seeds and increase growth in the Areas of your Life. Page 310

Personality Development and Spiritual Growth – Time tested faith-based steps to grow in your personality, Life Areas, and spirituality. Page 311

The Holy Spirit as Your Guide – The vital roles the Holy Spirit plays as your Guide and Helper in your preparation for your New Year and continual support in your daily life. Page 312

Divine Assurances to Edify Your Life - Scripture-based assurances to read or speak aloud each day to build faith in God and ourselves. Page 313

Scripture Birthday Blessings - Blessings that can be personalized and spoken over Your Life at Your Birthday Celebration. Page 314

Your Birthday Promise Supporting Scripture - Scriptures to meditate on pertaining to God's purpose, plan, and provision for our lives. Page 315

Your Personal Experience

Your Birthday activation and celebration is a personal experience. There is not just one way to do it. The following are suggestions on how to make your celebration meaningful to you as you end one Year and begin the next.

Design Your Own Ritual

Plan a time specifically to meet with Father God through the Holy Spirit to celebrate and activate Your Birthday Promise for this Year. Design a ritual, or way of doing this, to organize this time as you are led. Look over the Aides in Part Three, *Personal and Spiritual Growth Aides,* to provide inspiration and direction.

On or around Your Birthday, in your time with the Spirit, suggestions are…

- Set aside a quiet time, light a candle. Have your Journal and pen at hand to write down your insights.

- Invite the Holy Spirit. *"Holy Spirit, I invite you to this Yearly Review of my life. Guide our time together. Cleanse this space from anything that does not belong. Let me feel your presence, comfort, insight, and protection. Open my heart, my mind, my soul, so I may hear You clearly."*

- *"Show me what I need to see about My Birthday Promise at this time. Give me understanding. Bring growth from the experiences of this past Year, and clarity into the plans, hope and vision for the coming Year. Let God's Light reveal what needs to be seen at this time. May the plans of my heart be only for the highest good for my life."*

- Reflect on the ratings you gave yourself while working through the various Birthday Month Life Reviews. Identify the areas you want to focus on for the New Year.

- Celebrate. Give thanks for the past Year. Thanks for the victories and the lessons learned through the challenges. Thanks for the new revelations you received. Thanks for the opportunity to continue on through this next Year. Thanks for the healing. Thanks for the blessings.

- Ask God to remove what is no longer needed in your life in this New Year; to help you remove the patterns of protection you put into place that you no longer need in the Areas where you have been healed.

- Identify traits that you want to express more of in the coming Year and receive them into your life. Together with the Lord, set fresh intentions for the Your New Year. Set intentions to be able to adjust to new routines and habits to accommodate what is needed now. Endeavor to purify your thoughts and actions.

- Activate. Ask God to fill you with the gifts, talents, and experiences you need for the New Year. Ask Him to equip, activate, heal and build, especially in challenging areas. Ask for guidance on what you need to move forward. Ask to know God better.

- Be still. Take time to sit quietly and listen for what God has to say through His Holy Spirit. Feel His love. Receive His assurance. Receive His peace. Jurnal your experience.

- Pray to God: *"Father God, I ask that you help me remember, revive, and renew the purpose for which I was born, activate the gifts given to me at birth, give me Your Wisdom and guide me through life's circumstances."*

- Seal and protect this time together with the Spirit and the new vision for the Year: *"Heavenly Father, I seal this time and all that was accomplished and agreed to in our time together. I receive the plan for my life for this Year. Bless this Year. Draw me closer to You and Your ways of love and peace."*

You have searched me, Lord, and you know me. You know when I sit and when I rise; you perceive my thoughts from afar. You discern my going out and my lying down; you are familiar with all my ways. Psalm 139:1-3

My prayer to Father God for the Coming Year

Pray this Prayer or Personalize it for Yourself

Father God,

Thank You for this time we have had together and for all that You have shown me. I am thankful that I am Your child, that You have a plan for my life, and that it is unfolding just as it should.

Thank you for last Year. Thank You for all of the experiences and the lessons and blessings, good and bad. I learned a lot about myself and life in general. I learned that You are always there with me through Your Spirit to guide and direct.

I made it through many challenges, and came through stronger and better. I take the good Fruit from them into this New Year and leave the rest as memories and lessons.

I learned that life is an ongoing experience and I am thankful for every day. Empower me to make the most of each day this coming Year.

I look forward to this New Year and all of the opportunities it will bring.

Thank You that You have downloaded from the blueprint of my life that You designed, the experiences and opportunities that are planned for me this Year.

Fill me with the gifts and talents that I need for the Year ahead. The ones You prepared for me in advance and gave to me at my Birth that need to be activated this Year.

I receive them and fan them into flame for use in this New Year. I pray that what I do with them will edify the life You have given me. Activate them in my life in Your perfect timing. I want to become more aware of them and use them for the best and highest purposes.

In spite of my goals and dreams, I pray also to be able to just 'be.' To 'be' still in Your Presence, to 'be' me unapologetically.

Keep me in Your Presence throughout the Year, and teach me through all the Months and Seasons. I pray to receive the heavenly blessings of each Month throughout Your Seasonal Year for continued revelation and insight into my life as well as the lives of others.

I ask for peace and the assurance that I am where I need to be right now in my life.

Holy Spirit be my guide. I ask that this be a Year of growth in my Spiritual Fruit to become more like You and experience more of Your Love and Kingdom within me. Fill me with Your power and peace. Keep distractions away.

Help me to be a blessing to others, to carry out my role in the world, and to shine my particular light where I am needed. I pray to grow in faith, hope, and the greatest of these – love. Through it all I give You the glory, Almighty God.

Help me to know myself as I am known by You, God.

I Thank You in advance for Your work in my life.

I pray all this in the Name of Your Son, Yeshua. Amen.

For this reason I remind you to fan into flame the gift of God, which is in you through the laying on of my hands. For God has not given us a spirit of fear, but of power, love, and self-control. 2 Timothy 1:6-7 BSB

A Fresh Start Every Month!

Every Month provides opportunities to plant seeds and increase growth in the Areas of your Life. Suggestions to stimulate growth are:

Reflect: At the start of each Month, take a moment to reflect on the past and envision what you wish to attract for the future.

Reconnect: Remind yourself of the overall role of your life. Reconnect with your current goals and dreams and align your thoughts and activities to compliment them. Each Month is an opportunity to co-create with the Spirit.

Revise: What needs to change? Are there old goals that no longer fit, expectations that are no longer realistic, habits that are not rooted in love. Ask yourself, 'What do I need to let go of?"

Plan ahead: What do I want to move toward? What still matters to me? What small step can I take this Month to honor that? Where do I want to be more fully myself?

Reset: Use this insight to reset your mindset for the new chapter ahead. Review the traits of the current Month and reflect on how they are needed or active in your life.

Align With the Energies of the Month: Tailor your thoughts and activities where possible to receive the unique nourishment of each Month. Aries might call for being bold and taking the lead, mirroring the Spring season. Taurus could focus on building what was started, Leo could place more focus on recreation and creativity, mirroring the Summer season. Scorpio could focus on gratitude and letting go, mirroring the Fall season. Lastly, Capricorn could focus on career goals during the time of reflection encouraged throughout the cold Winter season.

Daily Ritual: Make reciting monthly affirmations a part of your daily ritual. Examples found in this Journal are - *Divine Assurances to Edify Your Life, Your Month's 'I Am' Personality Declarations. Biblical Affirmations to Declare Over Your Life*, and *Scripture*. Morning time with the Spirit and prayers whispered before the day unfolds or quiet evening prayers can create meaningful times of transformation.

Celebrate Your Progress! Reflect on the same Month a Year ago and compare your life then and now. How have you grown in certain traits? What have you learned about yourself and others? Have you grown in your relationship with the Spirit of the Living God? Acknowledge the growth and fulfillment that has occurred.

Personality Development and Spiritual Growth

Faith-based Steps to Take

Here are six time tested faith-based steps to take to grow in your personality, Life Areas, and spirituality.

Realize – that you can rise above. It is possible to rise above natural negative traits and struggles. The lessons learned from your mistakes and failures can become a source of strength. Realize that you cannot lose – you either win or you learn.

Repent – the power to transform your mind. Acknowledge that your thoughts and actions have contributed to the challenges you face and determine to walk away from that behavior. Repentance includes a change of heart and mind – changing the way you think. It involves remorse for past wrongs and a sincere movement toward God and His Divine principles for forgiveness and renewed purpose. This leads to a restoration of your relationship with the Divine and rewriting your path. This also includes forgiving yourself.

Pray – the ability to ask God to shift the course of events. Ask God to help. Send Him your prayers and petitions and believe that He hears you and will answer. Believe that the Spirit will successfully guide you on your path or if necessary change the course of events to get you to the next step of your journey.

Plant Seeds – start the process of change and growth. Set intentions and begin to act in faith toward the request you have. Act as if it has already happened. Begin with the end result in mind. See it already there.

Good Works – the power to transform the direction of your life. Do good works, help others, love yourself and others whenever possible to positively refine your traits and change the course of your life.

Faith – the belief that all things are working together for good. Believe in God and yourself and that the challenges you are going through will be resolved in just the right way for your life.

Give Thanks - thank God for your blessings. Take time to acknowledge the aspects of your life that comfort, support, and give you pleasure. There may be challenges in your life right now, but many times realizing 'things could be worse' can make you realize that the present challenges are blessings in comparison. Take time to think of the positives of your life and show gratitude.

The Holy Spirit as Your Guide

The Holy Spirit as your Guide and Helper is a part of your Spiritual walk and continually supports you in your daily life. He is very active in your preparation for your New Year. He plays several vital roles:

Guide and Counselor: He gives you guidance, comfort, counsel, and direction to help navigate each day of the Year. You just need to ask.

"When the Spirit of truth comes, he will guide you into all the truth, for he will not speak on his own authority, but whatever he hears he will speak, and he will declare to you the things that are to come." John 16:13 ESV

Supporter and Intercessor: He intercedes for you, praying on your behalf when you do not know what to pray for.

In the same way, the Spirit helps us in our weakness. We do not know what we ought to pray for, but the Spirit himself intercedes for us through wordless groans. Romans 8:26

"And he who searches our hearts knows the mind of the Spirit, because the Spirit intercedes for God's people in accordance with the will of God." Romans 8:27

Empowerer: The Holy Spirit gives you strength and empowers and supports you through the challenges of your spiritual journey.

For God has not given us a spirit of fear, but of power, love, and self-control. 2 Timothy 1:7 BSB

Teacher: He teaches and reminds you of God's Spiritual directions, helping you to understand and apply biblical truths.

But the Helper, the Holy Spirit, whom the Father will send in My name, He will teach you all things, and bring to your remembrance all things that I said to you. John 14:26 NKJV

"I will instruct you and teach you in the way you should go; I will counsel you with my loving eye on you." Psalm 32:8

Helper: The Holy Spirit serves as a Divine helper and guide leading and supporting you in your faith as well as your daily activities.

For those who are led by the Spirit of God are the children of God. Romans 8:14

# Divine Assurances to Edify Your Life

Scripture-based assurances build our faith in God and ourselves. Read or speak them aloud each day – twice if needed - once when you wake up and once before you go to sleep.

I AM NEVER ALONE

I am loved. (Romans 5:8)

I am never alone. (Matthew 28:20b)

I am set apart. (Psalm 4:3)

I am chosen. (1 Peter 1:2)

I AM EQUIPPED FOR EVERY GOOD WORK

God has given me everything I need to fulfill His purpose for me. (2 Timothy 3:17)

I am God's handiwork. (Ephesians 2:10)

I AM PROECTED

I am safe. (Psalm 91:1-2)

God will never leave me nor forsake me. (Deuteronomy 31:6)

I will not be anxious because God cares for me. (1 Peter 5:7)

I AM BEING TRANSFORMED DAILY

God is continually renewing my mind and shaping me into His image. (Romans 12:2)

I am made new. (2 Corinthians 5:17)

I AM A LIGHT IN THIS WORLD

I am approved. (1 Thessalonians 2:4)

I am a light to others, shining God's love and goodness. (Matthew 5:16)

I AM ENOUGH

I am competent. My competence comes from God. (2 Corinthians 3:5)

I am valuable to God. (Luke 12:6-7)

I AM STRONG

I am strong and powerful in the Lord. (Ephesians 6:10)

The joy of the Lord is my strength. (Nehemiah 8:10)

Scripture Birthday Blessings

Scripture blessings have the power to shape destinies, restore joy, and awaken Divine purpose. The following blessings can be personalized and spoken over your life at Your Birthday Celebration. As you speak the blessings, trust that God is listening and working behind the scenes to make this a truly blessed Year.

*The Lord bless you and keep you;
the Lord make his face to shine upon you and be gracious to you;
the Lord lift up his countenance upon you and give you peace. Numbers 6:24-26*

May the God of hope fill you with all joy and peace as you trust in him, so that you may overflow with hope by the power of the Holy Spirit. Romans 15:13

May he equip you with all you need for doing his will. May he produce in you, through the power of Jesus Christ, every good thing that is pleasing to him. All glory to him forever and ever! Amen. Hebrews 13:21 NLT

*Now to him who is able to do immeasurably more than all we ask or imagine, according to his power that is at work within us, to him be glory in the church and in Christ Jesus throughout all generations, for ever and ever! Amen.
Ephesians 3:20-21*

*For he will command his angels concerning you to guard you in all your ways.
Psalm 91:11*

Every good and perfect gift is from above, coming down from the Father of the heavenly lights, who does not change like shifting shadows. James 1:17

The LORD will open the heavens, the storehouse of his bounty, to send rain on your land in season and to bless all the work of your hands. Deuteronomy 28:12

And we know that in all things God works for the good of those who love him, who have been called according to his purpose. Romans 8:28

*May he give you the desire of your heart and make all your plans succeed.
Psalm 20:4*

Your Birthday Promise Supporting Scripture

Meditate on These Things

To everything there is a season, and a time to every purpose under the heaven:
A time to be born, and a time to die; a time to plant,
and a time to pluck up that which is planted. Ecclesiastes 3:1-2 ASV

In Him we were also chosen as God's own, having been predestined according to
the plan of Him who works out everything by the counsel of His will.
Ephesians 1:11 BSB

For we are God's handiwork, created in Christ Jesus to do good works, which God
prepared in advance for us to do. Ephesians 2:10

"Your kingdom come, Your will be done, on earth as it is in heaven." Matthew 6:10

The plans of the heart belong to man, but the reply of the tongue is from the LORD.
Proverbs 16:1 BSB

A man's heart plans his way, But the LORD directs his steps. Proverbs 16:9 NKJV

Many plans are in a man's heart, but the purpose of the LORD will prevail.
Proverbs 19:21 BSB

The steps of a man are ordered by the LORD who takes delight in his journey.
Though he falls, he will not be overwhelmed, for the LORD is holding his hand.
Psalm 37:23-24 BSB

A person's steps are directed by the LORD. How then can anyone
understand their own way? Proverbs 20:24

For it is God who works in you to will and to act on behalf of His good purpose.
Philippians 2:13

Your word is a lamp for my feet, a light on my path. Psalm 119:105

And over all these virtues put on love, which binds them all together
in perfect unity. Colossians 3:14

Let us not become weary in doing good, for at the proper time we will reap a harvest
if we do not give up. Galatians 6:9

And do not be conformed to this world, but be transformed
by the renewing of your mind. Romans 12:2

And this is the promise that he made to us—eternal life. 1 John 2:25 ESV

So we, though many, are one body in Christ
and individually members one of another. Romans 12:5 ESV

We have not received the spirit of the world, but the Spirit who is from God,
so that we may understand what God has freely given us. 1 Corinthians 2:12 BSB

Each person should live as a believer in whatever situation the Lord has assigned to
them, just as God has called them. 1 Corinthians 7:17

You make known to me the path of life; you will fill me with joy in your presence,
with eternal pleasures at your right hand. Psalm 16:11 NIV

Then the Lord God formed a man from the dust of the ground and breathed into his
nostrils the breath of life, and the man became a living being. Genesis 2:7

When Jesus spoke again to the people, he said,
"I am the light of the world. Whoever follows me will never walk in darkness,
but will have the light of life." John 8:12

This is the message we have heard from him and declare to you:
God is light; in him there is no darkness at all. 1 John 1:5

"I have come into the world as a light, so that no one who believes in me
should stay in darkness." John 12:46

Finally, brothers and sisters, whatever is true, whatever is noble, whatever is right,
whatever is pure, whatever is lovely, whatever is admirable—if anything is excellent
or praiseworthy—think about such things. Philippians 4:8

Author's Note

The viewpoint shared in *Your Birthday Promise Workbook, Planner, and Journal* is founded on my deeply held faith in the God introduced to me in the Bible. This is the Father God I have had a personal relationship with for over 40 Years through salvation in Yeshua, Jesus, and by following His spiritual teachings. There have been many dedicated hours of study, prayer, writing, teaching, and service, along with new revelations and insights into spirituality over the Years.

If God means something to you other than the God of the Bible, as you read this Journal, please relate to God as you know Him.

This Journal is designed to be used as you start your New Year at Your Birthday time and then to be continued on throughout the rest of the Year. In some cases it will introduce you to The GOD Who created YOU, and in all cases, it will show you how you can be more certain of your role and purpose in this life.

If you would like a deeper, closer, real relationship with God, you can have it too. God's Son Yeshua, Jesus, came to show us the ways and love of God. Believe in Him and your heart will be opened to receive Him. You will become an initiate into faith, a disciple of love. Ask the Holy Spirit to come into your life, through Yeshua, the bridge, the conduit to the Heavenly Kingdom.

When you open the door of your heart to God, when you believe and call on the Name of the Lord, He will answer, and your spiritual eyes will be opened and your relationship will begin. You will be given insight into the spiritual realm, which will help you overcome life's obstacles and live your life to the fullest.

> *"Behold, I stand at the door and knock; if anyone hears My voice and opens the door, I will come in to him and will dine with him, and he with Me."*
> *Revelation 3:20 NASB*

> *Call to me and I will answer you, and will tell you great and hidden things that you have not known. Jeremiah 33:3*

I pray you will be richly blessed as you spend time with The Most High. Through the downloads and discoveries you will receive as you reflect on your life as a whole, this past Year, and the goals and intentions you set for the Year ahead you will connect with Creator God, your role, and who you are in a deeper way. As you recognize and develop your core traits in the activities you are involved in at this moment you will see your life begin to unfold in a new way each day.

With Love, *Rose*

In Conclusion,

In conclusion, each Month offers valuable insight into our gifts, talents, roles, and purpose as well as spiritual lessons to guide us on our journey toward spiritual and personal growth. When you embrace these insights you not only understand yourself better but are also able to form deeper relationship with God, as well as more meaningful connections within your community.

As you reflect on your Month's traits, or explore those of others around you, remember that this serves as an insightful tool, inviting us all to get a richer understanding of our individual purpose on this Earth and our shared human experience.

God is exalted above all. He knows all about us and the life that is meant for each of us. We should learn to take the joys and trials that life brings us, and look at every circumstance of our lives, as a particular step necessary for our individual growth. While they are not all pleasant, they are all necessary.

To get to know ourselves and grasp the meaning of our life experiences, we must treat every occasion as a learning opportunity, believing that it has a positive value that can give meaning, growth and understanding to our lives. We need to continually make the adjustments to our lives based on what we have learned. The Fruit of this is a true vision, real insight, and reliable foresight that will advance our life's purpose and grow the Fruits of the Spirit as well.

To be fully receptive to the meaning of our daily experiences, we need to do our part and decide to reflect on them, understand them, and apply what we have learned. This will make known the Heavenly Kingdom which is already eternally embodied in our lives today.

"But seek first the kingdom of God and his righteousness, and all these things will be added to you." Matthew 6:33, ESV

Jesus said: ..."But the kingdom is within you, and it is outside of you. When you know yourselves, then you will be known, and you will know that you are the sons of the living Father." Gospel of Thomas Saying 3 BLATZ

God wants us to know Him and to know ourselves as the unique spark of His life that He created.

May the abundant blessings of God to be upon you this New Year and always.

Notable Reflections

The Greatest of These

Love is patient, love is kind.
It does not envy, it does not boast, it is not proud.
It does not dishonor others, it is not self-seeking, it is not easily angered,
it keeps no record of wrongs.
Love does not delight in evil but rejoices with the truth.
It always protects, always trusts, always hopes, always perseveres.
Love never fails. But where there are prophecies, they will cease;
where there are tongues, they will be stilled;
where there is knowledge, it will pass away.
For we know in part and we prophesy in part,
but when completeness comes, what is in part disappears.
When I was a child, I talked like a child, I thought like a child,
I reasoned like a child. When I became a man,
I put the ways of childhood behind me.
For now we see only a reflection as in a mirror;
then we shall see face to face.
Now I know in part; then I shall know fully, even as I am fully known.
And now these three remain:
faith, hope and love. But the greatest of these is love.
1 Corinthians 13:4-13

In life, you will realize there is a role for everyone you meet. Some will test you,
some will use you, some will love you, and some will teach you.

But the ones who are truly important are the ones who bring out the best in you.
they are the rare and amazing people who remind you why it's worth it.

~ Unknown ~

Know your role so you can stop playing the role of others.

Glossary

Traditional and Technical Terms Used in This Book

Your Birthday Promise: The Promise for your life between your Creator and you.

The Birthday Promise: The role, purpose and experiences one is guaranteed to encounter at some point in their life. It is a life plan that is believed to provide insights into various aspects of life including personality, strengths, weaknesses, relationships, career, life path, and life events that may occur, helping individuals understand their strengths and weaknesses and make choices aligned with their true potential. This Promise is between your Creator and you.

Constellations: The starry hosts that surround the Earth. The Constellations mark the beginning, middle, and end of the Spring, Summer, Fall, and Winter Seasons through the Months that are in each.

Fruit of the Tree of Life/Fruit of the Spirit: in the Book of Revelation 22:1-5, an angel shows John a river of life-giving water flowing down from heaven alongside a Tree which produces Fruit twelve times a Year, once each Month. From a Judeo-Christian viewpoint, these twelve Fruits from the Tree of Life are symbolic fruits, also called the Fruits of the Spirit, or virtues. They include the Fruits listed in the Book of Galatians 5:22-23. Each Fruit also reveals an aspect of God's nature.

Gregorian Calendar: Astronomers match the time of the entrance of the Sun into each Constellation with the calendar dates we use today, called the Gregorian Calendar. This is how the dates of the beginning and end of each Month in the Universe are identified.

Intentions: Goals and plans similar to resolutions

Names of Months: The names of the Seasonal Months are taken from the starry hosts, or Constellations, that surround the Earth. Each Month has its own name to identify it in the Universe. Their names in order beginning with the first Month of Spring are as follows: Aries, Taurus, Gemini, Cancer, Leo, Virgo, Libra, Scorpio, Sagittarius, Capricorn, Aquarius, and Pisces.

Role in the World/Contribution to Society: We each have a role to fill for ourselves and for humanity.

Spirit of the living God: The Holy Spirit, The Comforter, Who is always with us.

Your Birth Month: The Seasonal Month in which the Day of Your Birth falls.

Your Yearly Birthday Life Review: A deep dive into your life each Year at Your Birthday Celebration time.

Light of the Living God: Spiritual light, revelation, nourishment, life from God. Light of the Sun is a metaphor for the light of God. Nothing grows without the Sun, without God.

Journal:

Journal:

Journal:

Journal:

Journal:

Know Yourself and Your Life's Purpose

Your Birthday Promise

Workbook, Planner, and Journal

For more insight into Your Birthday Promise

Visit:

Website: www.YourBirthdayPromise.com

Email: YourBirthdayPromise@gmail.com

Made in the USA
Coppell, TX
30 January 2026

70555574R00188